MODERN
AMERICAN
DIPLOMACY

MODERN
AMERICAN
DIPLOMACY

Edited By
John M. Carroll
and
George C. Herring

SR *Scholarly Resources Inc.*
Wilmington, Delaware

The paper used in this publication meets the minimum requirements of the American National Standard for permanence of paper for printed library materials, Z39.48, 1984.

Scholarly Resources Inc.
104 Greenhill Avenue
Wilmington, Delaware 19805-1897

Library of Congress Cataloging-in-Publication Data

Modern American diplomacy.

    Bibliography: p.
    Includes index.
    1. United States—Foreign relations—20th century.
I. Carroll, John M. (John Martin), 1943–
II. Herring, George C., 1936–
E744.M589 1986   327.73   86-11918
ISBN 0-8420-2264-3 (alk. paper)
ISBN 0-8420-2263-5 (pbk.: alk. paper)

Contents

Preface / vii

Introduction / ix

In Search of an Orderly World: U.S. Imperialism, 1898–1912 / 1
By Joseph A. Fry
University of Nevada, Las Vegas

Woodrow Wilson and U.S. Intervention in World War I / 21
By Melvin Small
Wayne State University

The United States and the Versailles Peace Settlement / 35
By William C. Widenor
University of Illinois

American Diplomacy in the 1920s / 53
By John M. Carroll
Lamar University

The Diplomacy of the Depression / 71
By Jane Karoline Vieth
Michigan State University

The United States Enters World War II / 91
By Jonathan G. Utley
University of Tennessee, Knoxville

World War II and the Coming of the Cold War / 107
By Robert L. Messer
University of Illinois, Urbana

The Cold War in Asia / 127
By Carol Morris Petillo
Boston College

American Nuclear Policy / 147
  By George T. Mazuzan
  U.S. Nuclear Regulatory Commission

The Vietnam War / 165
  By George C. Herring
  University of Kentucky

Latin America from Cuba to El Salvador / 183
  By Lester D. Langley
  University of Georgia

The Middle East, Oil, and the Third World / 201
  By James W. Harper
  Texas Tech University

Afterword
  American Foreign Policy: Past and Future / 221

Index / 227

Contributors / 239

Preface

This book contains twelve original essays on the major issues in twentieth-century American diplomatic history. Although the authors are dealing with complex material, they have attempted to make their essays both meaningful and enjoyable for the undergraduate student. Designed to complement a standard textbook for courses in recent diplomatic history or in international relations, this volume presents interpretive material with new viewpoints, as well as traditional ones, and therefore should assist in stimulating class discussion. Specialists in their respective fields, the authors have not hesitated to express opinions or to pass judgments; thus, they provide an exciting, thought-provoking study rather than a mere collection of facts.

Modern American Diplomacy includes a general introduction and an afterword and focuses on three distinct periods. The first three essays deal with the formative era of America's recent diplomacy, the years between 1898 and 1919. These essays emphasize America's imperial adventure, its entrance into World War I, and Woodrow Wilson's attempt to shape the postwar settlement. The next three essays explore the interwar years between 1920 and 1941. During this era, America's hope for a lasting peace based on economic progress, political stability, and disarmament was destroyed by the Great Depression. By the end of the 1930s war again threatened to engulf the world. The largest section of the book highlights the problems, decisions, and challenges that have confronted American diplomats during and after World War II. The authors examine the origins and expansion of the Cold War, the nuclear arms race, the meaning of the Vietnam War, inter-American relations, and the rise of the Third World.

We would like to acknowledge the numerous people who contributed to the completion of this book. Many friends offered suggestions; colleagues read parts of the book in manuscript. To all our friends and colleagues, our thanks. A special thanks goes to Laquita

Stidham and her staff for preparing the essays for publication.

We wish finally to express our appreciation to the scholars who contributed to this book. They gave generously of their time and talents and accepted our editorial revisions with remarkable forbearance.

John M. Carroll
George C. Herring

Introduction

Beginning in the colonial era, Americans showed a strong interest in foreign policy in order to protect their survival against the larger French and Spanish empires in the New World. During the early years of the Republic, a wise and prudent diplomatic strategy was necessary to preserve independence. Presidents George Washington and John Adams were determined to avoid unnecessary European entanglements while the nation gained strength and stability in the decade after the American Revolution. Although the United States stumbled into war with Britain in 1812, it emerged from that conflict with its national territory intact and with a sense of pride and confidence that helped to stimulate an aggressive policy of continental expansion. This westward thrust consumed much of the nation's energy during the nineteenth century.

The end of the War of 1812 and the larger Napoleonic Wars in Europe marked a change in American and world history. Between 1815 and 1914 the world continued to experience a number of major wars but none matching the intensity and duration of the Napoleonic conflict. Isolated from the mainstream of world affairs by two oceans and the usually benevolent umbrella of the British navy, America enjoyed a period of growth and progress. Despite a costly and divisive Civil War during the 1860s, the country pulled together to complete the task of continental development and emerged as one of the leading industrial nations by the end of the century.

On the eve of the new century, the United States embarked on a course of imperial conquest. Certainly a policy of aggressive expansionism was not new for Americans. What was new was that the territories were noncontiguous lands abroad. JOSEPH A. FRY points out some of the factors that helped propel the United States along the road to imperialism. The economic boom of the late nineteenth century was extremely uneven, and it resulted in poor wages and working conditions for many factory laborers. Some capitalists feared a crisis as unemployment spread, workers became more militant, and production exceeded consumption. With the "safety valve" of the frontier supposedly closing, some industrialists looked to overseas markets as a way out of their predicament. Beyond this, American leaders were impressed by the attainments of European imperial powers and were convinced that the United States also had a mission to protect and uplift backward peoples. Religious groups, sea power enthusiasts, some businessmen, and a large segment of the social elite formed a small but powerful force in favor of overseas expansion. When conditions were ripe in the 1890s, Americans willingly embarked on an imperialistic adventure.

The "splendid little war" with Spain marked the emergence of the United States as a world power, and in just a few months it acquired a modest but sprawling empire. European nations recognized that the United States would play an increasingly important role in world affairs, and by the beginning of the new century America was making its power felt from the Caribbean to China. President Theodore Roosevelt epitomized the raw power and exuberant energy of the rising world power. He sometimes spoke brashly and acted impetuously, but for the most part he was as pragmatic and realistic as the nation itself. The young president bullied the weaker nations in Latin America but acted cautiously in confronting the major powers in Asia. William Howard Taft and Woodrow Wilson were not as successful as their predecessor in properly balancing both American objectives and power in these areas.

America's experience as an imperial nation produced mixed results. Some Americans basked in the prestige that accompanied great-power status. Others were more concerned with the negative side of imperialism: a brutal guerrilla war in the Philippines, the tarnishing of America's anticolonial heritage, the expense of maintaining colonies, and the failure of sizable foreign trade to develop in colonial areas. Above all, Fry maintains that the policies of imperialism often put the United States at cross-purposes with the current of nationalism, which would become the dominant international force in the twentieth century.

At the outset of the new century some optimistic Americans boasted that the next one hundred years would be a period of world leadership for their country. The beginning of World War I in August 1914 offered the United States the opportunity to exert increasing influence in international affairs. As the world's leading neutral, America could tip the balance between the evenly matched Allied and Central powers. MELVIN SMALL explores both the practical and idealistic reasons that caused President Wilson to lead the nation into war in 1917. The decision to intervene marked what Daniel Smith has called a "Great Departure" in American diplomacy. It reversed a century-long effort by the nation's leaders to remain largely aloof from European problems and conflicts. To mobilize the country for such a radical break with tradition, Wilson characterized the war effort in the most idealistic terms. He succeeded in bringing American power to bear on the western front at an early date and ensured the German defeat which came in November 1918. He also raised hopes and expectations that were difficult to realize at the Paris Peace Conference. WILLIAM C. WIDENOR focuses on the Versailles treaty of 1919, which he maintains proved disappointing for all the major powers involved. It was based on idealistic objectives that were simply unattainable amidst the bitterness and chaos of postwar Europe. Wilson came away from the peace conference in an optimistic mood because he believed that his League of Nations could rectify many of the injustices that had crept into the treaty. His design for world peace remains a hotly disputed issue. Historians continue to debate the merits of his League and the "what ifs" regarding Senate ratification of the Treaty of Versailles and U.S. participation in the world organization.

The defeat of the treaty by the Senate in 1919–20 marked still another shift in American diplomacy. America would attempt to remain aloof from European affairs, but policymakers could not ignore the fact that the United States had become the world's leading creditor nation. JOHN M. CARROLL examines how Republican administrations during the 1920s tried to bridge this gap between isolationism and activism in world affairs by emphasizing economic diplomacy and disarmament. Their hope was that general prosperity and stability, orchestrated through American leadership, would bring lasting peace. These hopes were dashed by the paralyzing effects that the Great Depression had on the victors of World War I. JANE KAROLINE VIETH explores why the 1930s were a decade characterized by an intense mood of isolationism in the United States. She maintains that even a staunch Wilsonian like Franklin D. Roosevelt seldom attempted to buck the prevailing currents of the depression years. Only the threat posed by the Axis powers allowed Roosevelt to move the nation toward war in 1940–41 to protect America's vital interests.

JONATHAN G. UTLEY traces the complex chain of events resulting in the Japanese attack on Pearl Harbor in December 1941, which swept away American isolationism and allied the nation with Britain and the Soviet Union against the Axis. This strange alliance between Communist Russia and the two capitalist powers was strained from the start, but it held together because of the mutual objective of defeating Nazi Germany. ROBERT L. MESSER views the origins of the Cold War as an outgrowth of the wartime tension between the Soviet Union and the United States. During the war it became clear that Roosevelt and Russian dictator Joseph Stalin were the senior partners in the alliance. Both leaders were content to postpone the discussion of difficult postwar problems in order to preserve a united front against the Axis. Roosevelt, who did not reveal his postwar plans, even to his closest aides, believed that he could successfully negotiate with Stalin after the war was over. His untimely death in April 1945 bequeathed to Harry S. Truman, who had not been kept well informed by Roosevelt, the awesome task of ending the war and negotiating a peace settlement. At the Yalta and Potsdam summit meetings and subsequent postwar conferences, it became evident that a wide gulf separated the British and Americans from the Soviets on a number of important issues, including the political future of eastern Europe.

During the next four years, political relations between the Western allies and the Soviet Union deteriorated rapidly, giving rise to what historians have termed the Cold War. As early as 1946 former British Prime Minister Winston Churchill described Europe as divided by an Iron Curtain which separated the free nations in the West from the captive peoples in the Communist-controlled East. By the early 1950s Soviet and American military forces confronted each other in Europe and exerted increasing influence in the Mediterranean region. Historians have vigorously debated the reasons for the outbreak of the Cold War. Some have traced the origins of the conflict to the long-standing ideological tension between the two powers and the political collapse of Europe in the wake of World War II. Others, such as Messer, have focused on the decisions made by wartime and postwar leaders in confronting the problems of negotiating a lasting peace.

The Cold War spread rapidly in the decade following World War II. CAROL MORRIS PETILLO examines the reasons for the expansion of the Cold War into Asia. She notes that, after the Communist takeover of China in 1949 and the outbreak of the Korean War the following year, the United States mobilized its resources to contain communism on a worldwide basis. American policymakers often assumed that nations that were pro-Marxist, or simply unfriendly to the interests and aspirations of the United States, were part of a Soviet-led Communist effort to overthrow capitalism.

This global confrontation between the United States and the Soviet Union became increasingly dangerous with the dawn of the atomic age. By 1949, when Russia exploded its first atomic bomb, both superpowers possessed the awesome nuclear weapons. During the past thirty-five years, America and the USSR have engaged in a frantic nuclear arms race that has made global destruction a real possibility. GEORGE T. MAZUZAN traces the evolution of U.S. nuclear policy and is less than optimistic about the future. He maintains that the proliferation of these weapons among lesser powers has increased the danger of nuclear war. To date, efforts to contain the nuclear arms race have met with only limited success.

During the past two decades the United States has been forced to reevaluate the extent to which its diplomatic, economic, and military power can influence and shape world events. At the height of the Cold War, American leaders assumed that the nation could and must pay any price to oppose international communism. Since that time they have begun to question the axiom that all pro-Marxist or unfriendly nations pose a threat to vital U.S. interests. The Vietnam War, America's longest and in some ways most tragic war, demonstrated the limits of American power. GEORGE C. HERRING focuses on the origins of U.S. involvement in Vietnam, why we gradually took over the war, and the consequences of the American war effort. He maintains that for more than a decade the nation fought to defeat a Communist-led nationalist movement in Southeast Asia. The protracted conflict resulted in divisiveness at home and a diminution of U.S. power and prestige abroad.

One lesson of the Vietnam War was that the world is not divided into two camps headed by the Soviet Union and the United States. A third camp or "Third World" of intensely nationalistic and neutralist-oriented nations has emerged since World War II. This phenomenon was apparent long before Vietnam, but that conflict dramatized the importance of the Third World for many Americans. In Latin America, Africa, the Middle East, and Asia, Third World nations, some rich and some poor, exerted an increasing influence on world affairs. The United States has been challenged to adjust its foreign policy to accommodate this sweeping change in international power relationships since 1945. LESTER D. LANGLEY and JAMES W. HARPER analyze American foreign policy in these Third World regions and maintain that the United States will face even more difficult problems and challenges in the near future.

American foreign policy in the twentieth century has undergone great changes which seem to be accelerating as the century progresses. The nation has achieved important successes in world affairs and also has experienced failures. It has progressed from the position of relative novice in international politics to world leader. There is no turning back to the tranquil period of American isolationism of the nineteenth century. The searching question is how America will use its energy and resources to confront the increasingly difficult international problems that will challenge the nation in the future.

Beaumont, Texas   J.M.C.
May 1986

In Search of an Orderly World:
U.S. Imperialism, 1898–1912

Joseph A. Fry

In 1900 Theodore Roosevelt responded to the critics of American efforts to subdue the Filipino insurgents by asserting that "every argument that can be made for the Filipinos could be made for the Apaches; every word that can be said for Aguinaldo could be said for Sitting Bull. As peace, order and prosperity followed our expansion over the lands of the Indians, so they will follow us in the Philippines." Roosevelt's assumptions of racial, cultural, and institutional superiority; his belief in American mission; his consciousness of economic considerations; and especially his conviction that order and stability were prerequisites for advancing and protecting U.S. interests abroad all typified the thinking that underpinned the nation's imperial policies from 1898 through 1912.

Not all Roosevelt's countrymen shared his enthusiasm for imperialism. Writing five years later, Moorfield Storey, president of the Anti-Imperialist League, incorrectly declared that "the wave of imperialism which reached this country in 1898 and for a while threatened to drown our people's faith in the great principles of free government has spent its force." Storey equated imperialism with the formal annexation of noncontiguous lands abroad, and this definition has allowed some historians to portray America's end-of-the-century territorial grab as a "great aberration," uncharacteristic of prior and subsequent national behavior. To be sure, the annexation of Guam, Hawaii, the Philippines, and Puerto Rico was unprecedented. Never before had the United States annexed territory located beyond the North American continent, and up until this time Americans generally had assumed that newly acquired lands would eventually become states and their inhabitants citizens.

Still, only by subscribing to this overly narrow definition of imperialism, and ignoring the aggressive, expansionist nature of

1

previous American actions, can one characterize late nineteenth-century expansion as an "aberration." Imperialism may more properly be defined as a relationship in which a stronger nation controls, or consciously attempts to control, the actions of a weaker country or group of people. Viewed from this perspective, the nation's relentless march to the Pacific coast, the subjugation of the Indians, and the bullying of Mexico in the 1840s provide compelling examples of earlier imperial actions. Similarly, subsequent U.S. economic domination of Cuba and the Philippines as well as the military, economic, and political hegemony over the Caribbean region, would contradict Storey's hope that U.S. imperialism was flagging by 1905.

American imperialism from 1898 through 1912 found its bases in diverse intellectual, economic, and strategic concerns. From the time John Winthrop pronounced the Massachusetts Bay Colony a "Citty upon a Hill," Americans have been convinced of their mission to mankind. The late nineteenth- and early twentieth-century sense of mission embodied a conviction of racial and institutional superiority. Americans, like many western Europeans, perceived a yawning gap between themselves (the "Anglo-Saxons") and peoples of Africa, Asia, and Latin America (the "barbarians"). Anglo-Saxonism received apparent scientific support from Social Darwinism, which emphasized the "survival of the fittest" and suggested that the United States had been climbing the evolutionary ladder more rapidly than less developed competitors. Accompanying this conviction of superiority was at least a verbal sense of obligation. According to William Jennings Bryan, the "advanced nations" were bound to put forth "conscious and constant effort for the promotion of the welfare of the nations which lag behind." How, asked Henry Demarest Lloyd, could America "progress from perfection to perfection while [the] Chinese ossified, and the Cubans and Philippine people were disembowelled, and Africans continued to eat each other?"

Others added a startlingly coercive dimension to this "duty." Professor John W. Burgess argued that there was "no human right to the status of barbarism"; uncivilized peoples who failed to cooperate would face coercion, expulsion, or even extermination. While many contemporary Americans opposed wars among Western, "civilized" nations, they found the use of force on weaker, "uncivilized" countries quite acceptable. In fact, the latter was necessary both to preserve peace and to lay the basis for progress. "In the long run," declared Roosevelt, "civilized man finds he can keep the peace only by subduing his barbarian neighbor." Moreover, he continued, "The most ultimately righteous of all wars is war with savages" since it cleared the path for enlightened progress.

Economic considerations reinforced these notions of mission. During the depression of the 1890s, Americans increasingly attributed the nation's economic problems and social tensions to the overproduction of manufactured and agricultural goods. The key to disposing of this "glut" and ensuring domestic prosperity and order was a vastly enlarged export trade. In 1893, the first year of the depression, the *New York Tribune* characteristically declared: "Today we produce of manufactures more than any two nations of Europe; of agriculture more than any three, and of minerals more than all together. The necessity for new markets is now upon us." Economic expansionists called for a variety of measures to capture world markets: an enlarged navy and merchant marine, island coaling stations, an isthmian canal, government aid for American businessmen, and overseas colonies. Expansionists emphasized that commerce coincided nicely with America's larger mission to mankind. As Albert Beveridge told the National Association of Manufacturers in 1908, every ship carried "American ideas and American ideals, more tangibly than all the speeches that were ever made."

Strategic concerns provided further impetus to U.S. imperialism. When Americans looked abroad in the 1890s, they saw the European states constructing empires throughout Asia and Africa; they saw a "world of empires." Some policymakers believed that to behave as a great power the United States needed to emulate the Europeans. Apprehension over the nation's economic and security interests led others to favor a preclusive or preemptive imperialism aimed at seizing the initiative from the Europeans. This was especially true in the Caribbean, where Americans had long been suspicious of British intentions and after 1898 came to see Germany as a threatening competitor. Few U.S. policymakers feared the establishment of an outright European colony in the Caribbean; however, the region's chronic financial and political instability provided European nations with the opportunity to impinge upon the independence of smaller nations, while ostensibly protecting property or collecting debts. America's minister to Cuba observed characteristically in 1904 that "the German government never loses an opportunity to impress itself on every community, whether economically or politically." Roosevelt spoke for a generation of U.S. civilian and military leaders when he agonized over the kaiser's attempt "to seize some Venezuelan harbor and turn it into a strongly fortified place of arms, . . . with a view to exercising some measure of control over the future of the

Isthmian Canal, and over South American affairs generally." Although Americans found no comparable interests in the Far East prior to 1899, U.S. leaders feared being denied access to the fabled but chimerical "China Market." After acquiring the Philippines, they were continually troubled by the strategic vulnerability of the archipelago.

The pursuit of these interlocking ideological, economic, and strategic objectives produced the central characteristic of U.S. imperial policy during the 1898–1912 period: the desire for an orderly and stable world. Policymakers deemed order and stability essential to transplanting American institutions successfully in uncivilized areas. Moreover, U.S. policy assumed a circular pattern as American leaders persistently defined the most acceptable "order" as one in which the nation's institutions were being recreated. This quest for orderly, political process was reinforced by America's aversion to violence as a vehicle for political change and a lack of understanding for societies, especially in Latin America, where opposition leaders found no other way to gain power. Economic expansion seemed to require similar conditions. Buoyed by the nation's burgeoning economic strength, Americans were confident of great commercial gains if the country were free to trade and invest in a peaceful, preferably capitalist, setting. Instability not only interrupted trade but also offered the occasion for European colonial powers to seize new colonies or restrict access to old ones. Most important, disorder and financial insolvency provided the excuse for European intervention in the strategically vital Caribbean region.

Ironically, the American pursuit of order almost invariably proved disruptive and destabilizing; a stark incongruity developed between imperial objectives and results. Remaking smaller nations in the image of the United States required the displacing of indigenous cultures and institutions and was inevitably a wrenching process. This was especially true when the United States coerced weaker countries into accepting its ideas of order and progress. Economic expansion often led to conflict with imperial rivals or produced explosive economic and social conditions in the exploited countries. Finally, U.S. imperial presence, whether it was based on strategic, economic, or ideological considerations, helped stimulate the revolutionary force of anti-imperial nationalism in colonial countries.

The Spanish-American War of 1898 brought the nation's imperial inclinations to the fore. The Cuban rebellion against Spanish rule had begun in 1895, with both sides pursuing strategies that destroyed crops and left thousands of Cubans dead of disease and starvation. The fighting not only devastated the Cuban economy and society, but it also impinged directly upon American interests and humanitarian sensibilities. The revolt jeopardized more than $50 million of American investments in Cuba, reduced Cuban exports to the United States from $79 million in 1892 to $15 million in 1898, led to the harassment and imprisonment of U.S. citizens, raised the prospect of European interference with American canal projects, and stirred the nation's concern for the Cuban people.

The search for an expeditious end to what Secretary of State Richard Olney termed the "anarchy, lawlessness and terrorism" in Cuba guided the official U.S. response to the rebellion. President Grover Cleveland and Olney believed that this could best be achieved under continued Spanish sovereignty. Dismissing the Cubans as incapable of self-government, Olney feared that a "war of races" would follow Spanish withdrawal. Therefore, in 1896 he wrote that the United States stood ready to support Spain in a policy combining force and reform in a mixture offering the "most potential for the termination of hostilities and the restoration of peace and order to the island." Despite this tacit American support, Spain failed to quell the rebellion, which raged on past William McKinley's inauguration in March 1897.

Elected on a vigorously expansionist platform, the new Republican president favored the annexation of Hawaii, an isthmian canal, a stronger navy, and the establishment of "American supremacy in world markets." Like his predecessor, McKinley deemed prolonged instability in Cuba intolerable, and he entered office with a definite policy: if Spain failed to restore order the United States would be forced to intervene. From his first note to Madrid in June 1897, McKinley's demands for rapid pacification of the island carried the implied threat of U.S. intervention, and his decision for war one year later followed logically from this policy.

Early 1898 brought clear evidence of Spain's inability to stop the fighting. Mobs rioted in Havana against Spanish autonomy proposals, the *New York Journal* published the letter of the Spanish minister to Washington which revealed his country's insincerity in talks with the United States, and the battleship *Maine* exploded and sank in Havana harbor. His patience exhausted, McKinley demanded an armistice, the right to mediate the conflict, and Cuban independence. Spain rejected these demands and war ensued. In calling for a declaration of war, the president based his decision squarely on the aforementioned U.S. interests; he would employ American forces to end the hostilities in Cuba and "to secure in the island the establishment of a stable government, capable of maintaining order and observing its international obligations, insuring peace and tranquility and the security of its citizens as well as our own." Lasting barely four months the "splendid little war" ended in early August, with the United States in possession of the Philippines, Puerto Rico, and Cuba. (Hawaii had been annexed in July, and Guam would be acquired later.)

Subsequent American actions in Cuba and the Philippines provide case studies of the workings of U.S. imperialism. In declaring war upon Spain, Congress had passed the Teller Amendment, which renounced any intention of annexing Cuba. As Whitelaw Reid wrote McKinley, however, there was a critical inconsistency in going to war to restore order in Cuba and simultaneously disclaiming any right of "sovereignty, jurisdiction, and control." To expel Spain and not establish U.S. authority would lead to another unstable "Hayti nearer our own coast." An American withdrawal, wrote one correspondent, would "give [Cuba] over to a reign of terror—to the machete and the torch, to insurrection and assassination."

McKinley agreed. Following the Spanish surrender he refused to recognize the Cuban insurgents as an independent government and left the U.S. Army in control of Cuba. In his annual message to Congress in December 1898, he called for close commercial relations with the island and promised that the United States would help build a "free and independent" state. Military occupation would continue, however, until there was "complete tranquility in the island and stable government."

McKinley and his secretary of war, Elihu Root, resolved the dilemma of control under the Teller Amendment by making Cuba an American protectorate. Inspired by Root, Senator Orville Platt of Connecticut offered an amendment to the Army Appropriations Bill of 1901. This amendment authorized the end of military occupation when Cuba had agreed to make no other financial or political agreements compromising its independence, to sell or lease naval bases to the United States, or to accept future U.S. intervention in its affairs. Under heavy American pressure, Cuba wrote the Platt Amendment into its constitution in 1901 and subsequently signed a treaty with the United States in 1903 embodying its terms. General Leonard Wood, the U.S. military commander in Cuba from 1899 to 1902, succinctly observed that Cuba retained "little or no independence." Although the American army withdrew in 1903, the marines would return in 1906, 1912, 1917, and over the first half of the century no Cuban government could survive without U.S. approval. Rather than ensuring stability, this foreboding U.S. presence actually prompted Cuban politicians to act on the probability of American intrusion and often to invite it.

While these intermittent military interventions starkly dramatized the American desire for order in Cuba, the U.S. occupation policy from 1899 to 1903 revealed similar objectives. In reform measures akin to the Progressive Movement under way in the United States, General Wood sought to remake Cuba in America's image by constructing a stable, middle-class, business-oriented society that would attract additional U.S. investors. He instituted a new school system, a revised legal code, a revamped structure for municipal governments, and extensive sanitary and public works projects. Few of these reforms had any lasting impact. Cuban students showed little interest in American textbooks that had been translated into Spanish with no regard for Cuban history or culture. Habeas corpus and jury trials found no place in the Spanish legal tradition, and the practice of smashing down doors and publicly whipping people to enforce sanitation measures hardly produced an enthusiastic response.

Wood's desire for continuing U.S. economic control proved more enduring. In 1903 President Theodore Roosevelt complemented the Platt Amendment with a reciprocity treaty that gave U.S. goods a substantial tariff preference in Cuba and funneled Cuban sugar exports to the United States. Over the ensuing twenty years, U.S. investments in Cuban sugar rose from $50 million to $600 million, and American companies came to dominate the island's public utilities, port facilities, and industries. This economic dominance contributed directly to Cuba's overdependence on sugar and to the growth of a large plantation system manned by hordes of impoverished workers. The economic and social discontent spawned by these conditions would ultimately fuse with nationalistic resentment against the United States to bring Fidel Castro to power.

In the Philippines, McKinley was unhampered by restrictive legislation, such as the Teller Amendment, and his decision to annex formally the archipelago embodied the various motives for American imperialism. He judged that returning the islands to Spain would have been "cowardly and dishonorable." Since they were located so close to the enticing China Market, abandoning them to "France or Germany—our commercial rivals in the Orient," would have been "bad business." McKinley also feared that casting any portion of the islands adrift might have created a "golden apple of [international] discord" and set off a scramble leading to war. Both his concern for order and stability and his low regard for the Filipinos further convinced him they could not be left to themselves; "they were unfit for self-government," which would soon degenerate into "anarchy and misrule." The only alternative, he concluded, was to take all the islands and to "educate the Filipinos, and uplift and civilize and Christianize them."

When Emilio Aguinaldo and his followers proved none too eager to become "civilized," the U.S. quest for order and stability in the islands produced horrifyingly contradictory results. Fighting between the Filipino nationalists and American occupation troops began in February 1899, and three and one-half years of bloody guerrilla warfare followed. In a frank admission of American objectives, General William Shafter told correspondents it was necessary to kill the guerrillas so that "the remaining half of the population could be advanced to a higher plane of life." Following this dictum, U.S. soldiers tortured and killed captured Filipinos, herded civilians into concentration camps, burned crops, and slaughtered animals. The costs were staggering: 4,200 American lives lost and an expenditure of more than $400 million, approximately 18,000 Filipino battle casualties, at least 100,000 others dead from disease and starvation, and general devastation of land and crops. As historian Richard E. Welch has concluded, it is difficult to imagine that any disorder accompanying Philippine independence could have been so costly.

Having quelled the rebellion, the United States undertook a reform program even more ambitious than the one attempted in Cuba, but the results by 1913 were equally disappointing. Thousands of new schools and teachers failed to increase the literacy rate. In their average schooling of two years, few Filipino children were stimulated by, or benefited from, a curriculum that fluctuated between that of a Massachusetts elementary school and the contemporary industrial training for American blacks. Transplanted political institutions also floundered when restructured municipal and provincial governments and a new national assembly failed to alter previous patterns of corruption and elite rule. As in Cuba, economic measures were on the whole detrimental and unsettling. Miles of new roads and extensive harbor improvements did little to relieve the pervasive poverty. The long-range effect of the 1909 U.S. tariff was to tie the Philippines to the American economy, to promote large landholdings and overreliance on commercial crops, and to help fuel chronic agrarian unrest among landless rural workers. What Glenn A. May has called an "experiment in self-duplication" proved futile, leaving only economic domination and resentment of U.S. control.

Even as the United States was annexing and pacifying the Philippines, the China Market appeared to be in jeopardy. The McKinley administration had watched anxiously in late 1897 and early 1898 as France, Germany, Great Britain, Japan, and Russia forced a weak and vulnerable China to grant them spheres of influence and lease-

EXECUTION. The American military hangs Filipino rebels in the early 1900s.
(National Archives)

holds within its territory. If these countries were to obstruct U.S.
trade within their areas of control, the value of the Philippines as an
"American Hong Kong" would be rendered negligible. To avoid this
possibility, Secretary of State John Hay dispatched his first Open
Door Note in September 1899. He called upon the European countries and Japan to treat all trading nations equally with regard to
tariff rates and transportation facilities in their areas of influence.

The ambiguous European responses to Hay's note were hardly
reassuring, and McKinley and his secretary soon had reason to be
even more apprehensive over the fate of both American commerce
and Far Eastern stability. In June 1900 the Boxers, a secret society
devoted to ridding China of foreign domination, besieged the diplomatic compound in Peking. McKinley readily joined with the
European powers in sending an expeditionary force to restore order.
The president sought not only to protect endangered American

diplomats and businessmen but also to prevent the European powers from utilizing their armies to secure further commercial or strategic advantages. Hay's closest adviser, William Rockhill, typified administration thinking when he pronounced Far Eastern stability essential to American economic interests and expressed concern that China's complete collapse might even produce the ultimate instability: a war among the rapacious, imperial rivals.

This combination of fears prompted Hay to dispatch his second Open Door Note on July 3, 1900, in which he urged a solution to preserve "Chinese territorial and administrative entity" and to safeguard "the principle of equal and impartial trade with all parts of the Chinese Empire." Aware that the United States lacked the power to restrain the European nations, Hay hoped that a clear statement of U.S. policy might moderate their actions. When the precariously balanced European rivalry in China prevented a division of the country, Americans renewed their vision of potentially great economic gains.

With McKinley's assassination in September 1901, Theodore Roosevelt assumed the management of the nation's evolving imperial interests. The very embodiment of U.S. imperialism, the Rough Rider had enthusiastically endorsed McKinley's more assertive policies. Once in office he carried these policies to their logical conclusion in the Caribbean; however, he could locate no interests worthy of comparable effort in the Far East.

Carefully balancing foreign policy objectives against the power available to achieve them, Roosevelt pursued a restrained Far Eastern policy. Demanding the Open Door for American trade and investment in Manchuria (the Chinese province of greatest commercial interest), or actively supporting Chinese territorial integrity, would have necessitated confronting Japan. As he later told William Howard Taft, the Japanese had vital interests in Korea and Manchuria; the United States did not. Moreover, the Open Door was an "excellent thing,... so far as it could be maintained by general diplomatic agreement." But, Roosevelt cautioned, Manchuria's history demonstrated that "the 'open door' policy ... completely disappears as soon as a powerful nation determines to disregard it and is willing to run the risk of war." For Roosevelt an orderly and stable relationship with Japan outweighed the prospect of the persistently elusive economic gains in China.

When he turned to the Caribbean, Roosevelt exercised no such restraint; he believed that both American interests and power warranted vigorous action. His acquisition of the Panama Canal route provides the most vivid illustration of both this vigor and the often disruptive effect of his quest for order. By 1900 Roosevelt and the nation considered an isthmian canal essential. Reducing the sailing time between the two coasts by one-third would enhance the power of the navy and facilitate commercial access to both the new island empire and the beckoning Asian market. After securing British agreement to exclusive American control and fortification of a canal, Roosevelt decided that the Panama route was superior to an alternate one through Nicaragua.

To Roosevelt's disgust, Colombia balked at granting a right-of-way through its northernmost province. After threatening to nego-tiate with Nicaragua, Secretary of State Hay wrung a treaty from Colombian chargé to Washington Tomás Herrán. Signed in January 1903, the Hay-Herrán Treaty granted the United States sovereign control over a six-mile-wide zone for ninety-nine years. In return, Colombia was to receive $10 million and a rent of $250,000 per year. Eager to "make the dirt fly," Roosevelt became irate when Colombia rejected the treaty, demanding an additional $5 million from the United States and $10 million from the French-owned New Panama Canal Company. After fulminating privately that the "foolish and homicidal corruptionists in Bogota" could not "be allowed perma-nently to bar one of the future highways of civilization," he later emphasized publicly: "the Government of Colombia, though wholly unable to maintain order on the Isthmus, has nevertheless declined to ratify a treaty . . . which opened the only chance to secure its own stability and to guarantee permanent peace on, and construction of a canal across, the Isthmus."

Even though Colombia had simply exercised its right as an inde-pendent nation, Roosevelt seriously considered forceful interven-tion to seize the coveted passage. This proved unnecessary when a most opportune revolution occurred in Panama against Colombian rule. Prior to the bloodless coup of November 3, 1903, Philippe Bunau-Varilla, a Frenchman with interests in the New Panama Canal Company and contacts with the Panamanian conspirators, had talked with Roosevelt and several members of the State De-partment. In all of these conversations, he received the unmistakable impression that the United States would aid the revolution. Roose-velt made no explicit guarantees, but he later admitted that Bunau-Varilla "would have been a very dull man had he been unable to make such a guess." Indeed, an American battleship arrived prompt-ly on November 2, ostensibly to discourage European intervention but actually to prevent Colombia from suppressing the rebellion. Roosevelt justified this action on the basis of an 1846 treaty with Colombia, in which the United States had pledged to uphold, rather

"HELD UP THE WRONG MAN." President Theodore Roosevelt deals with Colombia on the canal issue. (*Harper's Weekly,* 1903, Library of Congress)

than destroy, Colombian sovereignty on the isthmus.

Roosevelt's support for this revolution was only a momentary deviation from his persistent pursuit of order and stability in the Caribbean. Acting with unseemly haste, he recognized the new

Panamanian government on November 6, 1903 and put Secretary Hay to work on a new canal treaty. The product (later characterized as "The Treaty No Panamanian Signed") was negotiated with Bunau-Varilla and placed Panama alongside Cuba as a U.S. protectorate. For the same payments that originally were offered to Colombia, the United States received a zone ten miles wide (up from six) to administer as if "it were the sovereign." The new lease was to run in perpetuity and included the right to use any rivers, bodies of water, or land outside the canal zone that were necessary to the canal's construction. Taft correctly observed that the treaty empowered the United States "to prevent revolutions" in this "Opera Bouffe republic." With this goal in mind, Roosevelt promptly shored up the white-dominated Conservative party's rule and dismantled the Panamanian army. From now on both domestic politics and external security would be dependent on decisions made in Washington. Once again, however, this hardly guaranteed stability. Panamanian opposition to U.S. sovereignty arose immediately and continued unabated into the 1970s.

"The inevitable effect of our building the canal," Secretary of War Root recognized, "requires us to police the surrounding premises. In the nature of things, trade and control, and the obligation to keep order which go with them, must come our way." Roosevelt agreed; disorder disrupted trade, interrupted America's civilizing mission, and invited European intervention. While still vice president, he had thought it necessary periodically to "spank" unruly Caribbean nations, and in October 1902 the U.S. Navy established a Caribbean squadron charged with enforcing political order. Referring to Venezuela in 1901, one naval officer expressed a general American perception. Diplomacy, he said, had little impact on "the semi-enlightened and uncultivated members of the present administration ... but they can appreciate the potential presence of a squadron of battleships."

It was the threatening presence of European battleships in Venezuelan waters that strengthened Roosevelt's resolve to impose order on the Caribbean. The ruthless Venezuelan dictator, Cipriano Castro, had provoked a combined British-German-Italian blockade and occupation on December 1902 by refusing either to pay or to arbitrate debts owed these nations. While Roosevelt cared nothing for Castro, whom he dismissed as a "villainous monkey," he feared the Germans would use the incident or similar ones to establish a permanent presence in the Western Hemisphere. The Venezuelan crisis was arbitrated in February 1903, but Roosevelt remained apprehensive.

His apprehension intensified as he watched the Dominican Republic "drifting into chaos." Plagued by chronic financial and political difficulties, the country had incurred millions of dollars in debts to both European and American creditors. Roosevelt was reluctant to allow Germany and Great Britain "to act as the policeman of the Caribbean." However, he confided to Root that, "if we intend to say 'Hands off' to the powers of Europe, sooner or later we must keep order ourselves." He put his solution before Congress in December 1904 in what came to be known as the "Roosevelt corollary" to the Monroe Doctrine: "Chronic wrongdoing" in the Americas could "require intervention by some civilized nation," and adherence to the Monroe Doctrine could force the United States "in flagrant cases of such wrongdoing or impotence" to serve as an "international police power."

Armed with this rationale, he pressured the Dominicans into accepting American loans and permitting the United States to administer its customs system, giving 45 percent of the receipts to the Dominican government and the remainder to its creditors. When the U.S. Senate rejected a treaty embodying this arrangement, Roosevelt ignored the legislators and implemented the plan through an executive agreement. Secretary of War Root reinforced American domination of the country and clearly foreshadowed subsequent attempts to fasten a sterile status quo on Latin America when he assigned U.S. military officers to train a rural police force. Having combined these measures with the presence of the U.S. Navy, Roosevelt announced in December 1905 that "all revolutionary movements" had been "completely discouraged" and that "stability and order and all the benefits of peace" were "at last coming to Santo Domingo."

The imposition of order and stability on the tumultuous Caribbean region also constituted one of the central goals of Roosevelt's handpicked successor, William Howard Taft. Genial and well intentioned, the corpulent Taft had helped oversee the growth of the American empire while serving as governor of the Philippines and as secretary of war, but he lacked both Roosevelt's grasp of and inclination to dominate his administration's foreign policy. As a result, Secretary of State Philander C. Knox played a prominent role.

Taft termed the policy that resulted from this collaboration "dollar diplomacy." Acutely aware of the nation's ever-expanding industrial production, he unabashedly declared "that the Government of the United States shall extend all proper support to every legitimate and beneficial enterprise abroad." While he emphasized the economic aspects of American imperialism more than either McKinley or

Roosevelt had done, the quest for order and stability remained central. Taft explained that he preferred to substitute dollars for bullets, and Knox elaborated concerning the Caribbean: "True stability is best established not by military, but by economic and social forces.... The problem of good government is inextricably interwoven with that of economic prosperity and sound finance; financial stability contributes perhaps more than any one factor to political stability." Similarly, Taft planned to secure a stable balance of power in China through economic means.

Both Taft and Knox would have preferred "some formal right" such as the Platt Amendment "to compel peace" by knocking Central American "heads together"; failing that, they turned to Roosevelt's Dominican formula. While the Taft administration meddled in Mexico and Honduras, its most ambitious attempt at stabilizing Caribbean affairs centered on Nicaragua and that country's aggressive dictator, José Santos Zelaya. Termed by Knox as a "blot upon the history of Nicaragua," Zelaya had attacked Honduras militarily in 1907 and thereafter sought to foment revolutions in El Salvador and Costa Rica. He had further aroused American ire by arbitrarily canceling two concessions held by U.S. citizens and by concluding a disturbing financial agreement with a European syndicate in May 1909. This agreement refinanced Nicaragua's national debt and provided for European control of the country's customs receipts in case of default. Undergirding all of Zelaya's actions was a fierce nationalism and defiance well summarized by his boast: "I ridicule the United States, laugh at Germany, and spit on England."

When a revolution, partially inspired by American firms, broke out against Zelaya's rule in October 1909, Taft and Knox could hardly conceal their glee. The execution of two captured Americans who had been fighting with the revolutionaries provided the pretext for intervention. Knox accused Zelaya of personally ordering the killings and declared that the revolution represented the majority of Nicaraguans. After Knox implicitly recognized Juan J. Estrada, the rebellion's leader, Zelaya perceived the futility of further resistance to U.S. power and fled to Mexico.

Zelaya's departure did not bring stability. Washington refused to accept his successor, José Madriz, contending that he was a Zelaya puppet, and the fighting continued. American intervention became even more direct the following May when U.S. Navy vessels and marines cordoned off the port city of Bluefields to protect Estrada's forces. After regrouping behind American defenses, Estrada gained tenuous control of the country in August 1910.

The Taft administration eagerly stood ready to apply dollar diplomacy. In return for diplomatic recognition, Washington demanded that Estrada request a loan guaranteed by Nicaragua's customs receipts and appoint customs officers approved by the United States. Estrada reluctantly consented, but, before the treaty was signed in May 1911, he was replaced as president by Adolfo Díaz, formerly the bookkeeper of an American mining company. All Taft's efforts went for naught when the U.S. Senate rejected the treaty and the application of the Dominican formula to Nicaragua.

Unable to make Nicaragua an official protectorate, as had been done with Cuba, Panama, and the Dominican Republic, Taft and Knox persuaded American bankers to advance funds, intercede with Nicaragua's European creditors, and administer the customs system. But order and stability remained elusive, and in July 1912 a revolution began against Díaz's rule. Dollar diplomacy having failed, Taft resorted to force, the ultimate American tactic in the Caribbean. He dispatched 2,500 marines and eight warships, stifled the rebellion, and ensured Díaz's reelection in 1913. As an ongoing symbol of Taft's failure to substitute dollars for bullets, American marines remained in Nicaragua until 1925.

Dollar diplomacy proved no more successful in China. At the time of Taft's election, one wag suggested that TAFT might well have stood for "Take Advice From Theodore." Nothing could have been less descriptive of his Far Eastern policy. Unlike his predecessor, Taft aggressively sought to enforce the Open Door and to increase American investments and trade in China, viewing this as good business. Together with Knox and key State Department members Willard Straight and Francis M. Huntington Wilson, the president also believed that large doses of American capital would contribute to a more stable balance of power by strengthening China and countering growing Japanese influence in Manchuria.

The administration initiated this policy in the summer of 1909 by demanding that American bankers be included in the Hukuang Railway loan. China had concluded an agreement in June with English, French, and German bankers for funds to build this road. After nearly one year of pressuring both the Europeans and the Chinese, Taft obtained reluctant agreement for American involvement. Knox explained this persistence, stating that he envisioned both economic benefits and "the right to proportional representation in the influence which attaches to the holding of the credits of the Chinese government." When internal Chinese opposition blocked the project, Knox succeeded only in exasperating the Europeans.

Undeterred, the secretary of state concocted another scheme, described by a British diplomat as "so vast and fantastic as almost to stagger the imagination." In October 1910, Straight, having left the State Department, negotiated an agreement with China to have an Anglo-American banking group finance a trans-Manchurian railway from Chinchou to Aigun. Hoping this agreement would furnish the leverage he needed to "smoke Japan out" of Manchuria, Knox called for an international syndicate to neutralize or internationalize all Manchurian railways. Most particularly, he sought to wrest the East Manchurian Railway from Russia and the South Manchurian Railway from Japan. If these countries refused to cooperate, he planned to proceed with the Chinchou-Aigun railroad. Japan and Russia responded by agreeing in July 1910 to defend the status quo in Manchuria. Knox's plan garnered only conflict with Russia and Japan; he had driven the two rivals together and prodded them to close the Open Door a bit more tightly. When he reverted to the Chinchou-Aigun railroad, he found the Chinese had not ratified the agreement and the British were unwilling to alienate Japan, their primary Asian ally.

In violating his earlier resolve not to let anything as "unimportant as China interfere" with his golf game, Knox made a final attempt to apply the Dominican formula. In September 1910 the Chinese approached American bankers for a loan to finance currency reform and Manchurian development. Knox consented but with the stipulation that an American be made the official financial adviser to China. At the urging of U.S. bankers, who had begun to harbor reservations about the Taft-Knox strategies, Britain, France, and Germany were invited to join the consortium. Each country assented but vetoed an American financial adviser to the Chinese government. Combined Japanese-Russian opposition further delayed implementation of the agreement until it fell victim to the revolution that overthrew China's Manchu dynasty in October 1911.

That a revolution had thwarted the loan carried both short- and long-term significance. In an immediate sense it starkly symbolized dollar diplomacy's failure either to stabilize China or to increase America's trade and investments. From a longer historical perspective, opposition to foreign domination constituted the primary component of the evolving Chinese nationalism. Anti-imperialism sparked the revolution of 1911 and would continue to be an integral part of the revolutionary process which ultimately brought Mao Zedong's victory in 1949.

As the Taft administration ended, the United States looked back over a decade and a half of intense imperial activity. From Cleveland through Taft, American policymakers had translated U.S. economic, ideological, and strategic objectives into the quest for an orderly and stable world. However, these policymakers never seemed to grasp the fact that U.S. actions as often as not caused disruption and instability. Throughout the period a persistent dichotomy had haunted U.S. imperial policy, a dichotomy between the goal of order and stability and the frequent result of disorder and conflict.

Indeed, American policies yielded mixed returns. In the Caribbean, the United States had expelled the Spanish, stifled European interventions, seized a canal route, begun construction of the waterway, increased investments from $100 million in 1902 to $1.5 billion in 1912, and imposed a tenuous peace by curbing the warfare between Central American states and reducing the incidence of revolutions. These goals, however, were accompanied by marked failures. Sanitary measures, new roads and buildings, and reformed customs services did little to relieve the pervasive poverty. Efforts to impose a conservative status quo through training rural guards and crushing revolutions did nothing to further representative governments and at best led only to autocratic, one-party rule. These economic and political failures were part of the larger, futile effort to export American institutions to Cuba and the Philippines. More importantly, the U.S. contemptuous and coercive treatment of the Latin Americans ignored their pride and nationalistic aspirations, confused stability with progress, and left a legacy of hatred and distrust. José Vargas-Villa, a well-known Colombian writer, graphically conveyed these sentiments when he referred to "the barbarians of the North," whose imperial policies were "the sport of savages," and the "doctrine of plundering, robbery, and conquest."

Far Eastern policies were even less successful. The costs of imposing order on the Philippines were appalling and the returns negligible. Neither the acquisition of these islands nor the proclamation of the Open Door policy increased trade with China. In fact, U.S. exports to China actually decreased from $53 million to $24 million between 1905 and 1912. Perceptive statesmen like Roosevelt recognized that the United States lacked both the power and the interests for a policy comparable to the Caribbean efforts. When others, such as Taft and Knox, failed to understand this, their attempts to strengthen China and augment American commerce served only to alienate European and Japanese competitors.

Perhaps most significantly the U.S. search for an orderly, stable world continued well beyond 1912. This emphasis on a status quo patterned after American institutions helped place the United States on a collision course with those twentieth-century nations and forces that found existing conditions unacceptable: modern, developed nations such as Germany, Japan, and Russia and revolutionary Third World nations like China, Cuba, and Vietnam.

Sources and Suggested Readings

Beisner, Robert L. *From the Old Diplomacy to the New, 1865–1900.* Arlington Heights, Illinois, 1986.

Burton, David H. *Theodore Roosevelt: Confident Imperialist.* Philadelphia, 1969.

Challener, Richard D. *Admirals, Generals, and American Foreign Policy, 1898–1914.* Princeton, 1975.

Cooper, John Milton, Jr. *The Warrior and the Priest: Woodrow Wilson and Theodore Roosevelt.* Cambridge, Massachusetts, 1983.

Field, James A., Jr. "American Imperialism: The Worst Chapter in Almost Any Book." *American Historical Review* 83 (1978): 644–68.

Gillette, Howard. "The Military Occupation of Cuba, 1899–1902: Workshop for American Progressivism." *American Quarterly* 25 (1973): 411–25.

Healy, David F. *The United States in Cuba, 1898–1902: Generals, Politicians, and the Search for Policy.* Madison, 1963.

————. *U.S. Expansionism: The Imperialist Urge in the 1890s.* Madison, 1970.

Hunt, Michael H. *The Making of a Special Relationship: The United States and China to 1914.* New York, 1983.

Israel, Jerry. *Progressivism and the Open Door: America and China, 1905–1921.* Pittsburgh, 1971.

LaFeber, Walter. *Inevitable Revolutions: The United States in Central America.* New York, 1983.

————. *The New Empire: An Interpretation of American Expansion, 1860–1898.* Ithaca, 1963.

Langley, Lester D. *The Banana Wars: United States Intervention in the Caribbean, 1898–1954.* Lexington, Kentucky, 1985.

Markowitz, Gerald E. "Progressivism and Imperialism: A Return to First Principles." *Historian* 37 (1975): 257–75.

Marks, Frederick W., III. *Velvet on Iron: The Diplomacy of Theodore Roosevelt.* Lincoln, 1979.

May, Ernest R. *American Imperialism: A Speculative Essay.* New York, 1968.

May, Glenn A. *Social Engineering in the Philippines: The Aims, Execution, and Impact of American Colonial Policy, 1900–1913.* Westport, 1980.

Miller, Stuart C. *"Benevolent Assimilation": The Conquest of the Philippines, 1899–1903.* New Haven, 1982.

Munro, Dana G. *Intervention and Dollar Diplomacy in the Caribbean, 1900–1921.* Princeton, 1964.

Pérez, Louis A. *Cuba Between Empires, 1878–1902.* Pittsburgh, 1983.
Scholes, Walter V., and Scholes, Marie V. *The Foreign Policies of the Taft Administration.* Columbia, 1970.
Trask, David F. *The War with Spain in 1898.* New York, 1981.
Welch, Richard E., Jr. *Response to Imperialism: The United States and the Philippine-American War, 1899–1902.* Chapel Hill, 1979.
Williams, William Appleman. *The Tragedy of American Diplomacy.* New York, 1962.

Woodrow Wilson
and U.S. Intervention
in World War I

Melvin Small

When World War I began in August 1914, those Americans who read the front pages of their newspapers clucked their tongues over the latest folly of the Old World. A few even began rooting for their favorites in the lethal contest: the Franco-British-Russian coalition or the Austro-German side. Most Americans, however, went on with their summertime activities and paid scant attention to the cataclysmic events on the Continent.

To a people insulated from the turmoil of Europe by the Atlantic Ocean and unencumbered by alliances, such nonchalance was understandable. American memories, however, were short. The last time Europe had been at war, from 1792 to 1815, the remote and weak United States became deeply involved economically, politically, and ultimately (in 1812) militarily. In 1914, no longer remote and weak, the United States was emerging as the most powerful country in the world and was the most important neutral for the major belligerents.

In 1917 the United States would enter the Great War. This involvement would have far greater impact on Americans than the War of 1812. When the guns finally fell silent on November 11, 1918, the United States would be the preeminent power in the world, its president a towering international figure, bringing his influence to bear in such far-flung places as Shantung and Siberia.

How this all came about has been a topic that has intrigued Americans almost from the day that President Woodrow Wilson went before Congress to ask for a declaration of war. The minority that had opposed intervention swelled in the 1920s when the world did not turn out as Wilson had promised and when the archives began to reveal that the "democratic" Allies were almost as disreputable as their enemies. When war clouds again appeared on the European horizon in the late 1930s, so many Americans looked back with distaste to the alleged blunder of April 1917 that Congress passed a series of neutrality acts that, in effect, were to keep the country out of the *First* World War.

The eddies of controversy that once swirled around the question of Wilson and his diplomacy from 1914 through 1917 have been forgotten today by all but a few historians. At the same time, the issues of that controversy are still salient, for they involve definitions of national security, the proper role of the president in foreign policy, and indeed, the control citizens have over that foreign policy. Much of the controversy centers around Woodrow Wilson.

Wilson was one of the best prepared of American presidents. A college professor and administrator before he entered politics in 1910, he had written a major textbook on U.S. government and was a noted historian. When he took office in 1913, he anticipated answering the call for reform from the Progressive Movement and devoting himself primarily to domestic politics, an area in which he felt most comfortable. As he commented, "It would be an irony of fate if my administration had to deal chiefly with foreign affairs."

Not the typical American politician, Wilson was a deep thinker with a well-developed view of the world and the nature of human interaction. His father was a minister and his mother the daughter of a minister. Although he did not enter the clergy, the spirituality and idealism that infused his thought made him the country's most prominent lay preacher. Concerned above all with principle, he understood the amorality of the game of international politics but never accepted it as the proper way for Christian nations to conduct their business.

Strong-willed and confident in his own vision, Wilson was a powerful leader who by war's end was looked to by people the world over as the person to guide them out of the ruinous cycle of imperial rivalries, arms races, and war. His idealism and his belief in a world without empires and alliance systems could also be interpreted as a highly realistic policy. That is, in breaking down the barriers to free economic interaction, he could enhance the peaceful expansion of America's informal empire.

Wilson understood the power of the presidency in foreign policy. The Constitution's checks and balances worked fairly well in apportioning power between Congress and the president on the domestic scene. When it came to international relations, the president held most of the cards. With Wilson's power to interpret neutrality law, his command of the armed forces, and the "bully pulpit" that he controlled, it was no contest in the conflict with Congress over American posture toward the belligerents.

At the start of the war, however, a war that many Americans believed would be over before the first snow fell, Wilson did not foresee that his administration would be dominated by foreign adventures. After all, most of the recent European wars had been limited affairs of several weeks or a few months. Thus, the United States could proclaim its traditional neutrality, and Europe would be back to normal in a short time.

America's "traditional neutrality" was easier to proclaim than to practice. In the abstract, neutrality could take three forms. A nation could be strictly neutral in a legalistic sense, apply its laws, treaties, and precedents to specific incidents, and let the chips fall where they may. In this case, legalistic neutrality might aid one belligerent more than another to a point where a neutral could tip the balance in the war. On the other hand, a nation could try to be fair to both sides, not allow its actions to determine the military outcome, and, consequently, decide to ignore legal precedents on occasion. A third, and rather unrealistic, option would be to close up one's ports and economy to belligerents and refuse to have anything to do with them until after the war, in which case a nation would be giving up the bonanza of increased trade that is normally available to neutrals during wartime. Moreover, this third option would be unfair to those belligerents that had every reason to expect that they would be able to buy needed materials in the neutral country.

Throughout the war Wilson maintained that he had selected the first option, that of scrupulous legal neutrality. In reality, although he would not admit it, he also was concerned with the impact of his policy on the military fortunes of the belligerents and, more importantly, with the maintenance of the U.S. lucrative war trade with the Continent.

When Wilson took office in March 1913, the United States was in a recession that spiraled down toward a depression by the summer of 1914. The war trade presented a much needed shot in the arm to the ailing American economy and, naturally, to Wilson's political fortunes. By 1915 hard times were over, and the economy boomed through the end of the war. When confronted with major assaults against American neutrality by the British on the high seas, Wilson could not lose sight of the fact that most of the war trade was with them. Any punitive severance of the economic link to Britain could lead to a drastic diminution of that trade which, in turn, could lead to a recession or depression.

The impact of economic variables is unmeasurable. Suffice it to say that for whatever reasons, fair-minded observers could conclude that Wilson tolerated many more violations of his country's neutrality from the British, with whom the United States had a most lucrative trading relationship, than he tolerated from the Germans. In his defense, it was true that, while British violations involved the loss of property and, to some degree, national prestige, German violations often involved the loss of human life.

Wilson's pursuit of neutrality was affected by general American attitudes toward the belligerents. When the war began the vast majority of his countrymen, perhaps as many as 80 percent, preferred a British to a German victory. At the same time, those who supported British arms did not feel as strongly about their favorites as did the minority that was fervently anti-British. This minority included many German-Americans, Irish-Americans who hated England, Jewish-Americans who hated England's ally Russia, and Scandinavian-Americans who feared Russian domination of their homelands. In many cases in a democracy, a minority that backs an issue strongly can compete with a majority that is only lukewarm in its support of the opposite side of that issue. In this case, the majority also included the powerful American intellectual, economic, and political elites, almost all of whom were pro-British. For many analysts this is the only group that counts in the formation of opinion, for its views must ultimately influence those of everyone else.

As the war progressed more and more Americans, who were relatively neutral or mildly pro-British, became strongly anti-German, owing to the influence of those American elites, British propaganda, real and fabricated German atrocities on land, submarine outrages at sea, and bumbling German spies caught in the United States. By 1917 the vast majority of the American population was prepared to join a crusade that would defeat Germany and make the world safe for democracy.

Interestingly, Wilson's attitudes toward the belligerents did not follow those of the general population. At the onset of the conflict, he instinctively blamed Germany for initiating a war against the England that he loved. Upon reflection, he realized that all of the blame was not on one side, and that the system was at fault more than any one single nation. Through the end of 1916, Wilson was relatively balanced in his judgment, although he never wavered from a fundamental Anglophilia. Yet, when he finally decided on war, he returned full circle to his original position and seemed to catch up with the rest of the population. In the spring of 1917, Wilson again blamed Germany for the entire war. Perhaps he had to convince himself of the rectitude of the British cause before he led his nation into war.

Whatever his personal feelings in the late summer of 1914, Wilson's early neutrality policies appeared to be both neutral and even-handed in their impact on the belligerents. Rulings that were in the German interest included a refusal to speak out against alleged German atrocities in occupied Belgium, an attempt to increase the number of neutral vessels plying the Atlantic by permitting the sale of German merchant ships bottled up in American waters when the war began, and a ban on the sale of submarine parts to England. Rulings that were in the British interest included the seizure of two German wireless stations in the United States and the refusal to demand that England adhere to the London Naval Treaty of 1909, a treaty it had not signed because it permitted neutral merchant vessels far more freedom to trade with belligerents than Britain could accept.

As the war dragged on, three other major policies tipped the balance toward England. The first is the most controversial. When the war began, Wilson adopted an unusual policy for a neutral. He banned private American loans to belligerents since money, "the worst of all contrabands," bought all others. Historically, it had always been proper for neutral bankers to make loans to belligerents. Now Wilson took the high road and forbade those loans. Unfortunately for his claim to consistency, he took a lower road in 1915 when the British, whose orders for food and war materials had catapulted the United States from recession to boom, began to run out of cash. Confronted with the prospect of a new recession, Wilson reversed himself and permitted credits and loans which the British used to buy U.S. materials essential to their war effort. On the surface, this policy was entirely legal; all belligerents could make loans in the United States. It was not Wilson's fault that American bankers much preferred doing business with England than with Germany. However, Wilson had gone on record earlier against this sort of traffic, and his reversal belied his claim to a new, highly moral brand of neutrality.

A second major neutrality policy that favored England involved Wilson's acceptance of the American arms trade with the belligerents. Since the British controlled the seas, most of this deadly material arrived in the Allied camp and ultimately was used to kill Germans. As with the American loan policy of 1915, trade in contraband was legal. Moreover, according to the president, were it not permitted, those belligerents that had been less militaristic, and thus not so well armed, prior to the war would have been at a disadvantage once the war began. As for the one-sided nature of the trade, Wilson noted coolly that the Atlantic Ocean had been around for a long time; it was too bad that the Germans had not taken account of that geographic fact.

Finally, when the British mined the North Sea and made it virtually impossible for neutral vessels to reach Germany without first stopping in England for sailing instructions through the minefields and for inspection, Wilson did not protest. Again, mining was a legal belligerent act, although no nation had ever mined an entire sea before. The Germans questioned the difference between mines, which Wilson accepted, and submarines, which he opposed. There was legal precedent for mining but none for submarine warfare, responded Wilson. More importantly, since mines were very effective, few neutral vessels dared to enter the fields without stopping in England; thus, loss of life attributable to mines was minimal. Submarine warfare was not as effective. Therefore, neutral vessels took their chances in the German war zone and occasionally were sunk, with consequent loss of life. Had more lives been lost as a result of the mining, Wilson might have been more receptive to German protests against American acceptance of that mining.

Wilson's interpretation of neutrality law was favorable to England. London was able to buy weapons in the United States, using American private loans to finance those purchases. Any neutral vessel that hoped to sell contraband to Germany risked the perils of the mined North Sea. Yet, what should Wilson have done? It was not his fault that the British controlled the Atlantic. Furthermore, the war trade with England was essential to American economic recovery. In any event, all of Wilson's measures could be defended as being within the bounds of international law and historical precedent. Throughout the war he maintained that America was scrupulously neutral and fair to both sides. The Germans were incredulous, for they could well see how the president's brand of neutrality was contributing significantly to the success of Allied arms. One can understand their frustration with Wilson and the United States in 1917 when they finally adopted a submarine policy that led the world's most prominent neutral into war against them.

From the Germans' perspective, Wilson not only erected a pro-British structure of neutrality law, but he also tolerated far too many violations of American rights on the high seas. In the quantitative sense, the Germans were absolutely correct, but how does one equate the loss of human life with the loss of property?

As in previous wars, Britain was mistress of the seas and controlled its domain imperiously. As usual, its navy's definition of neutral rights and the neutrals' definitions of their rights were at odds. Neutrals wanted to be able to sell almost anything to any belligerent without being subject to seizure by the British navy. For their part, the British tried to choke off neutral trade with Germany by using the broadest possible interpretation of contraband and by violating other nations' conceptions of the laws of search and seizure. Knowing the sensitivity of the Americans, the Admiralty did not tighten all of the screws at once. Indeed, had the British been violating American rights in 1914 in the manner in which they were in 1916, Wilson might have been forced to break relations at the outset of the war. Instead, they tightened the screws almost imperceptibly, first adding this item and then another to the contraband list, often changing the rules during periods of major German-American tension.

Such violations of American neutral rights were not ignored by Wilson. Each resulted in the filing of a formal protest, with such protests increasing in number and intensity until, as one wag noted, the State Department ran out of stationery. There was a point in late 1916 when British violations were so flagrant and frequent (the German submarine warfare was dormant) that Americans finally considered retaliatory legislation against London, including an embargo. In a classic case of cutting off one's nose to spite one's face, such action in late 1916 would not have caused England to cease and desist but would have brought about another American recession. Therefore, Wilson never went any further than strongly worded protests which London did not take seriously.

The British also were guilty of a variety of other offensive practices, including hovering just outside the three-mile limit in a most unsporting fashion, intercepting American mail on U.S. vessels, removing foreign nationals from those vessels, flying American flags on their own merchant ships to deceive German submarines, and, in 1916, issuing a blacklist of American firms that were trading with Germany and its allies. Protesting against all of these actions, Wilson blustered and threatened but never actually told the British to refrain from such behavior or else. "Or else" meant the closing down of Anglo-American trade, and by 1916 the United States needed that trade for economic stability as much as England needed U.S. supplies for the war.

To Wilson, the German assault upon American neutral rights was another story. When the war began, control of the seas belonged to

England, an island nation that depended upon oceangoing commerce to maintain its economy and supply lines. Even though the German surface fleet was the second largest in the world, it was no match for Britain's. Still, if only the Germans could attack the British on the high seas, their chances on land would improve immeasurably.

Germany did have several submarines in its naval arsenal, newfangled devices that had not been used in warfare to any extent until World War I. After some tentative experimentation in the fall of 1914, the Germans discovered that submarines were surprisingly effective; they had a new offensive naval weapon. In early February 1915, Berlin announced that as of February 18 England would be subjected to a submarine blockade. Within a clearly defined war zone, German submarines would attempt to sink all British vessels, including merchantmen. The Germans urged neutrals to keep their people and property off ships that flew British flags. As for neutral merchantmen, German submarine commanders would try their best to avoid mistakes.

The Germans thus began to employ a novel weapon for which no international laws existed. In the absence of precedent, Wilson argued that submarines had to follow the detailed etiquette of naval warfare that had long been applied to surface vessels. For example, when a submarine commander wanted to blow an enemy merchantman out of the water, the commander first had to surface and warn the merchantman of his intentions. A submarine was therefore virtually worthless once it relinquished attack by surprise and surfaced. Those small World War I submarines were quite vulnerable to being rammed by surface vessels and were so thin-skinned that the relatively small cannon mounted on merchantmen could destroy them. Obviously, if a submarine behaved like a surface vessel, its value would be significantly diminished. Nevertheless, Wilson maintained that submarines were no different from other ships of the line. If they struck without warning against nonmilitary targets, he would hold them to what he called "strict accountability." However, he never held the British strictly accountable for their violations of neutral rights.

Incidents involving Americans were bound to happen. In late March 1915, one American went down with a British steamer in the war zone, a victim of a German torpedo. While Wilson and his cabinet were hammering out a response, a much larger vessel, the British passenger liner *Lusitania*, was sunk on May 7. This time 128 Americans were among the almost 1,200 who lost their lives. At no point up to 1917 was the American population more outraged at the

Germans. To no avail the leaders in Berlin claimed that they had warned neutrals not to travel on the liner because they considered the *Lusitania* to be part of the British war machine. Furthermore, they pointed out that it carried munitions and was heavily armed. The latter charge has never been proved. Whether armed or not, the *Lusitania* was primarily a passenger vessel, and the German submarine commander, who had been publicly honored for his marksmanship, had struck without warning. The unpleasant image of the brutal Prussian, enhanced by atrocity stories associated with the occupation of Belgium, was indelibly etched in American memories. Although German submarines never again sank a passenger vessel with so much loss of civilian life, Americans never forgot the *Lusitania*.

Even before a furious Wilson was able to obtain an apology and settlement from the Germans for the celebrated sinking, the *Arabic*, another British liner, went down with the loss of two American lives. In response, a contrite German ambassador pledged that such occurrences would not happen again and that his nation would pay indemnities. For the remainder of 1915, German submarines operated cautiously and successfully avoided incidents that could enrage the United States. Germany's luck or circumspection ran out in March 1916 when the *Sussex* was sunk, in apparent violation of the *Arabic* Pledge. After strong threats from Wilson, Berlin produced a new pledge, the *Sussex* Pledge, in which Germany promised not to sink without warning vessels carrying passengers. This promise, however, was conditional upon British acceptance of neutral rights. Later, when the Germans violated the *Sussex* Pledge, they claimed they had every right to do so since the neutrals had not compelled London to alter its illegal practices on the high seas. Wilson rejected the argument, refusing to acknowledge the the *Sussex* Pledge was conditional. This pledge was observed through January 1917 when Berlin adopted a new submarine policy that forced Wilson's hand. The decision for unlimited submarine warfare was influenced by the failure to develop acceptable mediation plans.

Throughout the war, Wilson engaged in a variety of schemes in which he either would serve as an honest broker or at least bring the warring parties to the peace table. His task became more and more difficult as this first "total war" dragged on. Wilson proposed a peace without victors. How did one make such a compromise peace with an enemy that had to be painted as the devil incarnate in order to obtain the requisite sacrifices from one's citizenry?

In addition, the Germans were always slightly suspicious about the Anglophilic Wilson's professed evenhandedness. For example,

his most serious mediation proposal was the House-Grey Memorandum of February 1916. Colonel Edward M. House, Wilson's
chief diplomatic adviser, journeyed to London, Paris, and Berlin. In
London, House tried to lure the British to the peace table with a plan
that suggested possible American entry into the war if the British
agreed to talks and the Germans did not. Berlin was not given the
same bargain.

Wilson offered his final and most impartial mediation proposal in
late 1916 when he was far more exasperated with the British than
with the Germans. At almost the same time, the German government
gave peace one last chance and floated its own program. When the
American and German proposals failed, Berlin decided to go for
broke.

In January 1917 the German High Command made its fateful
decision to move from limited to unlimited submarine warfare. As of
February 1 all vessels carrying contraband, enemy and neutral alike,
were declared fair game in the German war zone around the British
Isles. Up to this point, submarine commanders had been relatively
genteel in the use of their weapons. With hopes for a German victory
fading, the submarine was to be unleashed in a desperate attempt to
bring England to its knees. According to the decision makers in
Berlin, the balance of power was slowly shifting toward the Allies,
especially considering their relative economic strength. The time had
come to do all that was needed to obtain a swift victory in 1917.

As for the most prominent neutral, from the Germans' perspective, the United States had discriminated against them in its unequal
application of neutrality laws. The *Sussex* Pledge had not been
violated, they contended, since it was conditional. The Germans
knew that unlimited submarine warfare was likely to move the
United States from neutrality to belligerency, but they thought that
the war would be over before a single American doughboy arrived in
France. Their timetable was correct in one respect in that U.S.
soldiers did not have an impact until 1918. They erred, however, in
thinking that the unleashed submarine would cripple England in a
matter of months.

Significantly, Wilson opposed preparedness measures in 1914 and
1915. Only in 1916 did he launch programs to increase America's
military and naval strength. Thus the Germans knew that the United
States was woefully unprepared for war in 1917. Had the nation been
better prepared, had American soldiers been ready to jump into
troop ships that would take them to the battlefields of France, the
Germans might have thought twice about risking American
belligerency.

Whatever marginal fault one can find with Wilson for not preparing his nation better, he was confronted with a serious crisis not of his own making. He had gone on record against the use of the submarine in the manner announced by the Germans and was wholeheartedly supported in that position by most Americans. Through 1917 ten American vessels had been sunk by mistake; in March nine were sunk on purpose. Each day's newspaper brought a new horror story about Americans lost at sea.

Wilson's move toward war was aided by two other events. First, the Russian revolution of February–March 1917 meant that the tyrannical czar was no longer a member of the alliance led by democratic England and France. The new Russian government was at first decidedly democratic and reformist, according to Wilson a "fit partner" for the United States.

The second and more important event was the Zimmermann Telegram. German Foreign Minister Arthur Zimmermann sent a message to his embassy in Mexico City, urging his diplomats to try to induce Mexico to join the German side in exchange for the territories taken by the United States in 1848. The telegram was intercepted by the British intelligence service and handed over to the Americans. To make matters worse, when the story leaked out, Zimmermann admitted that he had been the author of the dispatch. Wilson compounded Germany's public relations problem when he released the infamous document to the American press. Undoubtedly, by the time he decided to go public with it, he wanted to obtain strong popular backing for his increasingly tough line toward Berlin.

President Wilson had three options in February 1917. The first was to acquiesce in the German policy and ban American vessels and citizens from the war zone. Such a move would have kept the United States out of war. It also would have crippled Anglo-American commerce, and, more importantly, for Wilson and many Americans, it would have represented an unconscionable truckling to an allegedly immoral weapon wielded by a brutal people. In the latter respect, Wilson believed that he not only had to defend American national honor but the honor of all of the civilized world as well.

Wilson's second option, midway between turning the other cheek and entering the war, was armed neutrality. Although he was unable to obtain congressional authority to arm American merchantmen, he did use executive authority to effect that policy. Armed neutrality, however, was only a stopgap measure. The cannons mounted on American vessels could not contend with submarines that no longer adhered to naval etiquette.

By the middle of March, Wilson became convinced that national security could be protected only by entering the war on the Allied side. Moreover, he argued, once on the Allied side, he could use his influence to construct a peace that would establish a new international order. On April 2 he went before Congress to ask for a declaration of war. The six senators and fifty representatives who refused to go along with their colleagues on April 6, the date war was formally declared, reflected accurately the sizable antiwar minority in the nation at large.

Most of Congress and the country thrilled to Wilson's stirring war message. He took the high ground with the immediate cause for his decision—the submarine—serving only as a symbol of the immorality of the German leadership. In oversimplified terms, Wilson blamed Germany for starting and prolonging the war and promised that democracy would be made safe once the Prussian menace was destroyed. What Wilson did not choose to discuss in his speech was revealing. He did not mention the European balance of power, the significance of American trade with Britain, the heavy investments U.S. financiers had made in the Allied cause, or the secret imperialist designs of France and England, among others, in the "democratic" coalition.

On the other hand, by choosing to emphasize the idealistic nature of U.S. entry into war, Wilson increased the number of Americans who accepted the dramatic deviation from their country's tradition of isolation. It is impossible to determine how much of Wilson's personal rationale was presented in his public request for war. Undoubtedly, he was convinced that German submarine warfare reflected the innate inhumanity of the Prussian character as compared to the Anglo-Saxon. Surely he could not have forgotten his earlier, more sophisticated analyses that emphasized the structural failings of the European international system and British violations of neutral rights.

Whatever Wilson really believed, unlimited submarine warfare was the catalyst that moved him to ask for a declaration of war. One can sympathize with the Germans who were frustrated with Wilson's acceptance of neutrality policies that were skewed toward Britain. After all, unlimited submarine warfare can be interpreted as an understandable response to Britain's unlawful behavior in the Atlantic, unlawful behavior that greatly enhanced its capacity to make war on the Continent against Germany and the Central Powers.

A genuinely pacific man who abhorred war, Wilson was convinced that his country's honor and security, and indeed, the honor and security of the civilized world, were at stake. From today's perspective, the picture is less clear, especially when we remember how the Germans linked their policies to Wilson's perceived unneutrality.

According to most analysts, national security can involve three components: a military dimension, an economic dimension, and a prestige dimension. (A fourth, the moral dimension, must be dismissed as irrelevant in the real world of international politics.) In the spring of 1917 the Germans did not pose an immediate military threat to the United States. To be sure, American civilians were assaulted on the Atlantic, but there was no direct threat to U.S. territory and none to American vessels had they chosen to stay out of the submarine-blockaded area. A national security justification for war must be found elsewhere.

The German submarine blockade did pose an economic threat. The health of the American economy was dependent upon trade with Britain. A diminution of that trade could have resulted in a recession. Yet, how much of an economic downturn merited the resort to arms? That is a deep philosophical question for which each observer may have his own answer.

In the same vein, the submarine blockade was a clear challenge to American prestige or honor. Supported by his constituents, Wilson had proclaimed early on that his country could never accept unlimited submarine warfare. To back down, according to those who can justify war on the grounds of honor, would be to sully the name of the United States and to make the country look so weak that aggressors might try to get away with even more direct challenges to national sovereignty. Most wars originate in perceived threats to national honor. American involvement in World War I was no exception.

With Wilson's decision for war the United States at last became a full participant in the international system, a position into which it had been slowly moving since the turn of the century. Doubtless, the nation would have taken its place at the table of the mighty sooner or later, given its immense economic power and political and cultural influence. Still, the manner of entry into the system had a major impact on future U.S. behavior.

For the short run, Wilson's simplistic and idealistic public presentation of American policies led to disillusionment and partial retreat from the system once the world did not turn out as he had promised. Also, the perceived mistakes of 1917 crippled the hands of U.S. leaders in the 1930s who wanted to curb Axis aggression before it was too late. Finally, the manner in which Wilson almost single-handedly determined neutrality policy and defined the international situation for the public served as a dramatic lesson for later presidents who exerted enormous power over their countrymen as they involved them in crises in every corner of the globe. In most cases, American money, diplomats, and sometimes soldiers were sent in the name of Wilson's policy of making the world safe for democracy.

Sources and Suggested Readings

Buehrig, Edward H. *Woodrow Wilson and the Balance of Power.* Bloomington, Indiana, 1955.

Coogan, John W. *The End of Neutrality: The United States, Britain, and Maritime Rights, 1899–1915.* Ithaca, 1981.

Devlin, Patrick. *Too Proud to Fight: Woodrow Wilson's Neutrality.* New York, 1975.

Gregory, Ross. *The Origins of American Intervention in the First World War.* New York, 1971.

Karp, Walter. *The Politics of War: The Story of Two Wars Which Altered Forever the Political Life of the American Republic (1890–1920).* New York, 1979.

Link, Arthur S. *Wilson.* 5 vols. Princeton, 1947–1965.

———— *Woodrow Wilson: Revolution, War, and Peace.* Arlington Heights, Illinois, 1979.

May, Ernest R. *The World War and American Isolation, 1914–1917.* Cambridge, Massachusetts, 1959.

Small, Melvin. *Was War Necessary? National Security and US Entry Into War.* Beverly Hills, 1980.

Smith, Daniel M. *The Great Departure: The United States and World War I, 1914–1920.* New York, 1965.

————. "National Interest and American Intervention, 1917: An Historiographical Appraisal." *Journal of American History* 52 (June 1965): 5–25.

Tansill, Charles C. *America Goes to War.* Boston, 1938.

The United States and the
Versailles Peace Settlement

William C. Widenor

In the unstable and dangerous world in which we live, some of us have come to believe that the ethics of actions in international politics can be appraised only in terms of results and not in terms of intentions. No one has ever seriously questioned President Woodrow Wilson's devotion to securing a "just" peace to conclude World War I and constructing a better world. The more important question is whether he possessed true political wisdom, whether he understood how to attain the best results that circumstances would permit.

Whatever the shortcomings of the American peace commission that went to Paris in 1919 to negotiate a treaty to end World War I, it did not lack expert advice. Wilson's oft-heralded commission of expertise, frequently called The Inquiry, studied most of the international problems likely to arise in the course of peacemaking and supplied him with some two thousand reports. Such knowledge, however, never coalesced into a philosophy of international relations or a coherent approach to the construction of a lasting peace. Reports did not constitute plans, least of all blueprints for a workable international organization. In many ways the United States was as unprepared for bringing about peace as it originally had been unprepared for war. Historically, Americans had little experience in making other than bilateral peace treaties, and they were unaccustomed to thinking in terms of the requisites of a lasting peace.

Both the initial reaction of the American people to the outbreak of war in Europe, and their subsequent efforts to distance themselves from it and to arrange a "peace without victory," had much to do with the manner in which the United States finally went to war in April 1917. That in turn had a profound effect on the American view of a proper peace settlement. As Robert Osgood once put it, "Because neither war nor peace seemed related to any enduring self-interest, the motives which led to war were not adequate for the prosecution of war, and the objects for which the nation fought were not sufficiently compelling to sustain the break with isolation that was necessary for their fulfillment." Into this breach stepped the great American idealist and master propagandist, Woodrow Wilson. Essentially, the Wilsonian argument for war was that the United States as a participant, rather than as an onlooker, would be able to exert greater influence on behalf of its ideals in shaping a new world order and a just peace. It was Wilson's moral leadership that finally enabled America's pacifists and idealists to acquiesce in the unpleasant fact of U.S. participation in the war. Only the loftiest motives were capable of reconciling them to such organized violence.

The American people go to war in their own peculiar way. Messianism seems a recurrent propensity of American society in times of international conflict. Only high moral purposes can justify a supposedly moral society's engaging in war; all other wars are by definition immoral. As recent American history all too strongly attests, the United States has found it extremely difficult to fight wars that are limited in either scope or object. The pity of this is that in consequence only huge wars, and only those raising important ethical issues, are worthy of moral approbation. In 1917 a large minority in the country opposed American entry, and it was necessary to rally them to the cause. Woodrow Wilson knew how.

Both American war aims and expectations with respect to the peace—Wilson's Fourteen Points and Four Principles—were a function of these circumstances, but another important factor was involved. The kind of peace that was required developed rather naturally from one's view of the inception and character of the war itself. Take, for example, the various theories regarding the causes of the war. Merely to state the theories (the French theory that the war was completely Germany's fault, the British theory that it was the result of the breakdown of the Concert of Europe, and Wilson's belief that it was a function of the old order, of the political and social structure of the conservative regimes of Europe) is to understand what profound implications were contained therein for one's perspective as to the kind of settlement necessary for a lasting peace. Essentially, Wilson blamed the "old system," the old way of doing things, that included the traditional diplomacy of both England and France, countries on whose side the United States would fight but with whom Wilson would only "associate," not "ally," the United

States. The old system was variously particularized as the old diplomacy, the old balance-of-power system, and the absence of democratic control over foreign policy. In this view, because the fault lay in the system, however defined, attribution of guilt or innocence to individual belligerents was of little relevance. The need was to change the scheme of things entirely, to democratize and also, unfortunately, to Americanize it. The need was to set the world's peoples free and to encourage self-determination. Only a nation that determined its own destiny could be democratic, and only a democracy could be trusted to love peace and to make a new world order work. This was in essence the view held by Wilson in 1914 and one that he never really abandoned, but still another consideration led to his enunciation of the Fourteen Points. They were designed as a statement of war aims and as an instrument of propaganda, both at home and abroad, intended to cause the Allied peoples to quicken their efforts and to weaken enemy resistance by holding out the seductive hope of a just peace.

For all their obvious attractions and political popularity, Wilson's proposals were not quite the concrete plan for peace that his partisans later depicted them to be. As British economist John Maynard Keynes once complained, Wilson's ideas were very nebulous: "He could have preached a sermon on any of them or have addressed a stately prayer to the Almighty for their fulfillment, but he could not frame their concrete application to the actual state of Europe." His famous fourteenth point, calling for a universal collective security organization, was particularly undeveloped. It was difficult to oppose "a general association of nations to be formed under specific covenants for the purpose of affording mutual guarantees of political independence and territorial integrity to great and small states alike," but that did not mean that there was any agreement as to how those guarantees would be effected. Moreover, in enunciating his program, Wilson had sown many seeds of future difficulty. His extravagant promises of future world harmony were bound to come back to haunt him as it became clear that he had no magic formula for reconciling the claims of competitive nation-states. In addition, his was a peace program conceived in pacifist abstention from the war and probably much better suited to a "peace without victory," but the very act of entering the war meant that the United States would sit at the peace conference not as a disinterested mediator but as a victorious ally. The transition was a difficult one, and Wilson's task as peacemaker was formidable.

When in October 1918 the war was going badly for the Central Powers but (and this is important to note) before their armies had been completely defeated and before there were substantial Allied troops on German soil, the Central Powers sued for peace on the basis of the Fourteen Points. Their application was accepted by Wilson, and an armistice was finally concluded on November 11, 1918, even though the Allies themselves did not agree upon the meaning of the Fourteen Points (indeed, several of them had been drafted to be deliberately vague). The British insisted on an important modification and the French on a significant clarification. The modification was that the Allies should retain complete liberty in the matter of the freedom of the seas. In other words, they would not be bound by Wilson's pledge and would be free to institute blockades in the future. The clarification was that the restoration of evacuated territory by Germany should include compensation for damages to the civilian population. To any but the uninitiated that clearly meant reparations. These emerging ambiguities in the Allied peace program, portentous as they were, paled in significance before the fact that the manner in which the war was concluded left considerable doubt as to whether the peace was to be imposed or negotiated. The Germans certainly expected a negotiated peace, and in that they were to be gravely disappointed.

In what frame of mind and with what expectations did Wilson approach the peace conference? On November 18, 1918, two weeks after the mid-term election in which his party lost its majorities in both houses of Congress (with the result that Wilson's critics both at home and abroad could henceforth claim that he was the only one of the leading statesmen at Paris who did not command a legislative majority in his own country), Wilson startled the nation with the announcement that, contrary to American precedent, he personally was going to Paris as the head of the U.S. peace delegation. He apparently believed that only by appearing in person and using the weight of his enormous prestige could he secure the just and lasting peace which he had been advocating. What is unfortunately all too clear is that Wilson held an exalted view of both his own role and that of the United States. While en route to France in December, he not only claimed that "we would be the only disinterested people at the Peace Conference" but also boldly told the other members of the American delegation that the European leaders did not really represent their respective peoples (which was false) and that, if they did not do what he wanted, he would appeal to their people over their heads (which naturally did not work). Just as his partisans among historians would later depict the struggle, Wilson himself actually believed that he was engaged in a contest to determine whether his principles of a new world order would prevail over the dictates of reactionary nationalism. Americans are particularly inclined to think that they have principles, whereas other countries have only ambitions.

Wilson faced a task far more difficult than he knew. The war had destroyed the traditional European order and had resulted in what Raymond Sontag has so aptly called "a broken world." Unfortunately speed was at a premium. Europe was not only exhausted but also hungry. Anxiety was at a fever pitch. As Herbert Hoover put it, "The wolf is at the door of the world." The image was undoubtedly meant both figuratively and literally. There was a widespread fear, inflamed by temporary Bolshevik successes in both Bavaria and Hungary, that the Red menace was spreading westward, and there were many at the peace conference who sought to turn that fear to their own national advantage. As Ray Stannard Baker once claimed, "Paris cannot be understood without Moscow."

The changing nature of international politics also presented problems. Expectations ran dangerously high, and Wilson was not without responsibility for that state of affairs. This was to be the first great peace conference at which the diplomats were expected to conduct their negotiations in the open and with due consideration for public opinion. Wilson arrived in France on December 13 and was greeted with such an enthusiastic reception, not only in France but in England and Italy as well, that it was easy for him to misinterpret European public opinion and to assume that his version of a peace settlement would meet with nearly universal acclaim. Public opinion, however, was never unitary, and it was soon divided into thirty-two separate opinions, the number of nations in actual attendance at the peace conference.

The absence of Germany and Russia did not mean that harmony would prevail. Neither did Wilson's realization that open diplomacy was the enemy of negotiation and compromise, and that the important decisions had to be reserved for consideration by the Big Four (David Lloyd George of Great Britain, Georges Clemenceau of France, Vittorio Orlando of Italy, and Wilson himself). Both his ascendant popularity, which invited jealousy, and the feeling that Wilson and the United States did not deserve their preeminent position at the peace table, due to their tardy but crucial participation in the war, invited problems with the European leaders.

Moreover, those same leaders operated from an entirely different philosophical basis. They were suspicious of American intentions, believing that a conflict of interest was inevitable, both because all states had interests and could not be trusted to act contrary to them and because America, protected by the Atlantic, might be more interested in satisfying its self-righteous image of itself than in undertaking real commitments to enforce the peace in Europe. Clemenceau, remembering that the Germans had been turned back by bayonets and bullets, not by idealism, was particularly skeptical and could not think of Wilson without derogatory reference to his messianic complex. As he told Wilson's adviser and close friend Colonel Edward M. House, "You are practical, I understand you, but talking to Wilson is something like talking to Jesus Christ." In specific reference to the Fourteen Points, Clemenceau reportedly said that "God gave us his Ten Commandments and we broke them. Wilson gave us his 14 points—well, we shall see." The French and the Italians were, on the whole, much more skeptical than the British, but then they had a history of opposition to Anglo-Saxon cant. As Harold Nicolson, a member of the British delegation, once described their attitudes,

> They [the Latins] observed, for instance, that the United States in the course of their short but highly imperialistic history, had constantly proclaimed the highest virtue while as constantly violating their professions and resorting to the grossest materialism. They observed that all Americans liked to feel in terms of Thomas Jefferson but to act in terms of Alexander Hamilton. They observed that such principles as the equality of man were not applied either to the yellow man or to the black. They observed that the doctrine of self-determination had not been extended either to the Red Indians or even to the Southern States. They were apt to examine "American principles and American tendencies" not in terms of the Philadelphia declaration, but in terms of the Mexican War, of Louisiana, of those innumerable treaties with the Indians which had been violated shamelessly before the ink was dry. They observed that, almost within living memory, the great American Empire had been won by ruthless force. Can we blame them if they doubted, not so much the sincerity as the actual applicability of the gospel of Woodrow Wilson? Can we blame them if they feared lest American realism would, when it came to the point, reject the responsibility of making American idealism safe for Europe? Can we wonder that they preferred the precisions of their own old system to the vague idealism of a new system which America might refuse to apply even to her own continent?

The traditional and Wilsonian explanation emphasizes two essential goals. First, Wilson wanted a peace settlement of justice based, with respect to territorial adjustments, upon the principle of self-determination, a settlement that would leave no sores to serve as centers of infection productive of future wars. Second, he desired the creation of a League of Nations to ensure permanent peace. Revisionist critics have charged that his real interest lay in the construction of a peaceful, liberal, capitalist world order designed to assure both the moral and economic preeminence of the United States. Although one might quibble with the latter interpretation and insist that personally Wilson seemed much more intent on claiming moral preeminence, the virtue of the revisionist argument lies in its recognition that the United States was an ordinary country intent, as were all others, on the protection of its own interests. Moreover, it too was represented at Paris by men who had reputations to protect and constituencies to serve.

Wilson's principal antagonist at the peace conference, and his intellectual opposite in all matters pertaining to the assessment of the behavior of men and nations, was Clemenceau. From the French premier's conservative, skeptical point of view, conflicts among states were inevitable, and, although his country had prevailed over Germany on this particular occasion by assembling a powerful coalition against it, German resources and potential military power were such that even in victory France found itself in a precarious position. From the French perspective a Wilsonian peace would likely result in shortening the interval of Germany's recovery and hastening the day when that nation would seek to avenge its temporary defeat. The only security for France lay in the reduction of German power and the exaction of guarantees against its rising again. As Keynes once explained,

> So far as possible, therefore, it was the policy of France to set the clock back and to undo what, since 1870, the progress of Germany has accomplished. By loss of territory and other measures her population was to be curtailed; but chiefly the economic system, upon which she depended for her new strength, the vast fabric built upon iron, coal, and transport, must be destroyed. If France could seize, even in part, what Germany was compelled to drop, the inequality of strength between the two rivals for European hegemony might be remedied for many generations.

Such a program, Carthaginian in both philosophy and effect, represented a challenge to Wilson's conception of what was likely to make for a lasting peace at every fundamental point: disarmament of Germany as against general disarmament, a league of victors determined to prevent Germany from ever "breaking out" again as against a universal collective security organization, indemnities designed to cripple Germany as against simple reparations, and some dismemberment of Germany as against a peace based on the principle of self-determination. In fact, just beneath the surface of practically every problem confronting the peace conference lay the question of how France could best be protected against Germany.

Wilson had advantages on his side but also serious obstacles in his path. One advantage was the extraordinary position of moral leadership to which he had risen. His eloquent statements of idealistic war aims had made him a hero to liberals everywhere and had led war-weary and oppressed populations throughout the world to hail him as their deliverer, as the one person capable of making a just peace. This moral leadership, however, was bound to decline as ideals were forced to give way to practical considerations and as the aspirations of different national groups, such as the Italians and Yugoslavs, proved to be mutually incompatible. Inevitably, justice had a different face to every one of the nations concerned. But, in addition to this moral influence, all the traditional instruments of power lay in Wilson's hands. His severest critics, Keynes and Nicolson, always made much of this point. As Keynes expressed it,

> The American armies were at the height of their numbers, discipline, and equipment. Europe was in complete dependence on the food supplies of the United States; and financially she was even more at their mercy. Europe not only already owed the United States more than she could pay; but only a large measure of further assistance could save her from starvation and bankruptcy. Never had a philosopher held such weapons wherewith to bind the princes of this world.

One obstacle to a Wilsonian peace was the group of secret treaties and agreements that the Allies had made among themselves before the United States entered the war. France had been promised by Russia, although not by Great Britain, not only the return of Alsace-Lorraine but also possession of the Saar valley and the conversion of German territory west of the Rhine into an independent buffer state. Italy had been assured of large accessions of Austrian territory in the southern Tyrol and about the head of the Adriatic Sea, and Japan had been promised the German islands in the North Pacific and the inheritance of German rights in Shantung, a particularly important province of China. The French and Italian claims in Europe and Japan's claim to Shantung were destined to be the real headaches.

A second obstacle in Wilson's path was the vindictive spirit prevalent among the peoples of the Allied countries, including the United States, a spirit that, because these were democratic countries, had to be taken into account. The domestic politics of Britain (witness the so-called Khaki Election of December 1918) and France were such that few politicians could resist the temptation to seek domestic political advantage by upping the ante as to what should be demanded from the Germans by way of compensation. Thus the very democracy that Wilson thought a safeguard against war proved to be a barrier to a statesmanlike peace. The people were bloodthirsty and wanted retribution.

Still a third obstacle to Wilson's program was the awareness on the part of the other negotiators that he and his party were in political difficulty at home, and that Wilson had long ceased to be a prophet among his own people. As Nicolson once stated, "The tragedy of the American delegation in Paris was that they represented something which America had felt profoundly in 1915 and would again feel profoundly in 1922. They did not, however, represent what America was feeling in that January of 1919."

Perhaps the principal reason why Wilson was unable to translate American power into a settlement that would have conformed to the Fourteen Points was that he was not as disinterested as he pretended to be. All Wilson's actions in Paris point to the conclusion that the League of Nations was what he really cared about; all other considerations were secondary. To get the League Covenant adopted was an achievement so precious that he was willing to pay for it with concessions on other issues which in many cases contravened the principles of the Fourteen Points. He was almost obsessed by the conviction that the League Covenant was to be his personal monument and the solution to all human difficulties. What mattered some injustices here and there if the world had permanent machinery in the League to prevent war and to correct wrongs by peaceful process?

Clemenceau, first and foremost, but the other Allied leaders as well, let it be known, just as did the Soviets at the end of World War II, that they would swallow the American plan for international organization, but at a price. Therein may lie the key to understanding how to find the way through the labyrinthine negotiations that led to such a complex and inconsistent peace treaty. As Colonel House, who had to go about the dirty business of purchasing support for Wilson's league, once explained the ensuing pattern of negotiations,

> The fact is that the League of Nations in which he has been more deeply interested than anything else from the beginning ... has been played to the limit by the French and Japanese in extracting concessions from him; to a certain extent by the British too, and the Treaty as it stands is the result.

Before his vision of what could be achieved by a League of Nations he sacrificed his Fourteen Points one by one. Suffice it to say that at the outset Wilson conceded the South Tyrol to Italy for supposedly strategic reasons, thereby incorporating 225,000 Austrians into Italy and violating the principle of self-determination. From there on it was all downhill. In order to convince France to give up its plans for an independent buffer state on the Rhine, Wilson was forced to sign a special treaty pledging the United States to protect France against invasion, a treaty derogatory of the League idea since it implied that the League might not be effective and that separate and special guarantees were required. The Japanese threatened not to join, and as a result Wilson gave in on Shantung despite the long tradition of American concern for the preservation of the territorial integrity of China. The Germans were not only deprived of all their colonies and of considerable territory in Europe that contained large German populations, but they also were saddled with an exceptionally high bill for reparations and forced, in a war-guilt clause that was both anathema to the German people and ran contrary to the common sense of most Americans, to accept exclusive blame for starting the conflict.

Assessments of the peace settlement vary greatly. One of the most influential books of the post-World War I period was written by Keynes who had served as a member of the British delegation. It was a severe indictment of the Treaty of Versailles, particularly its economic sections. Keynes considered the treaty a failure and blamed Wilson, who was unsuited by qualities of character and temperament to overcome the guiles of the experienced European statesmen who demanded a vindictive peace. The president, according to Keynes, lacked sufficient intellectual equipment, had come to Paris without detailed proposals, demonstrated incompetence in the agilities of the council chamber, and had an arrogant, egotistical, and obstinate personality. This "blind and deaf Don Quixote," who before the treaty had appeared to the world as the savior of mankind, simply did not measure up to the challenge. Wilson, the Presbyterian theocrat, was easily "bamboozled" by Clemenceau and Lloyd George. Together, in Keynes's opinion, they wove a "web of sophistry and Jesuitical exegesis that was finally to clothe with insincerity the language and substance of the whole treaty."

Keynes's indictment of Wilson exhibits all the characteristics associated with the disappointed idealist, and it often has been dismissed on precisely those grounds. From our perspective in time it appears so harsh and personal that one is inclined to reject it out of hand. To do so, however, might be to deprive ourselves of the best explanation we have for the fact that a peace, which had so many Carthaginian features, was disguised by a kind of Wilsonian liberal rhetoric that even today creates an impression of fairness in unsophisticated readers. Wilson's attitude, as depicted by Keynes, was: "I see your difficulties and I should like to agree to what you propose; but I can do nothing that is not just and right, and you must first of all show me that what you want does really fall within the words of the pronouncements which are binding on me." Keynes's point is that European draftsmen were up to the challenge and that as a result a certain hypocrisy pervaded the whole treaty.

On the other hand, Paul Birdsall, an American scholar, in his book *Versailles Twenty Years After* (1941), called Keynes's account "caricature, not history." To Birdsall, Wilson was the only man of real stature at the peace conference. He insisted that the president had not failed; the League of Nations was, after all, to be accounted a victory for the Wilsonian approach to peace. Moreover, the record of what Wilson prevented was equally important. Had his moderating influence on Clemenceau and Lloyd George been removed, the treaty would indeed have been Carthaginian. Birdsall admits that the settlement contained many unfortunate provisions but claims they must be considered in the light of conditions over which Wilson had no control. He believes that on every major question, except that of reparations, the Treaty of Versailles would have been worse had Wilson remained in Washington. Pointing to the fact that the principle of self-determination prevailed to a considerable extent and that the political map of postsettlement Europe came closer to coinciding with an ethnographic map than ever before in European history, other scholars have observed that the surprising aspect of the negotiations is that Wilson was able to save as much of his program as he did. Even Birdsall admits that the treaty was a compromise between Anglo-American and French conceptions of a stable international order and contained Carthaginian as well as Wilsonian features. Although not going as far as Keynes, who stressed the Allies' economic subjugation of their defeated enemy and claimed that little was overlooked which might impoverish Germany or obstruct its future development, most scholars (Birdsall included) still condemn the reparations settlement, if not for its injustice then for its lack of economic sense and because "it combined an egregious breach of faith with an impolitic accusation of moral turpitude."

The question here is by what standards one assesses the treaty. If it is judged by the standards of American idealism, then Birdsall is probably right that without Wilson it would have been a worse treaty, but by any objective historical standard it is difficult to imagine how it could possibly have been worse. Certainly it did not last, and certainly it did not bring peace to Europe. In this regard, it compares unfavorably with the peace constructed at the Congress of Vienna in 1815, a peace that except for short and relatively minor wars lasted almost one hundred years.

As Julius Pratt once reminded us, Machiavelli, the Italian political philosopher, thought that there were only two prudent ways to deal with a defeated enemy: "Either destroy him altogether or treat him so generously that he will become your friend." Any middle course, Machiavelli believed, was perilous. It seems difficult to escape the conclusion that at Paris Wilson and the Allies chose a middle course. Either a hard Carthaginian peace or a peace of reconciliation probably would have stood a better chance of survival. It is not easy to read the German criticism of the treaty without deriving the impression that the Paris Peace Conference was indeed guilty of disguising a hard Carthaginian peace under the cloak of Wilsonian idealism and liberalism. Nicolson even went so far as to claim that "seldom in the history of man has such vindictiveness cloaked itself in such unctuous sophistry." Hypocrisy was the overwhelming and inescapable outcome, and as a result the settlement never had the moral authority so necessary to a lasting peace.

Moreover, as Henry Kissinger has argued, it also was unsuccessful from a balance-of-power viewpoint.

> If there was any real purpose to World War I, it was that of destroying German hegemony, but the Versailles peace settlement was probably more favorable to German expansion than the world that existed previously. Before the war Germany had France on one side and Russia on the other, with Britain commanding the seas. After the peace conference, Germany came to be surrounded by weak successor states of uncertain strength, none of whom were capable of resisting Germany.

In short, the diplomats paid precious little attention to the power structure of the postwar world. They made no provisions for the economic rehabilitation of Europe, ignored the Soviet Union, and did little to stabilize and strengthen the new states of eastern Europe.

Even Wilson's strongest defenders now agree that the treaty was imperfect and that it contained many unfortunate provisions, but they would insist that such problems pale before the great achievement of the League. Arthur Link, for example, has long argued that Wilson in the League of Nations was "able to create the machinery for the gradual attainment of the kind of settlement he would have liked to impose at once," and that things would have turned out very differently if only the United States had joined. As a result, in recent years the debate among scholars has tended to focus on the structure of the League and its capabilities with respect to preserving the peace and the reasons underlying the American failure to join.

It is probably true, as Wilsonians then claimed and have claimed ever since, that in the spring of 1919 the majority of the American people favored U.S. membership in a League of Nations. Thirty-two state legislatures had endorsed the idea, and thirty-three governors had gone on record in favor; a *Literary Digest* poll of newspaper editors indicated the same trend. It was very difficult to be against a league to preserve the world's peace.

What happened to change opinion and why did the United States never join the League? There have been several principal explanations. Many historians have argued that Americans wished to return to what President Warren G. Harding called "normalcy," the result of the slump in idealism which naturally follows in the wake of war. Wilson's inspiring leadership during the war raised the American people to a spirit of self-sacrifice that even brought them to accept the prohibition of alcoholic beverages, but with victory came an emotional letdown. America, many thought, had received little or nothing at the peace table but opposition and ill will. The country was weary of war. Hundreds of thousands of American boys were returning from Europe homesick, irritated by the treatment they had received in France, and generally disgusted with the whole affair. As one commentator wrote in the *New York Globe*, they were "only too glad to shut the front gate and stay at home for a while."

Another group of historians has accepted the explanation offered by Wilson and his friends and contained in the Democratic party platform of 1920. Henry Cabot Lodge, Republican majority leader in the Senate and chairman of the Senate Foreign Relations Committee, was singled out by name in that platform for his alleged inconsistency on the League and peace issue. The Republican Senate also was condemned for "its refusal to ratify the treaty merely because it was the product of Democratic statesmanship, thus interposing partisan envy and personal hatred in the way of peace and renewed prosperity of the world." It is true that the Republicans in the Senate, humiliated by six years of rather iron-handed Wilsonian rule and now again in the driver's seat politically, had their knives sharpened for Wilson. Congress, as invariably happens after a war during which the executive branch has run the show, also was determined to reexert its control over the nation's foreign policy.

These explanations are not necessarily wrong, but they may be incomplete. They tend to ignore the fact that it was no simple matter to construct a workable collective security organization. The Wilsonian interpretation has inhibited rational consideration of the real issues involved in Article X concerning the role of force in international affairs, and it is precisely on that point that American thinking has often tended to imprecision. We will, as Senator Lodge recognized, always have with us "those who wish to have the world's peace assured by force, without using force to do it." The best of recent American scholarship now concludes that differences of opinion as to how to achieve a lasting peace did play an imperfect, even decisive, role in the struggle over the League. It served the interests of many of those involved to present the struggle as essentially one of partisan politics and personal hatred, but the real problem seems to have been that Americans could not agree upon the nature of the League they wanted or upon the arrangements necessary to make it succeed.

Both Wilson and former President William Howard Taft, leader of the pressure group the League to Enforce Peace that advocated U.S. membership, occupied a position fraught with tension. As Walter Lippmann later came to recognize, "In them the idealism which prompts Americans to make large and resounding commitments was combined with the pacifism which causes Americans to shrink from the measures of force that are needed to support the commitments." Wilson, like many of his constituents, believed that idealism was a self-fulfilling proposition, and that the moral force of world public opinion was the best guarantee of peace. Consequently, he came to minimize the very exertions that were so important to the Europeans (the commitment to come to their aid with troops) and implied that the United States would never in practice be called upon to fulfill its commitment to use force on behalf of the territorial integrity of the other members of the League. He was trapped, in short, by the contradiction inherent in his own desires, a contradiction laid bare by Senator William E. Borah when he so pointedly asked: "What will your league amount to if it does not contain powers that no one dreams of giving it?"

Even the actual language of Article X of the League Covenant betrayed much of the ambiguity of Wilson's statements:

> The Members of the League undertake to respect and preserve as against external aggression the territorial integrity and existing independence of all Members of the League. In case of any such aggression the League Council shall advise upon the means by which this obligation shall be fulfilled.

That left the precise obligation of any particular individual state rather vague.

As Wilson's principal antagonist Lodge put it, the idea of a League was "all right—fine—but the details were vital." Lodge himself never thought that either world conditions or the nature of the American political system were conducive to the formation of an effective league. He believed in the necessity of enforcing the peace with Germany, as did other conservative internationalists like Theodore Roosevelt and Elihu Root, men who cannot be classed as isolationists because they were quite willing to support the French guarantee treaty and to undertake similar specific commitments. At the heart of their position was the conviction that there was no halfway house, no way of constructing an effective league without putting an international military force behind it. As Lodge told the Senate,

> If, however, there is to be a league of nations in order to enforce peace, one thing is clear. It must be either a mere assemblage of words, an exposition of vague ideals and encouraging hopes, or it must be a practical system. If such a league is to be practical and effective, it can not possibly be either unless it has authority to issue decrees and force to sustain them. It is at this point that the questions of great moment arise.

It was, Lodge insisted, "easy to talk" about a League of Nations and the beauty and necessity of peace, but the hard practical demand is: "Are you ready to put your soldiers and your sailors at the disposition of other nations?" In public he left the answer open, but, well aware of the strength of both the pacifist and isolationist blocs in Congress, Lodge was firmly convinced that a plan for an international army could never get through the Senate. It could not in 1919, it could not in 1945, and it could not today. There were insuperable obstacles to the formation of an effective collective security organization. Those obstacles lay deep in the American character and in the nature of the U.S. political system. What was required for the construction of an effective League of Nations was never politically feasible at home. It was a dilemma from which Wilson found it difficult to escape.

The Covenant that Wilson brought home was an uneasy compromise; it was not quite the "definite guarantee of peace" that Wilsonians, then and later, pictured it to be. It begged even the most basic of questions. It was not even clear whether it was meant to be an instrument of reconciliation or a means of giving permanence to the Allied victory, whether it was to be a truly universal association or only an organization of "free" nations. The fault was not entirely Wilson's but lay in the nature of things. As Brooks Adams once trenchantly observed, "To attain to a relation among its parts in which physical force could be used by a League, would imply an effort of collective thought of which we have no adequate notion." On the all-important question of the precise nature of the obligation incurred under Article X, the Covenant was particularly equivocal. This confusion was but the inevitable consequence of the peacemakers' efforts to preserve national sovereignty while nevertheless suppressing its consequences. This is the classic problem confronting those who would construct a universal collective security organization, and it was not solved either at Paris in 1919 or at San Francisco in 1945.

Wilson always found it difficult to give a compelling interpretation of American responsibilities under Article X. Although claiming that Article X was "the very backbone of the whole Covenant," he dared not claim that the League Council's advice derogated from "the right of our Congress under our Constitution to exercise its independent judgment in all matters of peace and war." Actually, either the council had the last word or Congress had it, but Wilson could not politically admit that. Consequently, he was left to try to resolve the contradictions inherent in American participation in the Covenant's version of universal collective security in the following unsatisfactory fashion. The engagement under Article X, he claimed,

> constitutes a very grave and solemn moral obligation. But it is a moral, not a legal obligation, and leaves our Congress absolutely free to put its own interpretation upon it in all cases that call for action. It is binding in conscience only, not in law.

To Wilson and his supporters the moral obligation was a real one, and their objection to Lodge's reservation to Article X was that it specifically removed that moral obligation. This was not a minor point but perhaps the obstacle to ratification, for the nature of the obligation assumed by member states would of necessity determine just what kind of organization the League was going to be. Since the success of a collective security organization would seem to rest on the absence of doubt as to the intentions of its members—that is, on the credibility of their commitments—Lodge's reservation stating that the United States assumed no obligation was, in effect, a denial of the whole theory on which collective security rested. His reservations, although they would have preserved the League as a useful instrument of collaboration and international cooperation, would nevertheless have transformed the League into a noncoercive or intermediate type of international organization, which is essentially what it became. The problems involved in constructing a workable collective security organization without derogating from national sovereignty proved insuperable; Canada tried to have Article X suppressed in 1920, and in 1923 the League Council could not even decide whether its advice was binding. Like the United States, most of the countries involved were unwilling to sacrifice their traditional policies or vital interests to secure a more satisfactory peace. It seems doubtful that U.S. membership in the League, with or without the Lodge reservations, could have solved these fundamental constitutional questions.

The final argument of those who would defend the peace settlement and the American role therein is that it did manage, for all its imperfections, to create a new international order that functioned rather well for some years. Link would still insist that "it failed not because it was imperfect, but because it was not defended when challenges arose in the '30s." In this opinion, Link echoes the sentiments of Lloyd George, who once remarked that many of the ills blamed on the treaty were not intrinsic but rather the fault of the oncoming generations of leaders who failed to execute it. That argument, however, only raises the question of why the Versailles treaty was not defended. Root always believed that a great opportunity had been wasted at Paris, and that the American people could have been persuaded to undertake a specific and binding obligation to defend France, such as was incorporated in the French guarantee treaty, but that Wilson's league left too many loopholes to stand the test of time. Moreover, a good argument can be made that the treaty's hypocrisies and inconsistencies contributed much to its demise, instilling in the Germans the belief that they were being judged by standards that did not apply to other nations and hence lending a sense of righteousness to their revanchism and undermining in the minds of the Allies the idea that this was a legitimate and moral peace, deserving of respect and of being forcefully upheld.

The unhappy results can probably best be attributed to a confusion of purpose, to ongoing problems in the whole American approach to the conduct of foreign policy. Peace, a stable international order, and justice are not necessarily synonymous ends. Justice is a particularly troublesome and fleeting, time-bound concept. Wilson was sincerely determined to arrange a just peace, but that very preoccupation may have prevented both a peace of accommodation with Germany and a peace designed to keep Germany permanently in check. Either of those alternatives might have been preferable to the actual result.

Sources and Suggested Readings

Bailey, Thomas A. *Woodrow Wilson and the Great Betrayal.* New York, 1945.

———. *Woodrow Wilson and the Lost Peace.* New York, 1944.

Birdsall, Paul. *Versailles Twenty Years After.* New York, 1941.

Buehrig, Edward H., ed. *Wilson's Foreign Policy in Perspective.* Bloomington, 1957.

Floto, Inga. *Colonel House in Paris: A Study of American Policy at the Paris Peace Conference.* Aarhaus, 1973.

Gelfand, Lawrence E. *The Inquiry: American Preparations for Peace, 1917-1919.* New Haven, 1963.

Huthmacher, J. Joseph, and Susman, Warren, eds. *Wilson's Diplomacy: An International Symposium.* Cambridge, Massachusetts, 1973.

Keynes, John Maynard. *The Economic Consequences of the Peace.* New York, 1920.

Kuehl, Warren F. *Seeking World Order: The United States and International Organization to 1920.* Nashville, 1969.

Levin, N. Gordon, Jr. *Woodrow Wilson and World Politics: America's Response to War and Revolution.* New York, 1968.

Link, Arthur S. *Wilson the Diplomatist: A Look at His Major Foreign Policies.* Chicago, 1965.

Mayer, Arno. *Politics and Diplomacy of Peacemaking: Containment and Counterrevolution at Versailles, 1918-1919.* New York, 1967.

McDougall, Walter A. *France's Rhineland Policy, 1914-1924.* Princeton, 1978.

Nelson, Keith L. *Victors Divided: America and the Allies in Germany, 1918-1923.* Berkeley, 1975.

Nicolson, Harold. *Peacemaking, 1919: Being Reminiscences of the Paris Peace Conference.* Boston, 1933.

Smith, Daniel M. *The Great Departure: The United States and World War I, 1914-1920.* New York, 1965.

Stromberg, Roland. *Collective Security and American Foreign Policy: From the League of Nations to NATO.* New York, 1963.

Tillman, Seth P. *Anglo-American Relations at the Paris Peace Conference of 1919.* Princeton, 1961.

Trachtenberg, Marc. *Reparations in World Politics: France and European Economic Diplomacy, 1916-1923.* New York, 1980.

Vinson, John Chalmers. *Referendum for Isolation: The Defeat of Article Ten of the League of Nations Covenant.* Athens, Georgia, 1961.

Widenor, William C. *Henry Cabot Lodge and the Search for an American Foreign Policy.* Berkeley, 1980.

Yates, Louis A. *The United States and French Security, 1917-1921: A Study in American Diplomatic History.* New York, 1957.

American Diplomacy in the 1920s

John M. Carroll

In recent years a debate concerning the nature of American foreign policy in the 1920s has stirred considerable controversy among historians. Reduced to its simplest terms, the debate has centered on the question of whether or not America followed a policy of isolationism. Historians such as Selig Adler and Foster Rhea Dulles, who admire President Woodrow Wilson and his vision of a League of Nations that would ensure international peace and security through the collective action of its members, have argued that U.S. foreign policy was largely one of aloofness and withdrawal from world affairs during the 1920s. They maintain that the Senate's rejection of the Treaty of Versailles and membership in the League, as well as the subsequent refusal of Republican administrations to make political commitments to preserve the peace, led to a policy and sentiment that can be properly characterized as isolationism. These historians view American diplomacy in the 1920s as weak, halting, and timid and claim that it contributed significantly to the breakdown of the international order in the 1930s which, in turn, resulted in World War II.

Revisionists like Carl Parrini and Melvyn P. Leffler, who have followed the lead of radical historian William A. Williams, maintain that America was extremely active in international affairs in the 1920s and that U.S. diplomacy was not isolationist. American leaders, they claim, vigorously pursued international objectives of peace, stability, and prosperity but through economic diplomacy rather than through binding treaties and political commitments.

The debate over whether or not American diplomacy in the 1920s was isolationist is of limited usefulness because it is more semantic than real. The defeat of the treaty in the United States and the persistent instability in Europe after the war did cause the sense of despair and hopelessness that gripped the American public and prompted many citizens to reject Wilsonianism and its advocacy of political commitments. To this extent, a mood of isolationism existed in the United States which affected diplomacy and disappointed Wilsonian internationalists who wanted America to play a direct political role in world affairs. It is also clear, however, that except from 1917 to 1920 America was never more active in international affairs until the eve of World War II than it was during the 1920s. This apparent paradox helps to explain why the controversy focusing on isolationism has raged for so long without producing a consensus on the nature of American foreign policy in the 1920s.

Recent scholarship on the diplomacy of the postwar decade has provided several clues which help to clarify the nature of U.S. foreign policy. These studies indicate that the 1920s were a transitional decade in the shaping of twentieth-century American diplomacy. Republican policymakers rejected the traditional American aloofness from international affairs associated with the nineteenth and early twentieth centuries but were not prepared to embrace the kind of international commitment that has characterized the post-World War II era. American policy in the 1920s simply took on a new form, making it difficult for observers then, as well as now, to characterize: America was restrained yet active in foreign affairs during the 1920s. Three basic elements combined to shape Republican foreign policy. First, the treaty debacle in the United States and the public disillusionment with Wilsonianism created what Adler has called an "isolationist impulse." Policymakers were aware that close association with the League, or any indication of political commitment in international affairs, would bring a sharp reaction from Congress and the public. Thus, they avoided political commitments and what became known as collective security.

Second, American officials had great faith in the theory that economic, rather than political, forces would be the key to maintaining peace and stability in the postwar world. This view was based on the optimistic premise that advances in technology, communication, and transportation were making the world more interdependent and would lead to greater mutual trust among peoples. By solving economic problems and creating greater prosperity, American leaders hoped to build an international community in which the benefits of peace would be so evident that war would be unthinkable. The American strategy of economic diplomacy relied on two concepts which were evident throughout the decade: 1) that independent business experts should help shape American diplomacy because of their skill in this area and their objectivity in the face of political pressures; and 2) that economic and political agreements should be voluntary, based on mutual benefit and the enforcement power of public opinion.

Third, American policymakers believed that the United States enjoyed basic economic and military security and should not pursue any policy that might endanger either. This U.S. conception of its place in the world was a restraining force in foreign policy because it limited the sacrifices America would make or the risks it would take to ensure world stability. To many leaders of the era, the nation was an unassailable economic and military fortress. The United States would be active in international affairs in the 1920s so long as no political commitment was required or economic concession sought that might weaken its presumed security. The historian Joan Hoff-Wilson has aptly named this policy "independent internationalism," while others have called it "continentalism."

The debate over the Treaty of Versailles, with its controversial League of Nations section, dominated American foreign policy in the early 1920s. In retrospect, Wilson's decree that the 1920 election should be "a great and solemn referendum" on the League issue proved to be a costly error. The election results turned out to be not just a landslide for the Republicans but what Democratic National Chairman Joseph P. Tumulty termed an earthquake. Although Vice President-elect Calvin Coolidge doubted if Warren G. Harding's overwhelming victory meant that the American people opposed membership in the League of Nations, most politicians and media representatives believed otherwise. In early 1921, President Harding, who had equivocated on the issue during the recent campaign, declared that the question of U.S. membership in the League was as dead as slavery. Republican leaders realized that they would have to distance themselves from the tarnished mantle of Wilsonian internationalism or face the wrath of many in Congress who boasted with Senator Henry Cabot Lodge that they had "torn up Wilsonianism by its roots."

Republican presidential leadership during the 1920s reflected both the party and the public's desire to repudiate the missionary zeal and strong personal authority in foreign affairs associated with Wilson. Harding, who possessed at best a second-rate mind, made it clear that his secretary of state would run the department and make vital decisions. The Ohio president was content to allow Secretary of State Charles Evans Hughes (1921–1925), Secretary of Commerce Herbert Hoover (1921–1928), and Secretary of the Treasury Andrew

"WHY THIS CHICKEN CROSSED THE ROAD." (Rochester *Herald*, 1921, Library of Congress)

Mellon (1921–1932) to make most foreign policy decisions. Coolidge, who served as president for most of the decade, followed a similar policy, although his secretary of state, Frank B. Kellogg (1925–1929), was not as capable as Hughes. Both Harding and Coolidge were better informed and more astute in foreign affairs than historians have generally conceded, but they deliberately chose to play a subordinate role in that area. President Hoover, who is considered the most knowledgeable of all public officials in diplomatic matters during the 1920s, did not initiate any bold policies in foreign relations. For all his experience and expertise in diplomacy, Hoover, perhaps more than either Harding or Coolidge, feared and disliked encountering congressional opposition and usually avoided diplomatic measures likely to stir Congress against his administration. For the most part, presidential leadership in foreign affairs was weak in the 1920s, and most of the initiative in that field devolved on the secretary of state, his department, and other interested cabinet members who often confronted a suspicious Congress.

Secretary of State Hughes was largely responsible for shaping American diplomacy in the early part of the decade. A confirmed internationalist, he sought to reestablish American influence in the critical task of reconstructing Europe. Sensitive to charges that he was a "bewhiskered Wilson," Hughes appointed U.S. diplomats to sit on important League-affiliated bodies, such as the Reparations Commission and the Supreme Council, as "unofficial observers." These observers participated in discussions and outlined American policy but did not vote. Nevertheless, the influence of unofficial diplomats such as Roland Boyden was considerable because of America's dominant financial position in the world and the desire of European leaders to mobilize U.S. capital to help solve the pressing problems of reconstruction. After snubbing the League of Nations in the early days of the administration by failing to answer official communications from Geneva, Hughes and Harding began to cooperate with the League on a variety of humanitarian matters. By mid-decade American delegates served on committees and conferences relating to such problems as the opium trade, the white slavery traffic, and improving world health. Later in the decade the United States participated in League deliberations that were more clearly economic and political, including conferences on world disarmament.

The main thrust of America's European diplomacy, however, was directed toward the problem of postwar reconstruction. Europe had been devastated by the Great War. Its economy was shattered, political tensions were high, rearmament was under way, and the future political and economic stability of the Continent was in doubt. Hughes and other Republican leaders recognized that European instability directly affected U.S. interests. They addressed the question of European reconstruction by drawing on the experience gained in the Progressive Era, the war, and the recent peace settlement.

American foreign policy leaders in the 1920s placed great emphasis on economic diplomacy. Stunned by the tragedy of the recent
war, they questioned whether dependence on political commitments, military alliances, or large expenditures on armaments would
prevent a future world conflict. Many argued that these very policies
had led to the outbreak of the Great War. Instead, American policymakers held that economic prosperity and stability might lead to
future peace. Hughes emphasized this point when he stated that
"there will be no permanent peace unless economic satisfactions are
enjoyed." Business as well as political leaders stressed that the scientific advancement in communication, transportation, and technology made in the early part of the century and accelerated by the war
would lead to a prosperous world society linked together in peaceful
effort. Economic, rather than political, forces would shape the future, and governments should pursue policies that conformed to the
movement of economic forces rather than impeded them. As the
world's leading industrial and creditor nation, the United States
would play a vital role in shaping postwar events if a coherent policy
of economic diplomacy could be implemented.

American leaders also insisted that policy objectives should be
pursued through voluntary agreements and with the aid and counsel
of independent business experts. Both measures were brought about
in part by the defeat of the Versailles treaty and the reaction against
Wilsonianism. They were expedients designed to camouflage American diplomacy from the eyes of the Senate and deflect criticism that
the nation was entangled in the affairs of Europe. The use of voluntary agreements also reflected the view that political commitments
and military alliances did not prevent wars, or at least had not in
1914. Hughes once remarked that "the alternative of friendly settlements is resort to coercion, and if you wish peace you must pursue
the methods of friendly intercourse between governments ... there
is no other way." The use of independent business experts to implement American diplomacy was based in part on the experience of the
Progressive Era and the war, which showed that scientific management of governmental problems was more efficient, more equitable,
and served the public interest. As Michael Hogan has pointed out,
this form of public-private power sharing in diplomacy "conformed
with the American political economy, avoided wasteful and undemocratic state capitalism, and guaranteed a more efficient and peaceful
management of world affairs." In confronting the problem of European reconstruction, along with many other diplomatic issues of the
1920s, American leaders relied heavily on economic diplomacy,

voluntarism, and the use of business experts to achieve their goals.

This diplomatic strategy was first put to the test in confronting the problems associated with European reconstruction. Much of Europe was devastated by both the military and economic effects of the war. Parts of France and Belgium, as well as areas in eastern Europe, were destroyed by the advancing and retreating armies. The economies of most major nations were plagued by heavy indebtedness and persistent inflation. Germany, which had the strongest prewar economy, was saddled with a reparations debt under the Versailles treaty which was set in 1921 at $33 billion, an enormous sum at that time. Although some recent historians like Marc Trachtenberg maintain that Germany could have repaid the debt, American leaders were heavily influenced by the British economist John Maynard Keynes, who held that Germany was the key to European reconstruction, and that it could not recover unless the reparations debt was reduced substantially. The United States had a vital stake in German and European recovery because without it American trade, foreign investment, and eventually its entire economy were bound to suffer. Beyond this, the continuing economic paralysis in Europe might trigger social upheaval and the spread of bolshevism into central and western Europe. The unresolved reparations dispute also heightened political tension between Germany and France and indirectly threatened political stability in all parts of Europe.

The United States had an indirect stake in the reparations controversy in that major Allied nations owed America more than $10 billion in war debts. Beginning in 1919 Allied leaders urged the United States to cancel these debts in exchange for a commensurate reduction in German reparations. Although some reductions were made in the war debt payment agreements of the 1920s, American leaders refused to cancel them. Leffler has argued persuasively that domestic political considerations were the main cause of the U.S. stance on war debts. Cancellation would have meant higher taxes for Americans because the original war loans were raised by selling wartime bonds. The Republican administrations of the 1920s placed a high priority on aiding in the economic rehabilitation and political pacification of Europe but not to the extent that it might cause undue sacrifice or political turmoil in the United States. The refusal to cancel the war debts is an example of the domestic restraint under which American diplomats had to pursue foreign policy objectives.

The American approach to the problem of European reconstruction was to use patience and economic diplomacy. As the United States was the world's leading creditor nation, America's capital would be needed to bring about European recovery. Working in cooperation with U.S. international banking firms, the State Department made it clear that capital would not be available for European reconstruction until the German reparations debt had been scaled down to a reasonable figure. Although recent studies indicate that France's reparations policy was more flexible than previously thought, French leaders considered a substantial reparations debt as a kind of ransom to ensure French security and a safeguard to protect the Treaty of Versailles. The growing revisionist view of the treaty touched off by Keynes's *The Economic Consequences of the Peace* (1919), Germany's refusal or inability to meet reparations quotas, and the general British and American sympathy for the German position combined, however, to undermine French policy. In desperation, France jeopardized its entente with Britain by occupying the German Ruhr valley in January 1923 in order to collect reparations. During the months and days prior to the French military move, Hughes offered to establish an independent conference of business experts to set German reparations within what he described as Germany's "capacity to pay." The French military gamble temporarily sidelined the so-called Hughes Plan. Hughes responded philosophically by declaring "that each side would probably have to 'enjoy its own bit of chaos' until a disposition to a fair settlement had been created."

The Ruhr occupation resulted in the near collapse of the German economy and frustration for France's attempt to collect reparations. By November 1923, Premier Raymond Poincaré, with American encouragement, authorized the Reparations Commission to summon financial experts to study the reparations question. The Dawes Committee convened in Paris in January 1924 and included Americans Owen D. Young, chairman of both General Electric and RCA, and the Chicago banker, Charles G. Dawes, who were selected with the advice and consent of the State Department. Although ostensibly independent experts, Young and Dawes worked in close cooperation with the State and Commerce departments. During early 1924 the Dawes Committee turned out a report which suggested a major revision in the reparations system. The report called for a year-by-year schedule of payments, the reorganization of Germany's financial structure under an independent expert called the Agent General for Reparations, and a sizable private loan for Germany to help revitalize its economy. The plan was to be a temporary system to determine how much reparations Germany could actually pay.

During the summer of 1924 American leaders, including Young and Ambassador to Britain Frank B. Kellogg, lobbied to gain

French and German acceptance of the Dawes Plan. This was accomplished at the London Conference of July 1924. The powerful New York banking firm of J. P. Morgan and Company agreed to underwrite a substantial portion of the German Dawes loan after it was agreed that France would evacuate the Ruhr and that the power of the Reparations Commission to declare German defaults on reparations would be restricted.

The Dawes Plan, which went into effect in the fall, had an immediate positive impact on European economic and political conditions. American capital began to flow into Germany, and, through the office of the Agent General for Reparations, payments were transferred to the Allies. On the surface the German economy prospered, but its recovery was fueled by a torrent of short-term loans mainly from America which overly optimistic investors poured into the country. Contrary to the advice of Dawes Plan architect Young, German leaders failed to use the loans for productive purposes that would ensure a future trade surplus capable of meeting the reparations debt from solely German resources. Instead, the foreign loans were largely used for nonproductive purposes and to meet current reparations quotas. This created a dangerous situation because the Dawes Plan now rested squarely on the willingness of foreign investors to provide Germany with a continuous supply of short-term capital.

Despite the dangerous economic conditions developing in Germany, European leaders greeted the Dawes Plan and the anticipated economic recovery in the spirit of trust and conciliation. In 1925 Allied and German leaders met in Locarno to discuss a series of agreements designed to guarantee the existing borders in parts of Europe. During the course of the discussions, President Coolidge made it plain that the continued flow of American capital to Europe was dependent on some kind of security agreement in Europe. On December 1, 1925 the Locarno treaties were signed by German and Allied leaders. The most important of these treaties was an agreement confirming the inviolability of the Franco-German and Belgo-German frontiers and the demilitarized zone of the Rhineland. A feeling of euphoria swept Europe which contemporary observers hailed as the "spirit of Locarno." To many it appeared that the hatred and bitterness associated with the war was over, and a new era of peace and conciliation was at hand. For American policymakers the Dawes Plan and resulting Locarno pacts appeared to be a singular triumph of their economic diplomacy.

The new era of Locarno proved to be more an illusion than a reality. The spirit of Locarno only disguised the fact that Germany was thoroughly determined to revise the Versailles settlement by conciliation if possible, or by force if necessary. So long as Europe was relatively prosperous and the former enemies remained strong, Foreign Minister Gustav Stresemann was content to unchain Germany through diplomacy. German and European prosperity, however, largely depended on the Dawes Plan and the American short-term loans that supported it. By the end of the decade, Germany was finding it difficult to meet the increasing yearly reparations quotas stipulated in the plan. European leaders agreed in 1928 that it was time to establish a final reparations plan that would set Germany's total debt as well as a new yearly payment schedule. Such a plan would allow Germany to assess its total obligation to the Allies and presumably work harder to put its economic affairs in order.

In February 1929 the Young Committee of financial experts, which included Young and Thomas W. Lamont of J. P. Morgan and Company, met in Paris and hammered out a new reparations plan. The resulting Young Plan set German reparations at about $8 billion and reduced yearly payments below Dawes Plan levels. Subsequent agreements which helped implement the plan in 1930 called for the early military evacuation of the Rhineland and the establishment of the Bank for International Settlements, which would facilitate reparations transfers. German payments were to run for fifty-nine years, the same time span as the Allied war debt obligations to America, and during the last twenty-two years the two debts exactly corresponded. This linkage between war debts and reparations angered President Hoover, who became wary of the new reparations agreement and ultimately refused to ratify the Young Plan. Young, who had earlier urged Hoover to cancel the war debts and reduce American tariff barriers, was frustrated by the president's lack of support. He hoped that the new reparations plan, in combination with the Bank for International Settlements, might make it possible to commercialize all the wartime debts and thus put the whole issue out of the realm of future political conflict. Young maintained that Hoover was afraid to take the initiative on the war debt and tariff issues because he might incur the wrath of domestic interests that were well represented in Congress. The cancellation of war debts and tariff reductions, in Young's view, would stimulate world trade and facilitate the removal of the war debt and reparations questions from the political arena. Hoover held firm in his position and even signed a higher tariff law, the Hawley-Smoot Act, in 1930.

The conflict in views between Hoover and Young indicated one of the liabilities of using private business experts to carry out public policy. It also showed that Hoover, like Coolidge and Harding before him, pursued a policy of continentalism, which put domestic priorities far ahead of economic sacrifices that might have ameliorated international tensions during the 1920s. The Great Depression, which was triggered by the American stock market crash of 1929, curtailed short-term lending to Germany and undermined the Young Plan. By 1932 Germany defaulted on reparations, with Allied acquiescence, and this led to a series of German initiatives that struck at the heart of the Versailles system and destabilized international politics in the 1930s.

In addition to their reliance on economic diplomacy, American leaders believed that international disarmament would help guarantee worldwide security and stability. America's emphasis on disarmament in the 1920s was a reaction to the massive slaughter of the Great War and conformed to the prevailing view that economic progress, rather than military might, was the best safeguard against future wars. In fact, the two threads of American policy were linked. The cost of armaments in many countries caused both domestic and international economic problems and often led to political instability. Disarmament would help to eliminate wasteful expenditure and in the process promote commercial expansion and peace. Beyond this, most Americans believed that the prewar arms race had been a major cause of World War I.

The advocates of disarmament were active both in government and in the society as a whole. Reacting to the devastation of the war and its aftermath, disarmament advocates "fired the formation of the most dynamic peace movement in American history," Charles DeBenedetti has written. The peace seekers founded a variety of organizations supported by internationalists, pacifists, and liberal reformers. Such groups as the League of Nations Non-Partisan Association, the War Resisters League, and the National Council for Prevention of War thrived during the 1920s. One of the most striking successes in terms of publicity was the American Peace Award offered by millionaire publisher Edward W. Bok in 1923. The $100,000 award was to go to the author of the best brief plan to involve the United States in maintaining world peace. Veteran peace activist Charles H. Levermore won the award in 1924, but his plan was never adopted. Despite the lack of unity in the peace movement, it did have an impact on government policy.

In the spring of 1921 a coalition of peace groups, including feminists, Protestants, and internationalists, gathered to force President Harding to take the initiative in world disarmament. As a result of their efforts and with the support of Senator William E. Borah, Harding convened the Washington Conference of 1921-22. Although the agenda was limited, it offered an opportunity to stop the naval arms race and stabilize political affairs in the Far East. Delegates from the Big Three naval powers—America, Britain, and Japan, along with French and Italian representatives—assembled in Washington in late 1921 to open the first postwar disarmament conference.

Secretary of State Hughes stunned the delegates at the opening session by calling for an immediate end to the naval race. He proposed that Britain, America, and Japan reduce the number of their capital ships to conform to a relative power ratio of 5:5:3, respectively, and that no new battleships be constructed for ten years. France and Italy were assigned a ratio of 1.75 in the Hughes formula. In all, the secretary called for the major powers to scrap more than sixty ships. One British admiral was purported to have remarked that Hughes was preparing to scrap more English ships than the navies of the world had sunk in "a cycle of centuries." The Five-Power Treaty, signed the following year, incorporated the Hughes proposal and stipulated that neither the United States nor Britain could build new bases or strengthen existing ones in the Far East. The latter concession guaranteed Japan naval superiority in Asian waters. The delegates, largely because of French opposition, were unable to negotiate a disarmament agreement to cover submarines and cruisers.

Although the disarmament negotiations received most of the headlines, the conference was equally concerned with establishing a new order in Asia. As a result, two multination pacts were signed to replace the imperialistic system symbolized by the Anglo-Japanese alliance of 1902. A Four-Power Treaty, signed by Britain, France, America, and Japan, abrogated the former alliance and called for its signatories to maintain the status quo in Asia. Under the Nine-Power Treaty, signed by all nations having an interest in Asia with the exception of the Soviet Union, it was agreed to respect the integrity of China in conformity with the U.S. Open Door policy. The treaties contained no provisions for enforcement and thus rested on the goodwill of the signatories and the presumed weight of world opinion.

In light of the events of the 1930s and 1940s, many historians have criticized the noncoercive, voluntary nature of the Washington treaties. Since voluntarism was a vital aspect of Republican policy, which also included an emphasis on economic diplomacy and disarmament, it would be fairer to evaluate the Washington Conference in view of the totality of American foreign policy of the 1920s. It can be argued that the treaties failed to provide lasting security not because of their voluntary nature per se but because American economic diplomacy did not generate an expanding commercial system in which economic satisfactions were enjoyed by all nations. Japan, it should be remembered, started on its aggressive course mainly in response to the deteriorating state of the world's economy in the early 1930s.

Further attempts at naval disarmament were not as successful as the Five-Power Treaty. The Geneva Conference of 1927 failed to reach an agreement on cruisers because of an Anglo-American dispute over the desirability of limiting light, as opposed to heavy, cruisers. At the 1930 London Naval Conference the United States, Japan, and Britain reached an agreement concerning their relative strengths in terms of light and heavy cruisers and submarines, but it was seriously undermined by an escape clause that allowed any of the three powers to suspend the agreement if they felt threatened by a nonsignatory nation.

The most highly publicized peace initiative in the 1920s was the Kellogg-Briand Pact. This treaty, which called for nations to renounce war as an instrument of national policy and to settle all disputes by peaceful means, was eventually ratified by sixty-three powers. The origins of the pact can be traced to the early 1920s when Chicago lawyer Salmon Levinson organized the American Committee for the Outlawry of War and insisted that war was like collective murder and should be considered a crime before the law. In 1927 Columbia University Professor James T. Shotwell took up the theme and urged France to sign with the United States a bilateral treaty outlawing war. French Foreign Minister Aristide Briand, desiring an understanding with the United States that might bolster French security, cautiously endorsed Shotwell's plan. Pressured by various peace groups and the Franco-American amity resulting from Charles A. Lindbergh's solo flight to Paris in May 1927, the Coolidge administration began to consider the plan seriously. Secretary of State Kellogg took the lead in early 1928 by offering a treaty to outlaw offensive war as an instrument of national policy to France and other countries. The multilateral agreement was much less significant to the French, who had hoped for a private security understanding with America, but France, the United States, and thirteen other nations signed the officially named Paris Peace Pact in August 1928. The U.S. Senate ratified the treaty in January 1929 by a vote of 85 to 1.

By any standards the Kellogg-Briand Pact was a weak instrument for preventing future wars. Senator Carter Glass remarked that it was not "worth a postage stamp" in terms of maintaining permanent peace. The Kellogg Pact divided the numerous peace groups. Some peace activists like Shotwell maintained that it was the first step in revising American neutrality status in time of war and opening the way for cooperation with the League of Nations in imposing sanctions on aggressor nations. Other peace reformers noted that the pact was ratified at the same time that Congress was increasing naval strength and U.S. Marines were invading Nicaragua. They saw the pact as a smoke screen camouflaging the more pressing problems that stood in the way of maintaining a lasting peace. At best the Kellogg-Briand Pact was a voluntary agreement which the United States might interpret as a justification for taking indirect action against aggressors in time of war. Above all, the pact was a clear manifestation of America's independent internationalism in the 1920s.

The Latin American diplomacy of the United States stood in contrast to its relations with the rest of the world. American leaders still paid homage to the Monroe Doctrine and the Roosevelt Corollary to that document and considered Latin America a U.S. sphere of influence. As a result of the war, American trade and investments expanded rapidly and supplanted those of European powers that previously had had an important economic stake in Latin American republics. With the support of Secretary of Commerce Hoover's Bureau of Foreign and Domestic Commerce, American businessmen gained dominance over markets and economies in Latin America during the 1920s. In contrast to the open door style of economic diplomacy practiced in other parts of the world, however, the U.S. government encouraged closed door techniques in Latin America. The same cartels and special trading agreements that America objected to in Europe, the Middle East, or Asia formed the basis of inter-American trade. Under the doctrine of continentalism, Latin America was considered a special province of the United States, and different economic and political rules applied in that region.

During the early part of the century the United States had maintained stability and thwarted outside intervention in Latin America through the use of military force. By 1920 the Central American trouble spots—Santo Domingo, Cuba, Panama, Haiti, and Nicaragua—had been stabilized through U.S. military efforts. This policy of direct intervention and a commitment to preserve political stability contrasted sharply with America's economic diplomacy in other parts of the world.

By the early 1920s the threat of foreign intervention in Latin America receded, and this encouraged U.S. policymakers to pursue a less interventionist strategy in that region. The rise of intense nationalism and the undermining of old-style imperialism, which came about as a result of World War I, also caused the United States to reevaluate its interventionist policies in Latin America. Secretary of State Hughes took the initiative by making several goodwill tours in South America and by terminating the American military occupation in Santo Domingo. The American attempt to live down its image of the "Colossus of the North," however, was at best halting during the postwar decade. In 1926 President Coolidge ordered marines into Nicaragua to quell internal disturbances, even though American forces had been withdrawn as recently as the previous year. Under pressure from peace groups and congressional critics, he moderated his policy toward Nicaragua and appointed a special troubleshooter, Henry Stimson, to work out a nonmilitary solution to the crisis. Although U.S. forces remained in Nicaragua until 1933, Coolidge's action indicated a new direction in the nation's approach to Latin American problems. In a similar vein, he responded, with caution and restraint, to a crisis in Mexico triggered by the recent revolution in that country and to a dispute over subsoil mineral rights. Pressed again by peace activists and congressmen weary of the old-style interventionist tactics, the president appointed Amherst College classmate Dwight Morrow as ambassador to Mexico. Morrow charmed his Mexican hosts and negotiated a satisfactory settlement on the issue of subsoil mineral rights, thereby averting a serious crisis. Taken as a whole, the nation's Latin American policy conformed with the overall thrust of U.S. diplomacy in the 1920s, despite the important exceptions cited above. American policymakers, for the most part, eschewed the use of military force and attempted to stabilize the region through the use of economic diplomacy. Many historians have correctly noted that the roots of Franklin Roosevelt's Good Neighbor policy can be seen in the 1920s.

American foreign policy in the 1920s, with its emphasis on economic diplomacy, public-private power sharing, voluntarism, continental self-sufficiency, disarmament, and its rejection of direct military commitments, might seem strange and quaint to the contemporary observer. Yet, in the decade of the 1980s, American leaders are reconsidering and testing many of these same options in addressing international problems of the present. As a result of a long and costly Cold War struggle, in which military commitment and resort to the use of arms became a watchword of U.S. policy,

"GOODWILL." A critical view of U.S. policy in Nicaragua in the 1920s. (*New Masses*, Library of Congress)

many Americans now recognize the limits of the nation's vast military power. A seemingly futile nuclear arms race has rekindled interest in disarmament as a viable diplomatic option. The increasing interdependence of the world economy has reemphasized the importance of economic diplomacy and underscored the necessity of

public-private power sharing in solving many international economic as well as political problems. The oil crisis of the 1970s has stirred
renewed interest in continental self-sufficiency. Even the concept of
voluntarism, which was anathema to post-World War II leaders, is
again spoken of as a viable, although limited, strategy in the recent
era of détente.

The current reconsideration of diplomatic strategies associated
with the 1920s does not mean that U.S. foreign policy in that decade
can be termed a success. American leaders in the post-World War I
decade overvalued the usefulness of voluntary agreements and underestimated the value of military commitments. Attempts to bring
about meaningful disarmament in the 1920s were in many cases
naive and illusory. The reliance on public-private power sharing
worked well in some instances, most notably the Dawes Plan, but
was poorly coordinated in other cases, such as in the Young Plan
negotiations. America's strategy of continental self-sufficiency, in
both a military and economic sense, was narrowly conceived in the
1920s in light of the technological breakthroughs with possible
military applications and the emerging interdependent world economy. The nation's high tariffs and its refusal to cancel the war debts
ran counter to the larger policies of economic diplomacy designed to
ensure world peace and stability through an ever-expanding commercial network. In retrospect, the 1920s were a transitional decade
in American foreign policy in which new strategies in diplomacy
were attempted. Some were innovative and relatively successful, and
others proved to be shortsighted and ineffective.

Sources and Suggested Readings

Adler, Selig. *The Uncertain Giant, 1921–1941: American Foreign Policy
Between the Wars.* New York, 1965.

Buckley, Thomas H. *The United States and the Washington Conference,
1921–1922.* Knoxville, 1970.

Costigliola, Frank. *Awkward Dominion: American Political, Economic,
and Cultural Relations with Europe, 1919–1933.* Ithaca, 1984.

DeBenedetti, Charles. *The Origins of the Modern American Peace Movement, 1915–1929.* Millwood, New York, 1978.

————. *The Peace Reform in American History.* Bloomington, 1980.

DeConde, Alexander. *Herbert Hoover's Latin American Policy.* Stanford,
1951.

Dulles, Foster Rhea. *America's Rise to World Power: 1898–1954.* New
York, 1954.

Ellis, L. Ethan. *Republican Foreign Policy, 1921-1933.* New Brunswick, New Jersey, 1968.

Ferrell, Robert H. *Peace in Their Time: The Origins of the Kellogg-Briand Pact.* New Haven, 1952.

Grieb, Kenneth J. *The Latin American Policy of Warren G. Harding.* Fort Worth, 1977.

Hoff-Wilson, Joan. *American Business and Foreign Policy, 1920-1933.* Lexington, Kentucky, 1971.

Hogan, Michael J. *Informal Entente: The Private Structure of Cooperation in Anglo-American Economic Diplomacy, 1918-1928.* Columbia, 1977.

Iriye, Akira. *After Imperialism: The Search for a New Order in the Far East, 1921-1931.* Columbia, 1977.

Jones, Kenneth Paul, ed. *U.S. Diplomats in Europe, 1919-1941.* Santa Barbara, 1981.

Leffler, Melvyn P. *The Elusive Quest: America's Pursuit of European Stability and French Security, 1919-1933.* Chapel Hill, 1979.

Parrini, Carl. *Heir to Empire: United States Economic Diplomacy, 1916-1923.* Pittsburgh, 1969.

Schuker, Stephen A. *The End of French Predominance in Europe: The Financial Crisis of 1924 and the Adoption of the Dawes Plan.* Chapel Hill, 1976.

Trachtenberg, Marc. *Reparations in World Politics: France and European Economic Diplomacy, 1916-1923.* New York, 1980.

Tulchin, Joseph S. *The Aftermath of War: World War I and U.S. Policy Toward Latin America.* New York, 1971.

Williams, William Appleman. *The Tragedy of American Diplomacy.* New York, 1972.

Wood, Bryce. *The Making of the Good Neighbor Policy.* New York, 1961.

The Diplomacy of the Depression

Jane Karoline Vieth

From behind their broad ocean moats, many Americans in the 1920s and 1930s viewed international events with a certain aloofness, demanding that American foreign policy guarantee their political detachment from international squabbles. Consequently, through-out the 1920s they turned inward and rejected President Woodrow Wilson's dream of international cooperation and collective security through membership in the League of Nations.

The dogged public and congressional desire to abstain from for-eign political involvements forced even a staunch internationalist and big-navy man like Franklin D. Roosevelt to trim sail. His Wilsonian credentials were impeccable. As Wilson's devoted assis-tant secretary of the navy, Roosevelt shared the president's interna-tional perspective. Well traveled and experienced in foreign problems, he vigorously campaigned for an expanded navy, which he kept aggressively vigilant. By 1916 Roosevelt was calling for America's entrance into World War I and for the creation of an even greater military force than his superiors. When the United States did enter the war in 1917, FDR relished the important duties required of the Navy Department.

Roosevelt was an observer at the Versailles Peace Conference in 1919 and became an enthusiastic supporter of President Wilson's dream of American membership in the League of Nations. The League's ultimate rejection by the Senate in 1920, however, con-vinced Roosevelt that public opinion was shifting substantially. Once favorable, it was growing weary of Wilsonianism.

Despite the Republicans' political ascendancy throughout the decade, Roosevelt worked tirelessly to promote his own political fortunes. In 1920 he was chosen as a compromise running mate for the Democratic party's presidential candidate, Ohio's colorless governor, James M. Cox. Throughout the 1920s, FDR gingerly continued to support America's entry into the League of Nations and to offer leadership by writing magazine articles on foreign policy. He also loyally supported Al Smith's unsuccessful presidential ambitions and campaigned for his reelection as governor of New York. In 1928 Roosevelt again gained national recognition by successfully nominating Smith for the presidency. Although Smith lost the election, FDR emerged victorious as the new governor of New York and as a natural contender for some future presidential race. By the end of the decade he had cleverly achieved his personal goal. He had become a national figure and the beneficiary of the Wilsonian legacy.

Once Roosevelt decided to run for the presidency in 1932, he courted the support of isolationist elements within the Democratic party by aligning himself with the current nationalist mood and disavowing his Wilsonian past. Now he opposed American membership in the League and even refused to urge cooperation with it or to applaud its work. FDR also reversed himself on war debts and argued that the Allies and other European nations should pay back the American money borrowed to finance the war and relief and reconstruction efforts. After all, he reasoned, Europe's large expenditures for armaments illustrated that it could afford to meet its financial obligations. Such was the necessary political price for gaining his party's nomination. "A chameleon on plaid," grumbled his Republican opponent, Herbert Hoover.

During the 1932 national campaign, Roosevelt's strategy was to avoid the subject of foreign policy as much as possible, especially since his old Wilsonianism was unpopular and because he had few differences with Hoover. Anxious not to risk any of his political popularity, FDR even substantially moderated his earlier position in support of reciprocal trade agreements. By the end of the campaign, he was arguing for high protective tariffs. Actually, he made no major campaign speech exclusively on foreign policy, but his temporizing masked his true views. He continued to believe that the world was economically interdependent, that peace and prosperity were interrelated, and that a sound foreign policy required a national consensus, but he also worried that domestic problems would hinder his ability to achieve his foreign policy objectives. Nevertheless, Roosevelt was determined to try.

After the tremendous victory in which he swept forty-two out of the forty-eight states, the new president established an administration that was personal, centralized, and haphazard. Steeped in the aristocratic tradition of noblesse oblige, Roosevelt had an exalted sense of his own position and unlimited confidence in his personal influence and his own abilities. He fully regarded himself as the equal of foreign royalty and preferred personal conferences with foreign statesmen to indirect negotiations through official channels and subordinates. He supplemented his personal conduct in foreign affairs by keeping close contact with foreign representatives in Washington, by transacting business in a slipshod fashion over the telephone with his own representatives in foreign capitals, and by sending personal emissaries on diplomatic missions. He was not a systematic thinker but rather an on-the-spot improviser, pragmatic, even capricious. Frequently he accepted contradictory advice. Go "weave the two together," Roosevelt told a surprised adviser who presented him with two conflicting versions of a tariff proposal. Despite all that has been written about him, he remains an extremely enigmatic man, a reserved and self-sufficient figure, one not easily influenced, who quite independently made up his own mind and followed his own advice. "Never let your left hand know what your right is doing," he once told his close friend, Henry Morgenthau. "Which hand am I, Mr. President?" he asked. "My right hand, but I keep my left hand under the table," Roosevelt answered.

He failed to take congressional leadership into his confidence on foreign policy issues, and he often went over the head of Congress by appealing directly to the good sense of the country in his "homey" public addresses and fireside chats. Roosevelt's major speeches were all based on his own outlines, and his assistants were essentially executors, not formulators, who played a minor role in foreign policy design. His chief collaborators in foreign policy were Secretary of State Cordell Hull and Secretary of the Treasury Morgenthau, an avid New Dealer and a Dutchess County neighbor. "To Henry," Roosevelt's inscription on one of his photographs reads, "from one of two of a kind." Roosevelt's dependence on Morgenthau created friction between him and Hull and exacerbated FDR's already chaotic and uncoordinated, but still effective and well-informed, administration.

As disorganized an administrator as his chief, Hull complained about Roosevelt in his gently lisping manner as "that man across the street who never tells me anything." He was the conservative influence, discreet, inflexible, a man of high integrity and practical political experience. Roosevelt respected him, valued his opinions, and kept him as well informed as his personal habits permitted. One adventuresome and pliable, the other cautious and restrained, they complemented each other well. Behind the secretary's air of benevolent southern gentlemanliness lurked an avenging evangelical dogmatism on the subject of economic internationalism. He believed that "the king of evils" was the protective tariff, "the breeder of economic war." "We must eliminate these trade baa-yuhs, heah, theah, and ev'ywheah," mimicked his critics. Hull's presence in the administration indicated Roosevelt's long-range foreign policy objectives and the president's determination to return to the internationalism of his Wilsonian days, but all in his own good time.

Except for his own political appointees like Undersecretary Sumner Welles, a patrician from Boston and an experienced diplomat who headed the Latin American section at the age of twenty-eight, FDR particularly disliked the State Department and distrusted career officers as a class. He sarcastically referred to them as professional perfectionists. In a letter to Hull the president once wrote, "I am reminded of a remark made to me by an old career service man—'You can get to be a Minister if (a) you are loyal to the service, (b) you do nothing to offend people, (c) if you are not intoxicated at public functions.'" He also believed there was "a lot of dead wood in the top three grades that should never have got there."

By creating overlapping areas of authority in foreign policy, by setting various cabinet officials, personal envoys, and government agencies against each other, and by keeping them all jockeying with one another for influence and power, Roosevelt masked his intentions until he was ready to act. He set Morgenthau against Hull, Hull against Welles, Hull against his assistant secretary of state, New Dealer Raymond Moley, personal emissaries such as Norman Davis against career diplomats, and pitted a host of other bureaucrats and congressional groups against each other. By having the State Department espouse two mutually exclusive views at the same time, such as Hull's internationalism and Moley's self-protective program of independent economic nationalism—"intranationalism"—FDR undercut the department's ability to pursue a consistent course in international affairs and ensured his control of American foreign policy, just exactly as he wanted.

The president's major concern, as he told his inaugural audience in 1933, was to put "first things first." "Our international trade relations, though vastly important, are secondary ... to the establishment of a sound national economy." Yet, despite his tough inaugural address on avoiding foreign entanglements, there were vestiges of his old Wilsonianism. During FDR's first six weeks in office, he tried to prop up the disarmament conference in Geneva, supported Hull's reciprocal trade agreement program, and called for lowering barriers to world trade. By the fall of 1933, Roosevelt even extended official recognition to the Soviet Union, something that had been withheld since the Bolshevik Revolution of 1917. He did so by encouraging a consensus among businessmen and religious leaders who believed that recognition would increase the trade and prosperity in both countries and reduce the threat of Japanese aggression against Russia by enhancing Soviet prestige.

Actually, Roosevelt thought intranationalism was viable only in the short run and not as a long-range policy. He hoped that the nationalistic monetary and economic policies urged by advisers like Moley would work quickly enough to permit him to support currency stabilization and tariff agreements at the London World Economic Conference. But, after FDR torpedoed the conference in July 1933 with the famous "bombshell" message in which he reaffirmed the primacy of domestic recovery over Hull's arguments for international financial cooperation, he began to back away from decisive action in foreign affairs. Nevertheless, he still wanted the United States to play a role in reducing international tensions.

During the first two years of his administration, Roosevelt had a relatively free hand in fashioning American foreign policy. This was a period of general indifference throughout the country and of a widespread preoccupation with the problems created by the Great Depression. Roosevelt acted decisively in domestic affairs by extending government assistance to private bankers, cutting federal spending to balance the budget, taking the country off the gold standard, ending Prohibition, and stepping up economic recovery and unemployment relief by creating the New Deal's alphabet agencies: the National Recovery Administration (NRA), the Agricultural Adjustment Administration (AAA), and the Civilian Conservation Corps (CCC). Often indecisive in foreign affairs, however, FDR rambled back and forth, following a policy of internationalism and then of intranationalism and anti-imperialism, of self-determination, and of traditional power politics as events seemed to dictate. But, from late 1934 through 1935, events in Europe had frightened Americans and made them wary of foreign involvements and fearful of a general war. The tension caused by Germany's rearmament, the crisis unfolding between Italy and Ethiopia, France's doubling of the existing period of military service for conscripts, Japan's attempt to gain hegemony over China, and the League of Nations' consideration of sanctions against aggressive nations prompted FDR to write that "these are without a doubt the most hair-trigger times the world has gone through" in his lifetime.

Americans responded to these events by espousing isolationism, a policy that began to dominate national thinking and cost Roosevelt his flexibility in foreign affairs. Always FDR skirted controversial solutions which might undermine his political popularity and wreck his New Deal. He was also particularly sensitive to criticism that he favored radical departures in economic policy; consequently, he was eager to minimize charges that he supported major changes in America's traditional foreign policy. Such caution led him to steer a course of least resistance in international affairs, one of political expediency, economic nationalism, and political isolationism. Not only was he unwilling to take aggressive, unpopular stands, but he also seemed indifferent to the problems inherent in pursuing conflicting domestic and foreign policy objectives. To have resolved such contradictions would have been inconsistent with the philosophy of the early New Deal—one of short-term, quick, pragmatic solutions rather than of long-range, systematic planning.

Privately he was a loyal internationalist and believed in collective action to maintain peace; publicly, he frequently sounded and sometimes acted very much like an isolationist. In 1935 he wrote to Colonel Edward M. House, Wilson's trusted adviser, that he had several proposals by which American influence could help reduce the armaments race. His reason for rejecting these schemes was always the same: "I fear any suggestions ... would meet with [a] chilly, half-contemptuous reception." However, he frequently spoke of keeping America uncommitted. In his major campaign address in 1936, he mouthed the slogans of neutrality. "Despite what happens in continents overseas, the United States of America shall and must remain, as long ago the Father of our Country prayed that it might remain—unentangled and free."

In Congress key progressive Republican senators, such as William E. Borah of Idaho, Gerald P. Nye of North Dakota, Robert M. La Follette, Jr., of Wisconsin, California's crusty Hiram W. Johnson, and the powerful chairman of the Foreign Relations Committee, Key Pittman, staunchly defended a foreign policy of isolationism and opposed even symbolic American involvement in international affairs. Although few in number, they were extremely influential; Roosevelt believed he dare not alienate them on foreign policy issues since they warmly supported his New Deal legislation. It was they who urged a reluctant FDR in 1934 to support the Johnson Act, which forbade loans to any foreign government in default on its war debts. Roosevelt thereby cemented a valuable political relationship with these progressive Republican isolationists.

A further reason for FDR's caution in foreign affairs was provided by the sensational revelations of the Nye Committee in 1934. The hero of the drama was Nye, a stern young senator, whose committee investigated the influence of the armaments industry and the banking interests on American entry into World War I. It condemned these "merchants of death" for their lies and trickery. The timing was perfect. The committee's findings contributed to a general revulsion against intervening in Europe's squabbles.

Even a mild proposal that the United States not interfere with League sanctions against an aggressor nation was defeated because Johnson mobilized the Senate isolationists against it. So, too, was FDR's plan in 1935 for American entry into the World Court, the one internationalist gesture most likely to succeed. "To hell with Europe and the rest of those nations," announced one senatorial opponent. Roosevelt deeply resented this congressional defeat: "As to the 36 Senators who placed themselves on record against the principle of a World Court, I am inclined to think that if they ever get to Heaven, they will be doing a great deal of apologizing for a very long time—that is, if God is against war—and I think He is." The president and his advisers interpreted their defeat as a major crossroads in American foreign policy. It had aroused, they believed, a strong and vocal isolationist opposition, not just in Congress but in the country as a whole, which would temporarily hamstring the president's conduct of foreign affairs. "We shall go through a period of non-cooperation in everything ... for the next year or two," Roosevelt predicted.

By the summer of 1935 congressional isolationists responded to the growing threats to peace by demanding neutrality legislation that would define America's conduct toward a European war. They wanted an embargo on all armaments trade during wartime. Both Roosevelt and Hull approved the embargo scheme, but they wanted broad discretionary power to distinguish between victim and aggressor and the right to embargo arms only to the latter. Such executive authority, they reasoned, would provide a strong deterrent to aggression.

Congress resolutely opposed their request since it meant taking sides in a war and therefore implied American involvement. A compromise was drafted by Senators Pittman and Borah and accepted over the president's protest. It requested Roosevelt to declare a mandatory embargo on implements of war to all belligerents. The first Neutrality Act was signed in August 1935 and was applied against both Italy and Ethiopia after the Italian invasion of Ethiopia in the fall. The major weakness of the act, which Roosevelt and Hull previously had recognized, was that it embargoed only arms and munitions but not raw materials such as steel, coal, and oil, Italy's most vital imports. In attempting to undermine this unintentional aid to Italy, Roosevelt announced a "moral embargo," a voluntary agreement to cut back on the commodities sent to Italy. Predictably, however, Haile Selassie's soldiers were defeated in December 1935 by the Italian war machine, which was unintentionally aided by the inflexible provisions of the Neutrality Act.

By 1935 Roosevelt had almost given up any hope of conducting his own foreign policy. His attempts to gain congressional approval for his "moral" embargo on war materials and for executive discretion were repeatedly dashed by the congressional isolationists. Time was running out; the Neutrality Act was about to expire. After six weeks of debate, Roosevelt and Hull grudgingly faced defeat and accepted the second Neutrality Act in February 1936. Essentially, it was a continuation of the previous act, but it also prohibited loans to belligerents and required the president to embargo arms to any belligerent. It embodied the isolationists' major argument, the Nye thesis, that embargoes on arms and trade would prevent American involvement in war. Its application to the Spanish Civil War, however, ironically aided the spread of fascism by cutting off supplies to the democratically elected Spanish Republican government.

In the 1936 presidential election, Roosevelt devised a strategy of wooing isolationists and pacifists by reminding them of his administration's efforts on behalf of peace. "Peace, like charity," he told his audience, "begins at home and that's why we have begun at home. . . . But peace in the western world is not all we seek." He recited the administration's various attempts to maintain peace and concluded that all of this had come to naught. Therefore, he would now seek to "isolate America from war. . . . I have seen war. . . . I hate war." Once the election was behind him, Roosevelt believed that he could turn his attention to searching for peace, and his first major attempt at peacemaking was his decision to attend the Buenos Aires Conference in December 1936. He hoped to solidify the Good Neighbor policy, which had been initiated by his predecessor President Hoover on the principles of equality and partnership with the other American republics, the elimination of artificial economic barriers, and the union of the Americas against outside threats. He told his cabinet before leaving that, if he were successful in achieving an understanding of peace and disarmament at the conference, then perhaps a similar agreement could be reached in the Pacific and elsewhere. The Buenos Aires agreements had the effect of transforming the Monroe Doctrine from a unilateral declaration into a multilateral agreement.

"THANKSGIVING 1936." Uncle Sam reflects on the sentiment of American isolationism. (Library of Congress)

Even as Roosevelt attended the Buenos Aires Conference, he continued to mull over ways to help Europe maintain peace, but it seemed completely hopeless. Hitler had seized the Rhineland in violation of the Versailles treaty, the Spanish Civil War raged on, Japan and Germany had signed the Anti-Comintern Pact against the Soviet Union, and the aimless drift of the democracies, Britain and France, dictated a policy of watchful waiting. Despite his desire to avoid controversy on foreign policy, Roosevelt had to face the May 1 expiration date on the 1936 neutrality law and a new Congress that was even more suspicious of his intentions because of his tremendous landslide in the election. Two new provisions were part of the 1937 Neutrality Act. One prohibited Americans from traveling on belligerent ships, while the other established the "cash-and-carry" plan, under whose terms nations at war could buy American supplies and arms provided they paid cash and carried them away on their own ships. The president was given the authority to name the commodities to which cash-and-carry applied, although it was not nearly as much authority as Roosevelt would have liked. (This plan was limited to two years and was never applied under the act.) So overwhelming was America's desire for peace that the act was immensely popular.

The most serious congressional assault on the president's control of foreign policy was the Ludlow Amendment. Its debate in Congress was immediately prompted by the December 12, 1937 Japanese bombing of the USS *Panay,* which was anchored in the Yangtze River and prominently flying American flags. Roosevelt was indignant and discussed with his cabinet and the military high command the possibility of economic or military retaliation. He drew back, however, when he realized that there was no public outcry for such action and that, in fact, peace sentiment had been strengthened.

The *Panay* incident showed the precariousness of peace and stimulated congressional action on the Ludlow Amendment. Intended to be an amendment to the Constitution, it would provide that the government, except in the case of an attack on American soil, could declare war only when a majority voted to do so in a national referendum. Severe White House pressure prevented the passage of this amendment which would have deprived the president of control over foreign policy, one of his chief constitutional prerogatives. It was finally defeated in the House of Representatives in January 1938 by a vote of 209 to 188. The 188 votes illustrated Roosevelt's tenuous control over foreign policy, the intensity of congressional distrust and isolationist sentiment, and the national aversion to war.

Throughout the spring and summer of 1937 the president continued to pursue his dream of a world conference modeled on that held in Buenos Aires. Roosevelt sent Norman Davis, a respected internationalist and an adviser to both Wilson and Hoover, to Europe to discuss presidential plans informally with European leaders, and he invited Neville Chamberlain to the United States. Davis reported that most of the British and French politicians endorsed Roosevelt's ideas, but Chamberlain, the new British prime minister, was less sympathetic. Although he wanted the democracies and the dictatorships to work out a solution to their problems, Chamberlain did not like Roosevelt's suggestion for a comprehensive plan undertaken by many nations. He believed that foreign affairs were so fluid that any plans made would quickly become obsolete. Twice Roosevelt invited Chamberlain to visit him and discuss the international threats, and twice the prime minister refused.

Apparently Chamberlain's rejection of Roosevelt's invitation prompted the president to accept the advice of Davis and Secretary of State Hull. They had been urging him to give a speech stressing international cooperation and to do so in an isolationist stronghold. Roosevelt liked the dramatic gesture as it would give him an opportunity to criticize the aggressor nations publicly and to educate Americans to the threat of international lawlessness. On October 5, 1937 the president created an international sensation in Chicago by launching into a stern lecture on foreign affairs and doing so as no other president had dared for sixteen years. In an obvious but indirect reference to Japan's undeclared war against China, Roosevelt condemned the "present reign of terror and international lawlessness" and stated that unjustified interference in the international affairs of other countries "has now reached a stage where the very foundations of civilization are seriously threatened." If chaos continues, "let no one imagine that America will escape." Then, in a dramatic departure from the suggested State Department outline, came the Rooseveltian climax. "When an epidemic of physical disease starts to spread, the community approves and joins in a quarantine of the patients in order to protect the health of the community against the spread of the disease. . . . War is a contagion, whether it be declared or undeclared." He ended on a positive note, saying that "America hates war. America hopes for peace. Therefore, America actively engages in the search for peace."

The crowd cheered its approval, and most of the country responded favorably to Roosevelt's address, but not the outraged opposition. Some isolationist congressmen even threatened him with impeachment. Indignant at the lack of support from his own party leaders, the president complained that "it's a terrible thing to look over your shoulder when you are trying to lead and to find no one there." Afterward he shunned any further explanation of his speech. Perhaps he realized that a "quarantine" seemed to imply some kind of action without war, something beyond the usual political or military steps, and he knew that he had nothing more to offer and could not fulfill the expectations aroused by his speech. Regardless, the quarantine speech showed that he was still pursuing a variety of schemes for preserving the peace, and that this was simply one more in a series, as the Buenos Aires Conference had been.

The day after the speech the president asked Undersecretary Welles to outline a new peace program—the October Plan—to provide for American participation in collective action. Roosevelt intended to hold a dramatic meeting and appeal for a solution to international problems. Acting on Hull's cautious advice, he first sent a confidential outline of his proposal to Chamberlain who rejected it, arguing that it might jeopardize Britain's efforts to appease Italy and Germany. Disappointed at the prime minister's rebuff, Roosevelt nevertheless sent Chamberlain an obliging note, saying that he agreed to defer the proposal and await the outcome of Britain's appeasement policy. The president's proposal became one of history's "might have beens." Despite his rejection of the note, Chamberlain repeatedly tried, with mixed results, to secure Roosevelt's approval for his appeasement policy during the spring and summer of 1938. The wily FDR refused, however, to be taken in by Chamberlain's "game," as he called it.

The president's reaction to Germany's annexation of Austria also showed his refusal to make a commitment to Chamberlain's policy. When the British passively accepted the *Anschluss*, Roosevelt declined to do anything that might undermine their appeasement initiatives. In response to the crisis the U.S. government merely sent Hitler a meek note of protest. One State Department official succinctly summed up the American position: "We certainly can't be thought, whatever our sympathies may be, to assume any responsibility legal or moral in Europe at the moment."

During the winter and spring of 1938, Roosevelt's hopes for a revision of the neutrality legislation and its application to Spain were repeatedly dashed. He momentarily considered lifting the Spanish embargo but decided against it, in part out of fear of domestic repercussions and of alienating Catholics who supported it and in part because London and Paris intended to continue their policy of nonintervention regardless. Roosevelt further reasoned that lifting the embargo would probably not have helped the Spanish Loyalists (Republican forces). Ultimately, in February 1939, after the collapse of the Loyalist regime and the fall of Madrid, the American government recognized General Francisco Franco's new Fascist government, as did London and Paris.

Despite Spain, Roosevelt gave an "unofficial blessing" to a congressional push to allow greater presidential discretion in applying an embargo, but, when Congress refused to act, he drew back. Repeatedly, domestic political considerations restrained him from pressing too hard for revision. In the spring of 1938 he was preoccupied with a recovery program designed to end the seven-month

"GOOSE-STEPPING, NEVILLE?" An American view of the appeasement policy of British Prime Minister Neville Chamberlain. (Wilmington *Morning News*, 1938–39, Library of Congress)

recession and to help the 4 million unemployed Americans, many near starving, find jobs. In a fireside chat radio broadcast the president reminded his audience that several nations had rejected democracy "not because the people disliked democracy but because they had grown tired of unemployment and insecurity." Thus the priority given to economic and domestic considerations, the still seething political backlash over his attempt to enlarge the Supreme Court and to "pack" it with New Deal sympathizers, the fresh charges of "dictator" that sprang up over his ill-fated proposal to reorganize the executive agencies, and the continued opposition of conservative Democrats who disapproved of his New Deal legislation made FDR unwilling to risk spending his declining political capital on a fight for neutrality revision which, even if successful, he believed would probably have been ineffective.

The crisis over Czechoslovakia was the next European problem the president faced. His response was the same: "No risks, no commitments." It was a policy of "pinpricks and righteous protests." Although Secretary Hull stated publicly that the American government was following these critical events with "close and anxious attention," Roosevelt refused either to defend appeasement or to urge military resistance to Hitler's demands. As the crisis thickened and war seemed imminent, the president on several occasions appealed to the European powers not to break off negotiations over Czechoslovakia, but always he concluded with the traditional statement of American foreign policy: "The United States has no political entanglements."

In September 1938, Hitler invited Chamberlain to Munich to meet with him to discuss the Czech crisis. French Premier Edouard Daladier was also present as an uncomfortable witness, as was Italy's Benito Mussolini, the conference's self-styled mediator. The Czech representatives waited quietly at the British hotel throughout the thirteen-hour meeting in which four foreigners carved up their republic. After numerous arguments and conversations dominated by Mussolini, the only one of the four who could speak the others' languages, an agreement was reached at 2 A.M. Czechoslovakia was to be left defenseless and to cede its border fortresses and the Sudetenland to Germany. Roosevelt sent Chamberlain a terse, two-word message: "Good man." Although FDR has been given much credit for persuading Hitler to call the Munich Conference, his appeals actually were probably rather inconsequential. Hitler must have seen them as mere gestures, nothing more.

Munich marked a watershed in American foreign policy. A pair of shrewd observers, *New York Herald Tribune* columnists Joseph Alsop and Robert Kintner, wrote that "before Munich this country's role in world politics was chiefly that of a chorus, somewhat over-given to gloomy gesture and hortatory speech." After Munich, however, Roosevelt grew increasingly alarmed over European affairs since Hitler had proved once again that Germany could expand without encountering anything more than verbal protests from the democracies. Because of their increasing skepticism over America's policy of isolationism and their dislike of Chamberlain's appeasement policy, Roosevelt, Hull, and Welles began to reexamine American foreign policy assumptions. To the trio, U.S. interests dictated a firm, specific course. War must be prevented; if that proved impossible, then victory for the democracies must be ensured.

In his State of the Union address in January 1939, the president signaled a change in policy by calling for "methods short of war" and suggesting that these might curb aggression. At the very least, he wanted the neutrality law repealed, particularly its mandatory embargo section, so that he could make American arms available to friendly nations. Despite his appeals, Congress remained unmoved. Many politicians believed that Roosevelt would not run for a third term and viewed him as a lame-duck president. This, combined with the Republicans' gains in the 1938 congressional elections and their alliance with suspicious and rebellious anti-New Deal Democrats, explains his weakened political position. Furthermore, his confidential remarks to members of the Senate in which he was quoted as saying that "our frontier is on the Rhine"—a quote passed on to Washington columnists Alsop and Kintner and one that Roosevelt denied making—further alarmed suspicious senators already worried that he would drag the United States into a war. Reluctantly, FDR concluded that once again neutrality revision would have to be postponed.

Roosevelt's anxiety over the threat to peace in Europe was justified. Despite Hitler's promise at Munich not to acquire any more territory, in March 1939 he devoured the rest of the Czech nation and began a "war of nerves" against Poland by demanding that it cede the Free State of Danzig to Germany and permit the building of a German road across the Polish Corridor that divided East Prussia from the rest of Germany. Both Britain and France reversed their appeasement policy and guaranteed aid to Poland and later to Greece and Romania. The president denied recognition to Hitler's Czechoslovakian conquests and refused to acknowledge Mussolini's acquisition of Albania on April 7. Mussolini's latest venture created the impression that he would join with Hitler in a mutual enterprise. Roosevelt also sent the "Saturday Surprise" message to Hitler and Mussolini, asking them to guarantee thirty-one nations against attack. If they did so, the United States would join in international discussions of armaments and trade. The president's unconventional intervention had provoked tremendous popular response in the United States. Events in Europe were arousing Americans to the threat to peace.

Beginning in mid-April, Roosevelt quietly returned to the issue of neutrality revision. He met with lukewarm senators and representatives and explained that repealing the arms embargo was the best way to keep the peace and defend American interests. Hull helped him. According to Alsop and Kintner, the delightfully quotable secretary of state told the legislators that the coming struggle was hardly "another goddam piddling dispute over a boundary line." Not to repeal this "wretched little bobtailed sawed-off domestic statute," he said, was "just plain chuckle-headed." However, these arguments failed to persuade the isolationists who remained unalterably opposed to revision. Thus, Congress adjourned in early August without acting on neutrality legislation.

Roosevelt was angered by the opposition and privately told Morgenthau: "I will bet you an old hat ... that when [Hitler] wakes up and finds out what has happened, there will be great rejoicing in the Italian and German camps. I think we ought to introduce a bill for statues of [Senators] Austin, Vandenberg, Lodge, and Taft ... to be erected in Berlin and put the swastika on them." Actually, Roosevelt and Hull overestimated the extent to which Hitler cared for, or could be deterred by, an arms embargo. He had little regard for the United States and saw it as a "mongrel society," hopelessly weak and incapable of interfering with his plans. His desire to go to war with Poland depended not on American neutrality legislation but on British, French, and German negotiations with Moscow and the necessity of neutralizing Hitler's eastern border. The status of the neutrality law, despite Roosevelt's belief, therefore had almost no impact on the course of events in Europe or on Hitler's thinking.

By August 1939 all signs pointed toward a German-Polish crisis over Danzig, and on August 22 Hitler achieved one of his major foreign policy objectives when Moscow agreed to sign a Nazi-Soviet nonaggression pact. Now he would not have to fight a long two-front war since Soviet neutrality would be guaranteed when he invaded Poland. Roosevelt continued his last-minute efforts for peace, suggesting a settlement through direct negotiation and offering to be the mediator. His appeals were for domestic effect; he wanted to "put the bee on Germany," he said, which nobody had done in 1914. On September 1 the long-awaited crisis exploded as Nazi bombers and several divisions invaded Poland. Two days later France and Britain declared war on Germany. World War II had begun and still the United States remained shackled by its neutrality legislation. It was not fully repealed until October 1941, only two months before the Japanese bombing of Pearl Harbor and America's entrance into the war.

The nature of Roosevelt's leadership in foreign policy throughout the 1930s and its relationship to the outbreak of World War II are topics of complex and heated continuing historical discussions. Many official documents became available in the immediate postwar decade of the 1950s. Their accessibility to scholars has stimulated research, writing, and debate. Controversy rages over what FDR's intentions in foreign policy were and whether the president was deceitful or candid with Congress and the American public about his intentions.

One view of Roosevelt's leadership is critical of his conduct of foreign policy and argues that he pursued a number of insidious schemes to steer the country deliberately into war. Despite his awareness that the American public had consistently demonstrated its desire for peace, particularly in the 1940 election, isolationist and revisionist historians like Charles A. Beard contend that sometime around the outbreak of the war in Europe in 1939 the president decided that the United States must enter the conflict and deceitfully worked to bring this about as quickly as possible.

By contrast, another historical position, represented by William L. Langer and S. Everett Gleason, supports the view that by September 1940 most Americans were eager to approve of virtually any form of aid to the Allies. Actually, Roosevelt worked consistently to keep the country out of the war and was quite worried about America's ability to avoid the conflict. He underestimated popular support for his foreign policy, however, and was reluctant to be candid with the American public because he feared congressional opposition, which he was prone to exaggerate. Far from acting decisively and quickly, as isolationist and revisionist critics like Beard have charged, the president's keen sense of timing enabled him to wait patiently for the right moment. His acute political instincts made him realize that no leader could get too far ahead of his followers.

Another more recent historical view stresses America's contribution to Germany's appeasement throughout the 1930s. Critical historians have charged that the president failed to implement bold policies and to take decisive action, and that he was responsible for numerous tragic diplomatic blunders that culminated in the Munich Agreement. In fact, Roosevelt behaved little better than Chamberlain. Even at Munich, these critics have argued, FDR failed to grasp that more than the survival of Czechoslovakia was at stake.

Still another view, developed by historian Robert Dallek, states that Roosevelt acquiesced in the popular American preference for a passive foreign policy. He did so because he realistically concluded that at home he lacked the strong political consensus so essential to decisive and effective action abroad. He did not try to trick his country into war. On the contrary, Dallek has contended, the most striking aspect about Roosevelt was not his arbitrariness in pushing America into the conflict but rather his restraint. Thus the scholarly controversy concerning Roosevelt's diplomacy and World War II is filled with contradictions, which will no doubt stimulate further discussion and debate.

To summarize, in the early months of Roosevelt's first administration, he pursued a variety of schemes as circumstances dictated, from his old Wilsonianism to the economic nationalism of the New Deal, but his long-range plans called for internationalism, collective action, and reciprocal trade agreements. By 1935 his political flexibility was undercut by domestic isolationist sentiment. Consequently, he reluctantly acquiesced in the popular feeling and waited for events to educate the American public. During his second administration, however, the situation in Europe and the Far East convinced him that he must find some way to avert war, and he began the risky venture of trying to educate the public to the threats to its security. Cautious and prudent, Roosevelt was determined to build a consensus for his foreign policy and to maintain his political leadership.

Sources and Suggested Readings

Alsop, Joseph, and Kintner, Robert. *American White Paper.* New York, 1940.

Beard, Charles A. *American Foreign Policy in the Making, 1932–1940: A Study in Responsibilities.* New Haven, 1946.

Blum, John Morton. *From the Morgenthau Diaries.* Vol. 1, *Years of Crisis, 1928–1938.* Boston, 1959.

Burns, James MacGregor. *Roosevelt: The Lion and the Fox.* New York, 1956.

Dallek, Robert. *Franklin D. Roosevelt and American Foreign Policy, 1932–1945.* New York, 1979.

Hull, Cordell. *The Memoirs of Cordell Hull.* 2 vols. New York, 1948.

Langer, William L., and Gleason, S. Everett. *The Challenge to Isolation: The World Crisis of 1937–1940 and American Foreign Policy.* New York, 1952.

Leuchtenburg, William E. *Franklin D. Roosevelt and the New Deal, 1932–1940.* New York, 1963.

Moffat, J. C. *The Moffat Papers.* Cambridge, Massachusetts, 1956.

Moley, Raymond. *After Seven Years.* New York, 1939.

Offner, Arnold A. *American Appeasement: United States Foreign Policy and Germany, 1933-1938.* New York, 1969.

Roosevelt, Elliott, and Lash, Joseph P., eds. *F.D.R.: His Personal Letters, 1928-1945.* 2 vols. New York, 1950.

Rosenman, Samuel I. *Working with Roosevelt.* New York, 1952.

_____, ed. *The Public Papers and Addresses of Franklin D. Roosevelt, 1928-1945.* 13 vols. New York, 1938-50.

Schlesinger, Arthur M., Jr. *The Age of Roosevelt.* Vol. 2, *The Coming of the New Deal.* Boston, 1965.

U.S. Department of State. *Foreign Relations of the United States, 1938.*

The United States Enters World War II

Jonathan G. Utley

On Monday, December 8, 1941, President Franklin D. Roosevelt asked Congress to recognize that a state of war had existed following Japan's "unprovoked and dastardly attack" against American forces at Pearl Harbor. War had come to America. Why had it come? What series of events brought the United States into the war? The American people did not seek this war. There was none of the bravado of 1898 when Americans went off to trounce the hated Spaniard, nor was there the optimism of 1917 when the nation set forth to make the world safe for democracy. This time the mood was one of grim determination. Thus it is not the American people to whom we must look for an explanation of why the nation went to war but to their leaders, to President Roosevelt, Secretary of State Cordell Hull, and the rest of the Washington foreign policy establishment that led the country along a path ending in war.

Sometimes national leaders see a war coming, decide they should enter it, and resolutely direct their nation toward that end. At other times a nation stumbles into war because its leaders do not foresee a conflict and proceed blindly down a path they think will guide them to peace. With World War II and its leaders, both explanations apply. To see how, it is necessary first to survey what happened and then to explore why the U.S. government acted as it did.

In the 1930s two great military powers threatened to alter the world order. Increasingly militaristic and extremist, imperial Japan looked toward the establishment of a New Order in East Asia. In Europe, Adolf Hitler's Nazi Germany sought to establish a thousand-year Reich, uniting all the German-speaking peoples in Europe and dominating the rest of the Continent.

To this end, Germany annexed Austria in March 1938. Later in the year Hitler demanded that Czechoslovakia hand over the Sudetenland with its large German-speaking population. The Czechs wanted to fight and turned to their French and British allies for support, but neither of those nations was psychologically or militarily prepared for war. Instead, they sought to buy peace through appeasing Hitler with the Sudetenland.

Throughout these events Roosevelt kept an official silence. He did not trust Hitler and did not think that appeasement would work, but he too remembered the horrors of World War I. Like most Americans, the president was prepared to go to almost any length to avoid another war. Besides, given the isolationist mood of the people, there was little he could do.

Appeasement did not work. In the spring of 1939, Hitler took over the remainder of Czechoslovakia, and in September his armies blasted their way through Poland in less than one month. For Britain and France the loss of Poland was too much, and they declared war on Germany. That began the European phase of World War II.

With the outbreak of the war, Roosevelt invoked the Neutrality Act, a law prohibiting Americans from making loans or selling war materiel to any of the belligerents. The president, whose sympathies were with the Allies, quickly persuaded Congress to revise the law so that any nation could buy whatever it wanted in the United States so long as it paid cash and carried it away in its own ships. Roosevelt claimed his "cash-and-carry" program was totally neutral, but almost everyone understood that it favored the British, who had both the cash and the ships, and whose navy could keep Germany from taking advantage of the program.

During the winter of 1939–40, Britain and France used cash-and-carry to help prepare for the German spring offensive, but it was too little too late. German armies attacked Norway and Denmark in early April and moved against the Netherlands and Belgium one month later. In both cases the German blitzkrieg was spectacularly successful. In less than five weeks British armies were pushed off the Continent and France was conquered. By the end of June 1940, Hitler had made himself the master of western Europe, while a bloodied but not yet beaten Britain waited for the German invasion of the British Isles.

Shocked by these German victories the United States began to act. Roosevelt ordered a major preparedness program. Planes, tanks, and ships had to be built. Gasoline, copper, rubber, and all the other materiel needed for a modern industrial war had to be stockpiled. Congress appropriated vast sums for defense and even instituted the first peacetime draft in the nation's history. In an effort to help

Britain guard its ships from German submarines, Roosevelt "traded" fifty overage American destroyers for ninety-nine-year leases on a chain of British naval bases stretching from Newfoundland to British Guiana. Most Americans approved of these actions because they would help the nation to defend the Western Hemisphere should Germany try to cross the Atlantic. On the other hand, the American people were not prepared to cross the Atlantic themselves and confront German armies.

By the time Germany had crushed France, Japanese and Chinese armies had been fighting for three years. This Asian war began as an isolated incident in northern China but soon grew into a full-scale struggle for control of that country. In spite of its superior technology and mechanization, Japan could not defeat the poorly equipped, poorly trained, and even more poorly led Chinese armies. China lost battle after battle but did not surrender. Instead, the Chinese traded land for time, retreating farther and farther into the interior. Soon Japan found itself involved in a war it could not win but from which it could not extricate itself without humiliation.

During the first three years of the Sino-Japanese War the Roosevelt administration did little to help China or hinder Japan. It had given China a modest loan, protested many of Japan's actions, and implied that some form of commercial pressure might be applied against Japan if it did not mend its ways. In reality, however, no pressure was applied, Japan did not mend its ways, and the war dragged on with no end in sight. The German conquest of Europe changed all that.

Japan hoped to dominate East Asia politically, militarily, and economically. What held it back was its inability to conquer China and the British and U.S. presence in the region. Britain was the most formidable power because of its major investments in China, its colonies of Hong Kong and Malaya, and its large naval base at Singapore. But, by the fall of 1940, Britain was fighting for its life in Europe and was powerless to stop Japan in Asia.

Moreover, the German conquest of the Netherlands and France had left their Asian colonies vulnerable. Japan was interested in the French colony of Indochina because the northern part controlled the flow of supplies into China, while the southern half was an excellent base for launching an invasion against Singapore and the oil-rich Netherlands East Indies. That was a tempting target for a nation dependent upon the Western powers for its oil.

This situation was painfully apparent to Roosevelt and Hull even as the German offensive began. Consequently, when Japan showed a particular interest in the Netherlands East Indies, the secretary of state responded with a blunt warning that Japan should not cast a covetous eye on Southeast Asia. To emphasize American determination, Roosevelt and Hull ordered the U.S. fleet to remain in Hawaiian waters, where it was on maneuvers, rather than return to the fleet's home base in southern California two thousand miles farther away from Japan.

These warnings did not stop Japan. The magnitude of the German victories in Europe and the vulnerability of Southeast Asia led Japan further down the road of conquest. In September 1940, Japan joined a military alliance with Germany and Italy and occupied the northern half of French Indochina. The Roosevelt administration responded by embargoing all exports of scrap iron and steel to Japan. Such an embargo would not bring Japan to its knees, but Hull hoped it might bring Japan to its senses and stop its expansion into Southeast Asia. Had they wanted to, Roosevelt and Hull could have imposed far-reaching economic sanctions, even cutting off oil. Neither the president nor his secretary of state was willing to go that far, and trade with Japan continued in most items, especially oil.

Meanwhile, the United States moved closer to an alliance with Britain. When the British ran out of money for their cash-and-carry purchases, Roosevelt persuaded Congress to approve his Lend-Lease program. In his own sly way the president compared the program to lending your garden hose to a neighbor whose house was on fire. It was nothing of the kind. It placed the full economic and industrial resources of the United States behind Britain and marked the abandonment of even the pretense of American neutrality.

It did no good, however, to produce goods for Britain if they could not get past the German submarine wolf packs that prowled the Atlantic Ocean. In the first six months of 1941, Britain lost 3.5 million tons of shipping, with over 700 ships sunk and another 1,400 damaged. If those rates continued, Britain would be starved into defeat. Roosevelt had to do something.

Since the earliest days of the war the president had used the U.S. Navy to patrol waters around the Americas. These "neutrality patrols" were designed to locate German ships and broadcast their location to the British. During 1940 he had gradually increased the size and aggressiveness of the naval forces in the Atlantic. By February 1941, when Roosevelt formally created the Atlantic Fleet, it was a powerful force of 159 ships, including 2 aircraft carriers, 3 battleships, 8 cruisers, and 79 destroyers. Noting the direction the president was taking, Chief of Naval Operations Admiral Harold R. Stark commented that it was now a matter of when, not whether, the

United States would enter the war against Germany. In March, Roosevelt inched still closer to war by ordering the Atlantic Fleet to prepare for combat.

Although plans for convoying were ready by the start of 1941, Roosevelt hesitated to implement them. Once American warships began escorting American and British ships across the Atlantic, it would be impossible for a German submarine commander to distinguish between an American destroyer and a British destroyer. Inevitably, there would be casualties, and those casualties would lead to war. Rather than order convoying, Roosevelt aggressively extended his neutrality patrolling by ordering the navy to search for German submarines as far east as the 25th meridian, a line overlapping the German war zone surrounding the British Isles. With American destroyers looking for German submarines in a German war zone, it was only a matter of time until there was trouble. Surprisingly, it did not come until September when the USS *Greer* clashed with a German submarine. Although neither side drew blood in this engagement and the *Greer* was clearly the aggressor, Roosevelt went on nationwide radio to denounce the German submarines as the "rattlesnakes of the Atlantic" and promised that American ships would not wait for them to strike again. He ordered the U.S. Navy to begin convoying and to shoot at German warships on sight.

The war in the North Atlantic quickly escalated. In mid-October the *Kearny* entered a ferocious battle with a wolf pack of German submarines and received a torpedo in the side for its trouble. Through superior seamanship and good luck, the battered destroyer limped to safety with its dead and wounded. "America has been attacked," Roosevelt declared. "The U.S.S. *Kearny* is not just a Navy ship. She belongs to every man, woman, and child in this nation." Still, Roosevelt did not ask for a declaration of war; he knew Congress would not vote it. Even when over one hundred sailors died on the USS *Reuben James* at the end of October, the American people held back. The old fear of war that permeated the land was still too strong. Most Americans were willing to go along with the president when it came to Lend-Lease, neutrality patrolling, and even convoying or shooting on sight, but they were not willing to cross the Atlantic and engage in the war.

Meanwhile, Japanese-American relations were deteriorating at an alarming rate. To keep this spiral from ending in war, Secretary of State Hull and Japanese Ambassador Kichisaburo Nomura held many lengthy meetings during the spring of 1941 in a vain effort to find a basis for a Japanese-American agreement. By June, as the

Hull-Nomura talks dragged on, the European war took a startling turn, once again upsetting the Asian balance of power.

In a surprise move, Hitler unleashed his armies against the Soviet Union on June 22, 1941. As the German divisions pushed back the Red Army, Japan saw its chance. With Russia preoccupied in Europe, Japan could safely send its armies into the resource-rich areas of Southeast Asia. Ignoring the long series of American warnings, Japanese troops in late July moved into southern French Indochina and began preparations for an assault on British Malaya, Singapore, the Netherlands East Indies, and perhaps the U.S.-controlled Philippine Islands as well.

The United States reacted forcefully. It cut off all trade with Japan, including oil, and began a major buildup of American armed forces in the Philippines. Peace was slipping away in the Pacific. Denied oil, Japan could not allow negotiations to drag on indefinitely. Unless an agreement were reached with the United States, Japan would have to capitulate to the American demands or seize the oil in the East Indies. Japanese expansion had provoked American economic warfare, thereby forcing Japan to choose between abandoning its Asian ambitions or going to war against the United States.

In both Washington and Tokyo there were civilian and military leaders who recognized the seriousness of the situation and sought ways to avoid war. Their efforts failed and Japan chose to go to war. It needed to reach the oil wells of the Dutch East Indies but feared doing so because of the U.S. Pacific Fleet sitting menacingly at Pearl Harbor. Roosevelt and Hull had placed it there for the very purpose of deterring Japanese southern expansion. But, when Japan decided it had to go south no matter what the consequences would be, the fleet ceased to be a deterrent and became a target.

Thus, in a brilliant and daring maneuver, Japanese naval air units attacked and devastated the Pacific Fleet on the morning of December 7, 1941. At the same time, other Japanese forces pushed south into British Malaya and the Philippines. Germany honored its alliance with Japan and declared war on the United States, which responded in kind. The United States had entered World War II.

This narrative of events does not explain why American policy took the shape it did. Why did national leaders consider Germany a threat? Why did the Roosevelt administration challenge Japan's expansion into Southeast Asia when it refused to confront Japan in China? To what extent was American policy the product of idealistic principles, national self-interest, power realities, and stereotypical portrayals of the other side? To answer these questions the attitudes of the men who guided U.S. foreign policy must be examined.

In the twentieth century the United States emerged as the great industrial power of the world. Blessed with abundant raw materials, cheap labor, and dynamic corporate leadership, it became a wealthy nation, whose goods and investments spread around the world. American dollars, coupled with U.S. business and engineering skills, developed the resources of less developed states (known as developing nations today and what were referred to as "backward peoples" a half century ago).

It was a good world for the United States, and American leaders naturally sought to preserve it. They recognized and accepted the need for change but insisted that the change must be orderly and peaceful. Thus between the two world wars there was much talk of a world governed by international law and respect for the sanctity of treaties. Such principles appealed to Americans, who enjoyed the status quo, but offered no hope to nations like Japan and Germany, which each sought to improve its position in the world. Americans denounced German or Japanese aggression as unlawful or evil, forgetting that the United States climbed to its lofty position through the conquest of land belonging to Spain, Mexico, Hawaii, and a variety of North American Indian nations and ignoring a tendency toward gunboat diplomacy in Latin America and Asia. Although the German and Japanese attempt to revise the world order by force was only another in a long history of struggles for "a place in the sun," it was no less disturbing to the Roosevelt administration.

The most obvious aspect of the German-Japanese revisionism was that it used military conquest to achieve its end. Roosevelt and Hull were most disturbed, however, about what these nations sought to do with the territory they had conquered. In the 1930s both Germany and Japan had become autarchic powers—that is, they sought economic self-sufficiency by having the raw materials and the markets they needed within their own borders or spheres of influence. For Japan that meant undisputed control over East and Southeast Asia, from the iron ore of Manchuria to the oil in the Netherlands East Indies. For Germany it meant domination of the labor, raw materials, and industrial plants of Europe. Such control would be exclusive; neither Germany nor Japan would leave any room for American interests in their spheres of influence.

By contrast, U.S. leaders believed in a liberal commercial world order in which all nations would have equal opportunity to invest or trade in any country. Rather than exclusive spheres they talked of a fair field without favor for all nations, an "open door" to free competition. Not surprisingly, this liberal commercial philosophy favored the United States with its great masses of capital and business and technical skill. Americans also were convinced that their way of liberal commercialism benefited all the people of the world. Development in China, for example, helped the Chinese as much as it did the American company engaged in the project. Thus they viewed the challenge of Germany and Japan not only as a threat to American interests but also as a threat to world progress.

Militarily, the United States was not prepared to preserve a liberal commercial world order. In the Pacific, naval arms limitation treaties created a balance of power that prevented the United States from operating in the western Pacific and Japan from operating in the eastern Pacific. In the Atlantic the United States relied upon the presence of the mighty British navy to stop any hostile force from interfering in the Western Hemisphere.

Keeping these factors in mind, we can begin to see why Roosevelt responded as he did to German expansion. Both the president and the rest of his foreign policy staff made a clear distinction between what was undesirable and what was intolerable. The seizure of the Sudetenland by the Germans and their subsequent conquest of the remainder of Czechoslovakia were undesirable, but their control of Czechoslovakia did not significantly disrupt the liberal commercial world order and certainly did nothing to threaten the supremacy of the British fleet in the Atlantic. The same could be said of the German conquest of Poland. The fall of France in June 1940, however, was a totally different matter. Virtually all of western Europe had come under Germany's economic control and had been removed from the liberal commercial world order. Moreover, the future of Britain and its navy was very much in doubt.

By October the first test had been passed. The Royal Air Force had denied the *Luftwaffe* the air supremacy Hitler needed to launch an invasion of the British Isles, but the issue was still in doubt. Although Prime Minister Winston Churchill assured Roosevelt that the British would never surrender, no American president could be certain that the British people and economy could indefinitely withstand the strains of war. A new British leader might offer to buy peace with Germany in exchange for neutralization of the British fleet. For the United States it was hardly better to have the British fleet neutral than captured because in either case the Atlantic became a highway for German expansion rather than an obstacle to it. To keep Britain fighting, Germany would have to be pushed back, and Britain could not do that by itself. In other words, making sure that

Britain did not lose meant that Germany must be defeated, and that would require American involvement in the war.

German conquest posed not only a military threat to the United States but an economic one as well. Even as Hitler seized Czechoslovakia, Roosevelt showed his anxiety. He told a group of reporters that, if such aggression went unchecked, it would choke off free trade in the world and thus overburden the economies of the democratic states. One year later, as the 1940 German spring offensive began, the president repeated his warning. Washington foreign policy managers worried that, once Germany controlled Europe, it might use its economic leverage to demand political or military concessions from other nations. For example, Hitler might insist upon a submarine base in Argentina in exchange for allowing Argentine beef to be sold in Europe. If the United States tried to block these German designs by buying Argentine beef and the exports of every other nation in Latin America, it would place an unbearable strain on the U.S. economy.

Besides the danger that Germany could use its economic leverage to gain military advantages, German autarchic control of Europe threatened to destroy the progress and prosperity that the world had enjoyed for over a century. It was an argument stated eloquently by William A. Clayton, a wealthy cotton exporter who had joined the Roosevelt administration and sought to awaken the American business community to the perils Germany posed. Speaking early in 1941 he explained that, "to understand what is happening in the world today, one must go back to the Industrial Revolution which had its early beginnings in England a little over a century and a half ago." The Industrial Revolution brought in the age of the machine, which freed the world from excessive toil and fear of want, while it opened up great progress in intellectual, spiritual, and cultural growth. Clayton warned, however, that such progress could come only through the "basic, unchangeable laws of the machine . . . production and more production and the free movement thereof through the world." He denounced Hitler's autarchic system for denying this law by trying to put Europe under a centralized authority. With tentacles reaching into the Western Hemisphere, the führer's economic system sought to drive American trade from the world, thereby causing "severe strain on our traditional way of life."

The fall of France in June 1940 therefore established an intolerable situation. For both economic and military reasons it would be necessary to force Germany back to its original borders, or at least back to the situation in 1939. That could not be done without active

American participation in the war. Whether Roosevelt was willing to admit this as early as June 1940 is not clear; the president kept such observations to himself. What is clear is that he moved slower in confronting Germany than many of his advisers wanted. Roosevelt had seen the face of war in World War I and did not relish seeing it again. Besides, it would take time for the public to become angry enough with Germany to accept belligerent American actions. As late as April 1941 he refrained from ordering convoys and settled instead for the less provocative measure of aggressive neutrality patrolling. Still, Washington officials concluded that the United States and Germany would be at war before long, and the president did nothing to silence such speculation.

Developments in Asia followed much the same path as in Europe, although Japan never posed the same military threat as Germany. The early Japanese expansion was undesirable to American leaders but not intolerable. From July 1937 to the spring of 1940 most of Japan's expansion was confined to China. While the United States was sympathetic toward the Chinese, China was not strategically important to the United States, nor was its loss to the liberal commercial world order of any great consequence. The costs of war with Japan to preserve the Open Door in China would far outweigh any possible benefits that might be gained. The United States had never been willing to fight for China, except possibly fighting the Chinese, and it was not willing to do so now.

Only when Japan moved beyond China into Southeast Asia did the United States see its vital interests threatened and begin to offer strong resistance to Japanese expansion. One reason for this was economic. If China by itself was not a major loss to the liberal commercial world order, China and all of Southeast Asia would be. In the short run the United States could survive without the rubber, tin, and manganese that came from that region, but in the long run Washington policymakers believed that neither the United States nor the rest of the world could prosper with such a large part of the world monopolized by Japan. Just as in Europe, where the United States could live with the loss of Czechoslovakia and Poland but not all of Europe, so too the United States could tolerate the loss of China but not all of East and Southeast Asia as well.

A second reason was strategic. As Japan moved farther south it threatened areas important to Britain: the naval base at Singapore, the colony of Malaya, and the Commonwealth countries of Australia and New Zealand. Even a small Japanese advance into Southeast Asia would force Britain to divert desperately needed military forces from the European war in order to protect British interests. If Japan launched an all-out attack against the British and captured Singapore (as it did in 1942), Britain would be denied access to the men and materiel of its Asian colonies and allies. Moreover, if Germany should push into the Middle East and capture the Suez Canal, it could link up with Japan through the Indian Ocean and draw upon the resources of Asia to fuel its war machine. There was also the nagging problem of the Philippines. Militarily indefensible and economically insignificant, the islands stood as hostage to a fortune that could drag the United States into an Asian war if Japan moved south.

British strategic planners hoped to persuade Americans to protect Southeast Asia. As vital as that region was, however, U.S. policymakers were most concerned about Europe because they believed that once Germany was defeated the Americans and British could easily turn back Japan, while a war with Japan would leave the German threat still to be faced. Thus it was important to concentrate on the European theater and avoid war with Japan.

Avoiding war with Japan was not such an easy task. Secretary Hull worked diligently to find the basis for a lasting peace, but it was a futile effort. Japan was too committed to its autarchic New Order in East Asia to give it up, and the United States was too deeply devoted to the liberal commercial world order to tolerate Japan's New Order. Eventually these two systems would clash. Hull did not see any alternative and did not think that peace could come to Asia through a face-saving withdrawal of Japanese troops from China. That would only help the Japanese militarists extricate themselves from an embarrassing war and assure their continued control of Japan.

Like everyone else in Washington, Hull believed that the Japanese leaders were determined to dominate all of East and Southeast Asia, and, until Japan underwent a regeneration and purged itself of its extremist leaders, there was no hope for peace and therefore no reason to seek a short-term agreement with Japan. The events of July and August 1941 undercut the secretary's assumptions. Japan's decision to move south and the resulting American trade embargo meant that, if the United States hoped to avoid a war with Japan, it had to abandon the search for a lasting peace and begin negotiating a short-term, limited understanding, or what the diplomats call a modus vivendi.

Japanese Prime Minister Fumimaro Konoye realized this as well and urgently sought a meeting with Roosevelt during August and

September. He hoped that the two leaders could strip through the technicalities, which seemed to be the diplomats' stock in trade, and reach an agreement that at least, if it did not assure peace for all time, would postpone a war.

Roosevelt was interested—he always liked proposals that stressed personal diplomacy—but Hull and the State Department were strongly opposed. It was a trick, Hull warned the president. If the Japanese leaders were ready to live in peace, there was no need for a summit conference. If they were not, no amount of talk between the two national leaders would alter that fact. Therefore, during the critical months of September and October 1941, Hull spent his time looking for a comprehensive peace agreement that might postpone the war. Not until the middle of November during the eleventh hour of the negotiations did he consider a modus vivendi.

The agreement approved by State, War, and Navy department officials offered Japan moderate amounts of American oil if it would withdraw its forces from southern Indochina, limit the number of troops in northern Indochina to 25,000, and make no further advances in the South Pacific. The agreement was to last three months. Hull had to decide whether to offer Japan this modus vivendi or to admit that there was no diplomatic solution, issue a statement for the record, and turn the matter over to the army and navy. There were good arguments for both courses.

A variety of strategic factors favored an agreement with Japan, even one that would last only two or three months. The U.S. Army was building up its strength in the Philippines and believed that, once it was fortified with new American B-17 bombers, Japan would not dare move into Southeast Asia. Three months, army officers argued, would radically alter the balance of power in Asia. Moreover, by the spring of 1942 more American warships would be in service, and the bitter Russian winter might have stopped the German armies. In that situation, Japan might be more hesitant to expand south, and war might be averted indefinitely.

On the other hand, the American strategy for containing Japan in the Pacific assumed that Japan would continue to have 1 million soldiers bogged down in China. Army officers believed that Japan did not have the resources to fight both in China and against the well-defended Philippines. Yet, when Hull broached the modus vivendi with the Chinese government, it reacted with much vehemence, declaring that the Chinese people would consider it appeasement and might be so demoralized that they would be unable to continue the war against Japan.

There seemed to be no desirable choice before the Roosevelt administration. If by yielding to Chinese protests it abandoned the modus vivendi proposal, diplomacy would end and war would surely come. American intercepts of secret Japanese messages revealed that, unless an agreement were reached immediately, "things were automatically going to happen." But, if the administration went ahead with the proposal, China might collapse, with disastrous results for American interests in Asia.

To a remarkable degree the decision rested with Secretary Hull. While Roosevelt closely directed the policy toward Europe, Hull dominated the negotiations with Japan. For eight months he had sought an agreement. Early on November 26 he ended the search by recommending that the modus vivendi not be offered. In reaching this decision, he was greatly influenced by the possibility of the collapse of China, but there was more to it than a dispassionate weighing of the pros and cons. It was a decision made under great stress and after many months of lengthy and exhausting negotiations. Hull's determination to "kick the whole thing over" and to "wash his hands" of it reflected his fatigue and frustration at not being able to fashion a lasting agreement.

Important matters of state, especially those of war and peace, are supposed to be made by clear-minded leaders who, after weighing the evidence carefully, select the best option. But such decision makers are people, too, subject to stress and fatigue. When tired and under great pressure, they tend to avoid the complicated solutions and look for the simpler ones. Perhaps if Hull had not been so worn down by the months of negotiations, he could have summoned the energy to stand up to the Chinese leaders, assure them that they were not being abandoned, and insist that they continue the war while the United States tried to buy three months of peace, but he could not bring himself to do that. Instead, he phoned Secretary of War Henry L. Stimson and told him that it was now in the hands of the army and navy. Diplomacy had ended.

The War and Navy departments sent out warnings to their bases throughout the Pacific, notifying American commanders that, since diplomatic negotiations had ended, they could expect war with Japan at any time. When the attack came ten days later, U.S. forces in the Hawaiian Islands and the Philippines were not prepared. From that day to this, Americans have wondered how the Japanese navy could steam so far across the Pacific undetected and wreak such destruction upon the U.S. Navy at Pearl Harbor.

Implicit in many such questions was a racism which assumed that an Asian people were not capable of doing such damage to a Western nation without the complicity of someone within the United States. Unwilling to credit Japan's success to superior planning, American error, and just plain good Japanese luck, a variety of critics has accused Roosevelt and members of his administration of deliberately leading Japan to attack Pearl Harbor as a way of bringing the United States into the war. This "back door" thesis maintains that Roosevelt really wanted war with Germany, but, unable to provoke it in the Atlantic, he turned to the Pacific and Germany's ally, Japan.

Dozens of government and historical investigations have found no firm evidence to substantiate this point of view. What is clear is that Roosevelt and his administration knew Japan was about to attack. They even guessed some of the locations (the Isthmus of Kra, as Japan prepared to move toward the British naval base at Singapore, for example). What is in dispute is whether the president and his staff knew that the attack was coming against Pearl Harbor and did nothing about it. Roosevelt's critics charge that he withheld vital information from Pearl Harbor in order to keep the U.S. fleet in a state of unpreparedness and thus draw Japan into an attack. His defenders argue that the so-called vital information was actually fragments of intelligence, the meaning of which became clear only with hindsight. They maintain that the reason why so little of this information was shared with American commanders in the field was partially because of confusion over who already had access to it and partially out of fear of compromising the top-secret ways in which intelligence was gathered. Very few historians who have studied this issue accept the conspiratorial interpretation of the Pearl Harbor attack. Since it is impossible to provide positive proof that a conspiracy did not exist and since Americans are intrigued by conspiracies, the debate will certainly continue.

The debate over a conspiracy must not distract us from the more important question of how we got to the point where an attack would take place. If we concentrate not on December 7, 1941 but on the years from 1937 to 1941, we can learn much about the American nation and its role in world affairs. It was not out of an idealistic sympathy for the Chinese, French, Poles, or British that the United States moved toward war, nor was it the result of an emotional attachment to the ideal of international law and the sanctity of treaties. Instead, Roosevelt, Hull, and the others in Washington who crafted national policy moved the nation deliberately, but gradually, against the Axis because it sought to partition the world into autarchic spheres of influence, thereby destroying the liberal commercial world order on which the American people had built a good life.

Sources and Suggested Readings

Anderson, Irvine H., Jr. *The Standard-Vacuum Oil Company and United States East Asian Policy, 1933-1941.* Princeton, 1975.

Borg, Dorothy. *The United States and the Far Eastern Crisis of 1933-1938.* Cambridge, Massachusetts, 1964.

Borg, Dorothy, and Okamoto, Shumpei, eds. *Pearl Harbor as History: Japanese-American Relations, 1931-1941.* New York, 1973.

Compton, James V. *The Swastika and the Eagle: Hitler, the United States, and the Origins of World War II.* Boston, 1967.

Dallek, Robert. *Franklin D. Roosevelt and American Foreign Policy, 1932-1945.* New York, 1979.

Divine, Robert A. *Roosevelt and World War II.* Baltimore, 1969.

Feis, Herbert. *The Road to Pearl Harbor: The Coming of the War Between the United States and Japan.* Princeton, 1950.

Haglund, David G. *Latin America and the Transformation of U.S. Strategic Thought, 1936-1940.* Albuquerque, 1984.

Iriye, Akira. *Power and Culture: The Japanese-American War, 1941-1945.* Cambridge, Massachusetts, 1981.

Langer, William L., and Gleason, S. Everett. *The Challenge to Isolation: The World Crisis of 1937-1940 and American Foreign Policy.* New York, 1952.

————. *The Undeclared War, 1940-1941.* New York, 1953.

Layton, Edwin T. *"And I Was There": Pearl Harbor and Midway— Breaking the Secrets.* New York, 1985.

Leutze, James R. *Bargaining for Supremacy: Anglo-American Naval Collaboration, 1937-1941.* Chapel Hill, 1977.

Prange, Gordon W. *At Dawn We Slept: The Untold Story of Pearl Harbor.* New York, 1981.

————. *Pearl Harbor: The Verdict of History.* New York, 1985.

Reynolds, David. *The Creation of the Anglo-American Alliance: A Study in Competitive Cooperation.* Chapel Hill, 1982.

Utley, Jonathan G. *Going to War with Japan, 1937-1941.* Knoxville, 1985.

Wilson, Theodore A. *The First Summit: Roosevelt and Churchill at Placentia Bay, 1941.* Boston, 1969.

World War II and the Coming of the Cold War

Robert L. Messer

World War II has been called the "great divide" in modern American history. Certainly that conflict transformed American foreign policy. Ideas about national security and military preparedness were never the same after the "day of infamy" at Pearl Harbor. That generation's conclusions about the futility of appeasing aggression and the necessity of an active involvement in the world continued to instruct the nation's leaders long after the war. The experiences and lessons of that conflict formed the guiding principles of American diplomacy in the ensuing Cold War. These two global conflicts are inextricably linked. Any description of one would be incomplete without reference to the other.

Unlike World War II the Cold War between the United States and the Soviet Union had no formal declaration of hostilities to mark its beginning. Historians disagree not only about how or why the Cold War began but also when. However, most attempts to explain the origins of the Cold War begin with the American-Soviet alliance during World War II and then describe its deterioration. Mutual hostility and distrust predate World War II, but the breakup of the wartime alliance, coupled with the potential for direct or indirect military conflict between the two postwar superpowers, defines the Cold War.

How did these two allies, victors over the Axis aggressors, come to see one another as enemies? A partial answer to this complex question lies in the nature of their wartime partnership. British Prime Minister Winston Churchill christened the Allied coalition "the Grand Alliance." Others, including Adolf Hitler, considered this unlikely union of imperial Britain, democratic America, and Communist Russia an inherently unstable alignment of forces so alien that the strains of coalition warfare would surely pull it apart. However strange or unnatural, the combination of these three great powers was indeed grand. Only their combined resources of population, productive capacity, and armed might could have defeated the Axis alliance of Germany, Italy, Japan, and their satellite states. In the aftermath of that colossal military undertaking, these three victorious powers, acting together, had the capacity to exercise unprecedented control over a world ravaged and radically altered by the destruction of history's greatest war, a world wounded by the deaths of some 55 million people, and a world of chaos and ruin. Rebuilding a new international structure upon the rubble of World War II demanded the sort of combined, all-out effort expended in winning the war. That the victorious allies proved incapable of performing this formidable task is a reflection of the differences in the meaning of the war for each of the Big Three. Each fought a different war; each looked forward to a different peace.

Generalissimo Joseph Stalin did not even give his war the same name. In the West the conflict was first called the War for the United Nations and then the Second World War, but in the USSR it was officially named the Great Patriotic War of the Soviet Union. Stalin's war began on June 22, 1941 when Hitler launched a massive three-pronged invasion of Russia. For the next three years this war was fought largely on Soviet soil. In it the Soviet victors suffered by far the greatest losses of any of the combatants in World War II, including the losers. In a bloody struggle, made even more brutal by inhuman conditions of weather, guerrilla warfare, and the scorched-earth tactics of both sides, an estimated 20 million Russians perished, more than five times the total German casualties and twenty-five times the combined total of British and American war dead.

In Stalin's view the Western allies did not effectively enter his war until mid-1944. The Anglo-American invasion of France came less than one year before Germany's total collapse and more than one year after the decisive battles of Stalingrad and Kursk. Long before D-day at Normandy the Red Army had defeated the bulk of German armed strength, inflicting 80 percent of all German casualties. In its scale, timing, and strategic significance, Stalin's war on Russia's Eastern Front was very different from that waged in the west by the British and Americans.

Perhaps most important, Stalin's war differed fundamentally in its purpose. As its name implies, it was a war strictly of and for the Soviet Union. At first it was a battle for survival. By mid-1943, with the German armies in retreat, it became a war for revenge, both to justify the enormous losses suffered in the conflict and to make certain that such an onslaught never again could threaten the survival of the Russian people and the Soviet form of government. In this war the Soviet Union was not just a major victor; it was the only victor. Because he believed he had earned it, Stalin expected the lion's share of the spoils of this war. At the very least, he expected to recover the lands lost as a result of the German invasion and to maintain a controlling influence over any other territory wrested from the conquered enemy.

To Stalin that enemy was not just Hitler or Germany. It was prewar Europe and everything it stood for in the experience of that generation of Soviet leaders. Stalin and those around him remembered vividly the West's armed intervention in the Russian civil war of 1918–20 and the years of diplomatic isolation and ideological hostility. The prewar appeasement of Hitler by the British, French, and Americans seemed to him to have been motivated primarily by Western anticommunism. The war against Hitler and his Italian and eastern European allies only seemed to confirm Stalin's earlier experience in dealing with the rest of Europe. Anti-Soviet, Fascist Europe was the enemy that had to be defeated, punished, and permanently subdued. When Stalin insisted upon having only "friendly" governments on Russia's borders, he declared his refusal even to risk reestablishment of the prewar cordon sanitaire of non-Communist, anti-Soviet regimes.

Despite his hatred of Soviet communism, dating back to the Bolsheviks' separate peace with Germany in World War I, Churchill's approach to his war was not unlike that of Stalin. Churchill, too, had imperial ambitions. Rather than expanding his area of control, however, he sought only to hang on to as much of the prewar British empire as possible. To do this while defeating Hitler and at the same time avoiding the debilitating carnage of the First World War, Churchill had to rely upon the enormous manpower that only Stalin could provide. As the prime minister put it immediately after the outbreak of the Soviet-German war, "If Hitler invaded Hell, I would make at least a favorable reference to the Devil in the House of Commons." Harboring no illusions about the satanic qualities of Stalin and his dictatorial regime, Churchill nonetheless saw Hitler's Nazi Germany as the greater or more menacing evil in the world and publicly pledged British support for Soviet resistance.

A strategy of relying upon Stalin to help defeat Hitler had its price. Providing that the price of victory could be kept within acceptable limits, Churchill saw little choice but to pay it. The British leader's fatalistic acceptance of a Soviet "sphere of action" in eastern Europe was made explicit in October 1944 when he and Stalin concluded their secret "percentage deal." In return for a controlling interest in the affairs of Greece and equal shares in Yugoslavia and Hungary, Churchill, in effect, conceded the rest of eastern Europe to Stalin.

Conspicuously absent from this bargain was Poland, which for Churchill remained a special case. His war had begun in September 1939, in response to Hitler's invasion of Poland from the west, and was followed soon after by the Soviet occupation of the eastern portion of the country. This earlier Soviet participation in the partition of Poland, the revelation of the Katyn Forest massacre of 10,000 Polish officers captured by the Russians, and Stalin's later refusal to intervene in the abortive Warsaw uprising in order to save the non-Communist underground forces from annihilation at the hands of the retreating Germans all combined to make a mockery of the subsequent Soviet "liberation." The British, who had gone to war for Poland, hardly could be expected to endorse its subjugation by a second conqueror. For Churchill, Poland remained the "test case" of the Anglo-Soviet alliance.

That belated, mutually expedient alliance could not erase the memory of a time when Churchill and Stalin had been on opposite sides in the war over Poland. After the Nazi-Soviet nonaggression pact of August 1939 and the ensuing defeat of France, Britain had stood alone against Hitler. During its time of trial, Stalin not only collaborated in the destruction of Poland but also continued to ship vital raw materials to Germany until the very moment of Hitler's treacherous attack. Repeated British and American warnings of that betrayal went unheeded. Although historians disagree as to what extent, the rapid German advance deep into the Soviet heartland and the heavy price paid by the Russian people in losing and regaining that land were at least partly due to Stalin's miscalculations regarding Hitler's intentions. It therefore can be argued that Stalin's later claims for compensation, in return for his nation's great sacrifices during the war, were based on losses for which he was to some degree responsible. Certainly, from Churchill's perspective, Stalin's case for special treatment was reminiscent of the boy on trial for murdering his parents who asked for mercy on the grounds that he was an orphan.

In concluding his pact with Hitler, Stalin had attempted to buy time and some additional territory in anticipation of eventual war with Germany, but he did so at the expense of Britain and its allies. Thus, aside from the lack of sufficient manpower and equipment, Churchill was in no great hurry to mount an early cross-Channel invasion onto the beaches of France just to please his new "friend" Stalin. If Churchill had had his way, there might never have been such an invasion. He would have preferred penetrating what he optimistically called the "soft underbelly" of Europe with an invasion from the Mediterranean, intersecting Europe south to north and cutting off the Russians from Germany and the rest of Europe. This dubious military-political maneuver, however, was vetoed by the third and, in many ways, most important of the Big Three leaders.

President Franklin D. Roosevelt was the last member to join the wartime Big Three, but his involvement in both Churchill's and Stalin's wars began long before December 1941. From a prewar policy of isolationist self-interest and indirect support for appeasement, Roosevelt had moved warily toward an increasingly open and active policy of intervention to forestall an Axis victory.

Although the country remained officially neutral and fervently antiwar, from the beginning of the war in 1939 both Roosevelt and the overwhelming majority of Americans were morally committed to the forces opposing Hitler. Gradually that moral commitment was backed by a growing economic one as the United States took on the role of the "arsenal of democracy." War materiel from that arsenal went to the increasingly impoverished British under Lend-Lease, a unique aid program that authorized the president to "lend" ships, planes, tanks, guns—virtually anything needed to fight a war—to any country whose defense he deemed vital to American security. If not yet to the point of willingness to enter the war directly, by late 1941 Roosevelt had succeeded in convincing most Americans that Churchill's war was also their war.

An important part of that domestic sales effort was a joint declaration of Anglo-American war aims published after Roosevelt and Churchill's first summit meeting off Argentia, Newfoundland, in August 1941. In this eight-point communiqué, which the American press immediately dubbed the Atlantic Charter, the two leaders pledged to fight for "common principles," including the right of self-determination of all peoples "forcibly deprived" of it; free trade among all nations, "with due respect for their existing obligations"; and a mutual opposition to territorial "aggrandizement" or undemocratic territorial changes.

The qualifications were inserted to satisfy Churchill that these lofty goals would not interfere with the existing British imperial system of colonies and trade preferences. A few weeks after Pearl Harbor the rest of the twenty-six member anti-Axis alliance was called upon to endorse these same war aims in the UN Declaration. In affixing his signature to this document, Soviet ambassador to the United States Maxim Litvinov fashioned an even larger loophole by adding the stipulation that "the practical application of these principles will necessarily adapt itself to the circumstances, needs, and historic peculiarities of particular countries." Roosevelt's American audience, however, took public declarations, such as the Atlantic Charter, as guarantees that this time there would be no secret deals in violation of U.S. democratic principles. This sort of rhetoric also assured Americans that Britain was worthy of their support.

In the case of Stalin's war, Roosevelt encountered more resistance to any such American commitment. Memories of the Nazi-Soviet Pact, the Winter War against tiny Finland, the opposition of religious and ethnic groups, and the widespread antipathy toward communism and the Soviet dictatorship posed special problems in convincing Congress and the public that Russia, too, was a fitting recipient of the products of democracy's arsenal. Untroubled by the contradiction of waging a war for democracy in league with a totalitarian dictator, Roosevelt echoed both Churchill's priorities and his metaphor in explaining his private attitude toward Stalin as an ally: "I can't take communism . . . but to cross this bridge I would hold hands with the Devil."

Obviously, Churchill and Roosevelt looked upon their liaison with Stalin as a Faustian bargain and not as a marriage made in Heaven. But their concerns were of this world, a world threatened by Hitler more than by Stalin. Their first concern was how to win the war. At the beginning it was by no means clear that Soviet help would be decisive. Indeed, most Western military experts expected Russia to collapse in a matter of weeks. Roosevelt, however, was willing to gamble American money and supplies on the chance that such an investment would prolong the war on the Eastern Front, at least until the creation of an Anglo-American second front in the west.

The failure of that second front to materialize until late in the war was, in the words of Roosevelt's biographer James MacGregor Burns, "perhaps the most determining single factor" in the origins of the Cold War. The first cracks in the wartime alliance began over the issue of the second front and formed the gap between promise and reality that widened steadily during 1942 and 1943. Forced by British reluctance and military realities into repeated delays in launching a cross-Channel invasion, Roosevelt tried, with Lend-Lease supplies, to bridge that widened gap in the American-Soviet alliance. He was buying time with dollars and avoiding horrendous American casualties, while Stalin was buying territory with his most expendable resource, the lives of millions of Russian soldiers.

How significant was Lend-Lease to the Soviet war effort? As with so much else about the alliance, the answer is relative. From the American perspective the numbers speak for themselves. From late 1941 to the end of the war, the United States shipped to Russia over 18,000 planes, 10,000 tanks, 700 ships, 200,000 trucks, 5 million pairs of boots, millions of tons of food, and much more. Although the total cost of this aid was over $10 billion, Soviet historians point out that this impressive volume was less than 10 percent of the total Soviet war production and less than the amount provided to Britain. Moreover, most of these supplies arrived after the decisive phase of the war on the Eastern Front. It is clear, however, that Lend-Lease aid was an important qualitative contribution to the Red Army's fighting capabilities and formed a major link in American-Soviet relations during the war.

Determined to give the Russians every possible assistance, Roosevelt rejected suggestions that he use this aid as leverage to ensure good behavior on the part of the Soviets. His aid policy was based not upon any naive trust in Stalin's good intentions but upon his personal appreciation for the military burden Stalin was bearing on behalf of the Western allies. Roosevelt knew first hand, as he told General Douglas MacArthur in 1942, that "the Russian armies are killing more Axis personnel and destroying more Axis materiel than all the other twenty-five United Nations put together." The president also came to realize that this imbalance would continue not only for that year but also throughout the next and well into 1944.

First in 1942 and again in 1943, Roosevelt and Churchill had promised Stalin a second front in Europe, only to find that they could not make good on this pledge. Instead of a direct assault on Germany in a cross-Channel invasion of the Continent, the Western allies busied themselves on the periphery of the Axis empire, first with an invasion of North Africa in late 1942 and then the next summer by invading Sicily and Italy. Neither of these actions contributed directly to the defeat of Germany. Instead, they forced the postponement of a real second front; allowed Hitler to divert troops from the west to throw against the Russians in the east; and finally, in the unkindest cut of all, diverted supplies and shipping originally promised to the Soviet Union under Lend-Lease.

The reasons for the delay in the second front were sound enough from the British and American point of view: insufficient trained personnel, equipment and shipping shortages, and lack of air superiority. To Stalin, however, these excuses could not erase the fact that promises had been made and broken. The Western allies' concern that any attempt to breach Hitler's "Atlantic Wall" should have a reasonable chance for success and a reasonable cost in lives could only seem unreasonable to a leader whose nation was desperately struggling to maintain its very existence.

Roosevelt realized the seriousness of Stalin's position and worried that the Soviet Union might be forced out of the war. Raising hopes of an imminent second front, publicly declaring the Western allies' commitment to settle for nothing less than "unconditional surrender," and sending Stalin as much Lend-Lease aid as could be spared were all part of his effort to keep Russia in the war.

Like Churchill, Roosevelt needed Stalin to win in Europe, but the president also sought Stalin's support in other areas. The Allies were committed to a "Europe first" strategy, reflecting their agreement that Germany posed the greater and more urgent threat. Nonetheless, Roosevelt had to think ahead to winning the war against Japan. Following the defeat of Nazi Germany, the huge Red Army could relieve the Americans of the daunting task of expelling the Japanese from the mainland of Asia. The nearly 2 million battle-hardened Japanese troops in China, Manchuria, and Korea were a formidable force, against which the Chinese under Jiang Jieshi (Chiang Kaishek) had proved totally ineffective.

Roosevelt also sought Stalin's cooperation in the postwar peace. The president's plans for peace, following the defeat of Japan, envisioned a system of collective security designed to avoid the pitfalls of Woodrow Wilson's League of Nations. This revised version of the League, comprising the anti-Axis "United Nations," would be run by an executive council made up of all the world's major powers, including the Soviet Union and the United States, whose absence from the League had helped render it ineffective. To succeed, this new system would have to rely upon the enforcement or police power of the victorious major Allied powers. To gain Churchill and Stalin's cooperation in such a system, Roosevelt would have to make concessions to their war aims involving spheres of influence and violations of democratic principles. He considered such concessions as temporary expedients, made in response to Soviet security concerns and Victorian British ideas about the necessity of formal colonies. The need for such interim arrangements would decline once the new world organization was in full and effective operation.

A new international peace-keeping organization, however, could not begin to operate without the approval of the American people and Congress. Just one-third plus one of the Senate could veto this entire postwar system and with it destroy Roosevelt's hopes for a lasting peace. That all-important support at home could be jeopardized by premature revelation of any secret power politics that contradicted American ideals and public war aims. The ghost of Wilson and the fate of his League haunted Roosevelt as he prepared for the peace. He walked a diplomatic and political tightrope in his public versus private wartime policies.

Roosevelt's debut on the stage of Big Three summit diplomacy came in November 1943 when he, Stalin, and Churchill met for the first time at Tehran, Iran. There the three leaders set a final and this time firm date for the invasion of France. Roosevelt gained Stalin's verbal commitment to enter the war against Japan after the defeat of Germany. The president also put forth his plans for the peace.

Explaining the postwar role of the "Four Policemen," Roosevelt proposed that Britain and the Soviet Union police western and eastern Europe, respectively; the United States would be responsible for North and South America and the Pacific, presumably including Japan. Rather wistfully adding China to the big power club, Roosevelt expressed his hope that China would keep the peace on the mainland of Asia. Although Churchill remained concerned about the future of the British empire in such a system and Stalin expressed doubts about China's capacity and Europe's willingness to be policed, the three leaders agreed upon the broad outlines of the American proposal.

On other more politically sensitive agenda items, such as the postwar borders of Poland, Roosevelt had to be more cautious. He privately raised no objection to Churchill and Stalin's agreement that Poland be moved to the west at the expense of Germany, with the Soviet Union regaining much of the territory in eastern Poland occupied in 1939 under the Nazi-Soviet Pact. Referring to the more than 6 million Polish-Americans in the United States and his upcoming reelection campaign, Roosevelt pointed out that as a "practical man" he could not yet support such territorial changes. This sort of private acquiescence in a British and Soviet division of spoils in Europe, while publicly disavowing any such secret agreements, was characteristic of Roosevelt's dual, often contradictory, wartime diplomacy. One year later he again privately acquiesced in the

Churchill-Stalin percentage deal dividing political control of eastern Europe, but he reminded his allies that any final arrangements should be concluded when the three of them next met.

With the second front in Europe at last a reality and with the 1944 presidential race safely behind him, Roosevelt set out for what was to be his last meeting with Churchill and Stalin. This most important wartime Big Three summit was held in February 1945 at Yalta on the Crimean peninsula. The conference site is indicative of the relative bargaining position of the participants. The ill, in fact dying, Roosevelt was obliged to undertake an exhausting and dangerous trip to meet Stalin on Soviet soil. The president was willing to go this last mile in order to nail down the exact terms and timing of the Soviet entry into the war against Japan and to secure final agreement on just how the new peace-keeping international organization would operate. He succeeded in both these objectives.

THE ALLIED BIG THREE AT YALTA, FEBRUARY 1945. Fatigue and the ravages of declining health are clearly visible on the face of President Roosevelt as he sits with his wartime partners. (National Archives)

In return for two extra votes in the General Assembly, Stalin agreed to the American formula for the United Nations Organization. He also signed a secret protocol on the Far East, pledging to declare war on Japan three months after the defeat of Germany. The price for this much-needed help against Japan was essentially restoration of the tzarist spheres of influence in Manchuria and North China, including rights to naval bases and railroads.

On other conference issues involving eastern Europe, the military situation at the time gave Stalin a commanding bargaining position. The Red Army had occupied most of eastern Europe, and at that moment had advanced to within sixty miles of Berlin. The British and Americans were still recovering from the last German counteroffensive at the Battle of the Bulge and had not yet reached the Rhine. Under such unfavorable circumstances, putting some limits on what the Soviets already had gained on the battlefield was as much as Roosevelt and Churchill could hope to gain from the negotiations at Yalta.

The result was a private recognition of Soviet domination of the area already under its military occupation and a public Declaration on Liberated Europe which reiterated the Atlantic Charter's goals of self-determination and "free and unfettered elections," without providing an effective means to realize this goal. All Roosevelt came away with was Stalin's verbal assurance that some sort of pretense of democratic procedure would be carried out as soon as possible.

Upon his return from the conference, Roosevelt once again encouraged his domestic audience to focus upon the public myth rather than the private reality of Yalta. Responding to a carefully orchestrated White House public relations campaign, the American press immediately hailed the unenforceable Declaration on Liberated Europe as "the Crimean Charter," a triumph of American democratic war aims over selfish national interest and power politics. Roosevelt encouraged this illusion of diplomatic success in an attempt to garner support at home for a matter he considered more important: congressional approval of his peace plans. The temporary, politically useful gap between myth and reality was apparently something with which he was willing to live, but, within weeks after returning from Yalta, Roosevelt was dead of a brain hemorrhage. His successor had a very different perspective on the war and on the American-Soviet alliance.

Harry S. Truman's war was not the same one Roosevelt had waged in partnership with Churchill and Stalin. Truman's war in many ways more closely resembled the war experienced by most other Americans. His was one in which the American military and economic contribution had been decisive. Ignorant of the significance of the second front issue in Allied diplomacy, Truman assumed that the D-day landings in Normandy had been the decisive moment in the defeat of Nazi Germany. Although certainly aware through press accounts of the heavy fighting on the Russian front from 1941 to 1944, Truman, like many of his countrymen, thought that American Lend-Lease had been the key to Soviet survival. Unlike Roosevelt, who felt indebted to the Russians because they had borne the brunt of the fighting against Germany, Truman privately denigrated the Soviet contribution to the war. As he put it, "Without these [Lend-Lease] supplies furnished by the United States, Russia would have been ignominiously defeated." In Truman's mind the Soviets owed us; Americans did not owe them. This attitude influenced his views regarding the continuation of Lend-Lease after Germany's surrender and the denial of a Soviet request for a $6 billion postwar loan.

Whereas Roosevelt had moved during the war toward what Robert Dallek has termed a "regional internationalist" plan for a world peace-keeping system, Truman was much more a nationalist in his approach to both the war and peace. His views early on in the war reflected the isolationist self-interest common among his midwestern constituents. Immediately after the German invasion of the Soviet Union in mid-1941, the then obscure junior senator from Missouri publicly offered his opinion on the proper American policy toward the war on the Eastern Front: "If we see that Germany is winning the war we ought to help Russia, and if Russia is winning we ought to help Germany, and in that way let them kill as many as possible." Truman hastened to add that he did not want Hitler to win under any circumstances, but his basic position was very near that of other senators who saw no point in America helping "to make Europe safe for communism" and who publicly questioned whether a victory for Stalin was really any better than a German one. A loyal Democrat, Truman eventually fell into line and supported Lend-Lease for the Soviet Union, but his initial public reaction to the issue, before Roosevelt had made known his position, revealed Truman's more parochial view of national self-interest and his identification of Hitler and Stalin.

By the time he took over as president in 1945, Truman no longer sought to kill off the Russians. Like most Americans he had come to accept Stalin as an ally against Hitler. He was willing to get along with the Russians after the war. Truman's view of the basis of that postwar relationship, however, differed substantially from that of Roosevelt. He told his ambassador to Moscow, W. Averell Harriman, immediately after assuming the presidency, that "the Soviet Union needed us more than we needed them," and that, while he did not think we would be able to get 100 percent of what we wanted in dealing with them, he fully expected to receive at least 85 percent. This presumption of American preponderance resulted in a reversal of many of Roosevelt's wartime priorities.

At Yalta, Roosevelt traded what he did not have—temporary control of eastern Europe—for Soviet participation in the world-wide American peace-keeping system. At his first meeting with a high-ranking Soviet official, Truman bluntly gave Stalin's emissary, Vyacheslav Molotov, the choice of either fulfilling American expectations regarding free elections in the liberated areas, or dropping out of the United Nations Organization. Even on relatively minor procedural issues, such as whether France and China would participate in drafting preliminary peace treaties with Germany's eastern European satellites, Truman instructed his negotiators to tell the Russians "to go to Hell" if they refused to accept the Anglo-American position. Woefully unprepared and uninformed about Roosevelt's highly personal and secret wartime diplomacy, Truman tended to take public documents, such as the Atlantic Charter and the Yalta Declaration on Liberated Europe, at face value, and he expected the Soviets to live up to those agreements.

This changed perception of the war and the wartime alliance after Roosevelt's death was immediately evident when Truman, within days after taking office, delivered what he called "the old one-two to the jaw" of Molotov on the subject of the Yalta Polish agreement. Even Roosevelt had been disappointed by Stalin's performance in Poland following the Yalta meeting. Nonetheless, to the end of his life Roosevelt had urged upon Churchill the necessity to minimize such divisive issues. Therefore, Truman's verbal fisticuffs must have surprised and bewildered Molotov, but this sudden shift in presidential manner did not change Soviet policy in Poland.

After this initial bluster, Truman moderated his tone and sent Roosevelt's confidant Harry Hopkins to Moscow to work out an agreement that, after only cosmetic changes in its composition, led to American recognition of the Warsaw government. During this same period, Truman first abruptly cut off and then restored Soviet Lend-Lease shipments. As Truman struggled to gain a grip upon his office, Stalin was receiving conflicting signals from the new American president. Their first and only face-to-face meeting helped clarify for both men the image of the other.

Truman, Churchill, and Stalin met in July 1945 at Potsdam on the outskirts of the ruined city of Berlin. Truman's first and last Big Three summit conference was aptly code-named "Terminal." The war against Germany had ended more than one month before. Stalin would not enter the war against Japan until August, two days after the Americans dropped the first of two atomic bombs, and less than one week before Japan's surrender. Nonetheless, Potsdam marked the end of the wartime alliance.

THE BIG THREE CONFERENCE AT BERLIN (POTSDAM), JULY 1945. Seated (left to right): British Prime Minister Clement Attlee, President Harry S. Truman, Generalissimo Joseph Stalin. Standing (left to right): White House Chief of Staff Admiral William D. Leahy, British Foreign Secretary Ernest Bevin, Secretary of State James F. Byrnes, Soviet Foreign Minister V. M. Molotov. (Library of Congress)

The new president dreaded his initial encounter with "Mr. Britain" and "Mr. Russia." He put off the meeting as long as he could, probably in part because he wanted to know the results of the American attempt to build an atomic bomb but also because of his personal sense of insecurity and self-doubt. Privately, he repeatedly expressed his anxiety over having to fill Roosevelt's shoes. Once begun, the longest and least productive of the wartime conferences was plagued with difficulties. At its outset Stalin apparently suffered a mild heart attack, although Truman suspected a stalling tactic. Then, in the middle of the talks, Churchill was unexpectedly voted out of office and had to be replaced by the new prime minister, Clement Attlee.

Even before Churchill's stunning electoral defeat, Britain had been relegated to following the American lead in dealing with the Soviets. The war had reduced the once powerful British empire to the role of America's junior partner. Despite his subordinate status, Churchill had used the time between Roosevelt's death and the next Big Three meeting to impress upon Truman, in their frequent correspondence, the need for a united front against the Soviet Union. In contrast to Yalta, where Roosevelt often had sided with Stalin against Churchill, at Potsdam it was almost invariably Truman and the British aligned against Stalin. The American-Soviet formula on German reparations, agreed to at Yalta by Roosevelt and Stalin but temporarily blocked there by Churchill, was changed at Potsdam. The new American plan gave the Western allies effective control over how much the Soviets could expect to get out of Germany.

The single most important event during the Potsdam Conference occurred outside the negotiations just as the Big Three were about to begin their talks. From the War Department a radio message, couched in the terms of a birth announcement, informed Truman that the $2 billion gamble called the Manhattan Project had paid off beyond all expectations. The United States now possessed the world's first atomic bomb. In the words of the man who briefed him on the successful first test of the bomb, the news "tremendously pepped up" the president and gave him an entirely new sense of confidence in his approach to the conference. According to Truman, the bomb was both "the most terrible thing ever discovered" and "the greatest thing in history."

The news of the bomb dramatically altered American strategic thinking about the necessity of Soviet entry into the war against Japan. The president's military advisers now told him that, in view of this revolutionary new weapon, "the Russians were no longer needed" to defeat Japan. Indeed, Truman's foreign policy advisers suddenly viewed any Soviet declaration of war as an attempt to "get in on the kill." Truman concluded that one way or another Japan would soon "fold up," either as a result of Soviet entry or after the Americans used the atomic bomb. The terrible prospect of invading Japan had suddenly given way to the exhilarating vision of a quick, cheap American victory.

Aware of Japan's effort to seek peace through Moscow's mediation, Truman concluded that Soviet entry into the war would mean, in his words, "Fini Japs." The question for him was no longer if or even when the war would end but how and on whose terms. His highest priority remained ending the fighting by the quickest, surest method. The Manhattan Project scientists had given him a means for which Roosevelt only could have hoped. Truman did not hesitate to use it. In ordering the atomic attacks on two Japanese cities, his primary objective was to force Japan's surrender. A secondary consideration was that this surrender be on American terms, exclusive of Soviet involvement. What the Russians later called "atomic diplomacy" was conspicuously absent in the actual negotiations at Potsdam. Although not yet demonstrated to the Soviets and the world, the bomb nonetheless had a significant impact upon the American-Soviet alliance.

Stalin's spies had infiltrated the American atomic bomb project early on. He knew of its existence, and he knew that Roosevelt had deliberately kept that information secret from his Soviet ally. While Roosevelt had reserved the option of using the bomb militarily and diplomatically if and when it came into being, the entire project remained for him only a future possibility, or what he called an "ify" question. It was not something upon which he could base his wartime policy. How he might have handled the reality of the bomb at Potsdam is beyond knowing, but it seems unlikely that he would have played the sort of cat-and-mouse game Truman did. Truman went through an elaborate charade in order to be able to claim later that he had informed the Soviet leader of this important new development. Stalin feigned indifference and incomprehension about what Truman offhandedly referred to only as "a powerful new weapon." Knowing what the president was trying to say without actually saying it, Stalin reportedly remarked to his aides after the encounter that "they just want to raise the ante"; he immediately ordered a speedup in the two-year-old Soviet bomb project. The poker-playing Truman certainly believed that he had been dealt a winning hand at Potsdam. The bomb, as Secretary of War Henry L. Stimson put it, was his "master card" in ending the war on American terms and dealing with "the Russian problem" after the war.

The Grand Alliance was rapidly breaking up by the end of the Potsdam Conference, but the disaffection of allies at the end of a war is not the same thing as the outbreak of a cold war. Although incensed by "Bolsheviki land grabs," such as the Polish border changes, Truman still believed that he could work with the Soviet leader. As he wrote in his diary at Potsdam, "I can deal with Stalin. He is honest and smart as Hell."

After the stunning demonstrations of the bomb's power at Hiroshima and Nagasaki, Truman soon realized that Stalin refused to play by American rules. The anticipation that the bomb as America's "sacred trust" would be the "winning weapon" in war and peace proved only half right. Continued Soviet consolidation of its control of eastern Europe, the exposure of a Soviet atomic spy ring in Canada, and the Russians' total failure to be impressed by the American atomic monopoly in negotiating a series of outstanding disputes all prompted Truman to abandon his earlier optimism about being able to deal with that "son of a bitch" Stalin.

Declaring himself "tired of baying the Soviets," Truman personally set down in his own hand his outline of future American policy toward the Soviet Union. Since the Russians understood only the logic of force, they must be confronted with "an iron fist and strong language." He was convinced that Stalin's goal was to extend the area of Soviet military control from eastern Europe south to Iran as part of a larger scheme to invade Turkey, seize the Black Sea straits, and then break out into the Mediterranean. To counter this Soviet aggression, Truman proposed a global policy of containment that included consolidation of exclusive American control over Japan and the Pacific, creation of strong pro-Western governments in China and Korea, refusal to accept Soviet domination of eastern Europe, and the "forced settlement" of the Soviet Lend-Lease debt. This ambitious presidential checklist of countermoves to Soviet expansion came several weeks before George F. Kennan's "long telegram" from Moscow arrived in Washington. In that dispatch Kennan's analysis of the "neurotic" Soviet view of the world provided theoretical justification for Truman's Cold War policy of containment.

Although containment had his private blessing, Truman did not make this change of policy public at the time. There were still those Roosevelt holdovers within the administration and the Democratic party such as former Vice President Henry A. Wallace, who continued to advocate cooperation with the Russians, but, as one State Department insider recalled later, in early 1946 "the Cold War was on and we knew it." Although he could not yet publicly do so, Truman privately endorsed former Prime Minister Churchill's vivid description of the postwar world. With the president looking on, the wartime British leader announced the existence of a new cold war. An "iron curtain" had fallen between the wartime Big Three.

Another year would pass before the United States moved, with $400 million in aid to Greece and Turkey and Truman's public commitment to defend free peoples everywhere from subjugation by "armed minorities and outside pressures," to fill the breach in the Western defenses left by Britain's withdrawal from the eastern Mediterranean. The open-ended, urgent rhetoric was partly an effort, as one adviser put it, to "scare [the] Hell out of the American people," awakening them to the Soviet threat and the costs of combating it. The Truman Doctrine was also a public declaration of a global conflict, the Cold War with the Soviet Union.

Why the Cold War happened is an immensely more complicated question than when it began. The changes of perception and expectations that gave rise to the Cold War happened in the minds of different people at different times for various reasons. Focusing on the perceptions and expectations of the Allied leaders does not explain the total process. There are events that even dictators and "imperial" presidents cannot control. Nonetheless, the diversities among these leaders shed light on how the Cold War developed out of the wartime Grand Alliance.

Historian John Lewis Gaddis has pointed out that during the war Roosevelt attempted to contain Soviet postwar power by integrating it into an international system of big power cooperation. Truman abandoned that approach in favor of Churchill's containment by segregation. Whether either policy was better or more realistic is unprovable since Roosevelt did not live to continue his integrationist approach into the postwar period. Given the legacy of mutual distrust, the fundamental ideological disparities, and the vast differences of experience, it is doubtful that Roosevelt could have succeeded completely. Unlike Truman, however, he probably would have tried harder and longer, thereby at least clarifying an issue that continues to be debated among historians of American foreign policy.

Sources and Suggested Readings

Alperovitz, Gar. *Atomic Diplomacy: Hiroshima and Potsdam.* Rev ed. New York, 1985.

Anderson, Terry H. *The United States, Great Britain, and the Cold War, 1944–1947.* Columbia, 1981.

Burns, James MacGregor. *Roosevelt: The Soldier of Freedom.* New York, 1970.

Clemens, Diane Shaver. *Yalta.* New York, 1970.

Dallek, Robert. *Franklin D. Roosevelt and American Foreign Policy, 1932–1945.* New York, 1979.

Divine, Robert A. *Roosevelt and World War II.* Baltimore, 1969.

Donovan, Robert J. *Conflict and Crisis: The Presidency of Harry S. Truman, 1945–1948.* New York, 1977.

Eubank, Keith. *Summit at Teheran.* New York, 1985.

Ferrell, Robert H., ed. *Off the Record: The Private Papers of Harry S. Truman.* New York, 1980.

Gaddis, John Lewis. *Strategies of Containment: A Critical Appraisal of Postwar American National Security Policy.* New York, 1982.

Herken, Gregg. *The Winning Weapon: The Atomic Bomb in the Cold War, 1945-1950.* New York, 1980.

Larson, Deborah Welch. *Origins of Containment: A Psychological Explanation.* Princeton, 1985.

Mastny, Vojtech. *Russia's Road to the Cold War: Diplomacy, Strategy, and the Politics of Communism, 1941-1945.* New York, 1979.

Mee, Charles L., Jr. *Meeting at Potsdam.* New York, 1975.

Paterson, Thomas G. *On Every Front: The Making of the Cold War.* New York, 1979.

Sherwin, Martin J. *A World Destroyed: The Atomic Bomb and the Grand Alliance.* New York, 1975.

Sivachev, Nikolai V., and Yakovlev, Nikolai N. *Russia and the United States: U.S.-Soviet Relations from the Soviet Point of View.* Translated by Olga A. Titelbaum. Chicago, 1979.

Wilson, Theodore A. *The First Summit: Roosevelt and Churchill at Placentia Bay, 1941.* Boston, 1969.

Yergin, Daniel. *Shattered Peace: The Origins of the Cold War and the National Security State.* Boston, 1977.

The Cold War in Asia

Carol Morris Petillo

At the end of World War II, U.S. policymakers reexamined their government's agenda in Asia. Traditionally, Americans had distrusted the adaptable and competitive Japanese, hoped for extended markets and religious converts in China, and ignored the colonial holdings that made up most of the rest of the Far East. Pointing to their own intention to free the Philippine Islands, they held hopefully to a vague assumption that the other Western imperialist powers, long entrenched in Indochina, Indonesia, and Malaya, would retreat as willingly in the face of growing Asian nationalism. Beyond these occasional thoughts, the exigencies of wartime strategy and the higher priority assigned to Europe blurred the vision of most of those who faced the problems of U.S. policy in Asia after Japan surrendered. Nevertheless, a piecemeal policy emerged, which, although its major goals seemed clear, left much of its detail to tradition, convenience, and misunderstanding.

By early 1943 the Allies had agreed that Japanese expansion in Asia could not be tolerated. The policy of unconditional surrender was to include Japan as well as Germany. At meetings later that year a joint Southeast Asian command was established, and the Soviet Union agreed to enter the war against Japan shortly after the defeat of Germany. At Cairo, when Jiang Jieshi was included in consultations, the United States and Great Britain agreed that China would recover the territory it previously had lost in unequal treaty agreements with their governments, Korea would regain its independence, and Japan would be stripped of its Pacific island holdings.

Asian issues did not surface again in top-level negotiations until the Yalta meeting in February 1945. America's desire to persuade the Soviets to enter the war against Japan was predominant, and, as a result, earlier understandings with the Chinese were compromised.

In exchange for reaffirmation of its promise to join the Allied effort in Asia, the Soviet Union was guaranteed continued hegemony along its borders with China and access to the naval base at Port Arthur. Assuring Stalin of Jiang's agreement in these matters, Roosevelt confirmed the Soviets' "preeminent interests" in the Chinese East and South Manchurian railways and in the free port of Dairen. In addition, the Western powers conceded the Kuril Islands to the USSR. Since an aura of wartime trust still surrounded the Big Three, these promises seemed no threat to Western interests. In another year and a half, new personalities and new perspectives would redefine the implications of these agreements. In the meantime, the war in Asia came to a surprisingly early end, and the Russian alliance with the West reverted to the old antagonism based on conflicting ideologies and national interests. The principal goal of U.S. policy toward Asia in mid-1945 was to defeat Japan and, as a corollary, to negotiate with the USSR to the detriment of China. Significantly, neither the Soviets, the British, nor the Americans seemed to notice that once again Western leaders were assuming the power to determine Eastern fates.

Two realities would make this Eurocentric approach untenable. The first, one of those periodic great shifts in history, was simply that population growth in Asia during the entire twentieth century had far surpassed a relatively slower European increase. As a consequence, the nationalist movements, which had begun partly in response to the Wilsonian promise of self-determination after World War I, found ever-growing popular support. The second reality, far more evident to policymakers at the time, was the upsurge of patriotic fervor which indigenous peoples throughout Asia experienced in the face of the early Japanese victories. That Asians had defeated the Western imperialist powers in China and Southeast Asia spurred a new self-confidence among the colonized majorities. These ideas, along with the Western preoccupation with issues at home and in Europe, permitted nationalist movements to grow throughout the whole area at the end of the war. Although often weakened by internal power struggles, as in China, nationalism clearly presaged the end of European political domination of Asia. That these facts were not evident to policymakers in the West defines one dimension of the story of the Cold War in Asia for the next thirty years.

With the dropping of the atomic bomb on Hiroshima and Nagasaki in August 1945, power relationships in Asia shifted once again. Eager to ensure for themselves the promises made at Yalta, the Soviets declared war against Japan on August 8, two days after the bombing of Hiroshima. This exacerbated the already tense situation in China where the Chinese Communist Party (CCP) and the Kuomintang (Nationalist Chinese government) competed to accept the surrender and equipment of the defeated Japanese. The Russians continued to advance until the end of the month and soon controlled much of northeastern China where the CCP had wartime predominance. Other Soviet forces moved into Manchuria, an area of special interest to the Kuomintang. Observers wondered whether Moscow would honor the recently negotiated Treaty of Friendship and Alliance in which it promised to recognize and cooperate with Jiang's government or would ally itself with the ideologically more compatible Communists of Mao Zedong (Mao Tse-tung). Expectations in the United States were more often based on wartime evaluations of the CCP and Kuomintang than on any clear understanding of Soviet policy. Since President Harry S. Truman increasingly drew his advisers from that group which had supported Jiang and distrusted Stalin during the war, it is not surprising that official Washington expected, and therefore saw, Soviet duplicity at every turn.

Japan provided the United States with an advantage not available in Europe when Germany surrendered. Its abrupt collapse created a vacuum into which only one power was ready to flow. As a consequence, General Douglas MacArthur, named Supreme Commander for the Allied Powers but in reality representing U.S. interests as he saw them, took charge of the occupation and reconstruction of Japan. For the most part, he ignored the Far Eastern Advisory Commission and its Soviet member and began to make the Pacific the first line of American defense. Taking control of Micronesia and many other small Pacific islands, the United States soon made clear its intention to influence postwar developments in Asia. In Japan these goals seemed easily realizable; in China, the outcome was less sure. Although some attention was paid to the developing colonial conflicts in Southeast Asia and to Korea, America's immediate concern centered on the struggle in China.

Convinced that Europe and the Middle East were more vulnerable to the Soviet threat, U.S. policymakers, particularly Undersecretary of State Dean Acheson and Soviet expert George Kennan, at first paid less attention to Communist action in China. Certainly they agreed that the United States would continue to support Jiang, and that expanded trade with China could best be achieved through support of a non-Communist power in that part of the world. Still, China was considered somewhat less important than eastern Europe.

As is often true in democracies, however, domestic political pressures impinged on foreign policy. Led by Henry R. Luce's *Time-Life* media empire, a group of men and women, who had long been interested in China for a variety of reasons and who ultimately became known as "the China lobby," began to accuse the Truman administration of not paying the proper attention to the crisis in China. They argued that the United States was threatened as much by communism in Asia as in Europe, and that if China "fell" the administration would have to answer some serious questions. Their position seemed to be strengthened when Patrick J. Hurley, appointed by Roosevelt as ambassador to China in late 1944 and a longtime supporter of Jiang, brought Mao and Jiang together for a meeting in the fall of 1945. In conflict with his own staff, Hurley assured Washington that a coalition government could be established and that ultimately the Communist position would deteriorate. No sooner had he comforted his superiors with these promises, however, than Jiang's refusal to compromise broke up the negotiations. Hurley resigned, accusing his staff of disloyalty and his government of mismanagement. His argument that the State Department experts favored the CCP was inaccurate; they merely had pointed out that Mao and Zhou Enlai (Chou En-lai) headed a stronger, more efficient, less corrupt organization. Nonetheless, Hurley's opinions were widely repeated by those in the China lobby. By 1949 this group, supported by those who endorsed McCarthyism, would use the Hurley story as received gospel.

Late in 1945 President Truman asked General George C. Marshall to go to China and gather information upon which to base future U.S. policy in Asia. Marshall hoped to establish in China a new coalition government, preferably with non-Communist dominance. Until early in 1946 his quiet diplomacy calmed some of the violence that had long torn China apart. It did not, however, find long-term answers to the difficult questions presented by Chinese history and recent international developments.

Understanding the origin of the Cold War in Asia requires understanding the emergence of the Cold War in general. After August 1945, U.S.-Soviet relations changed drastically. By this time the trust necessitated by the war had foundered on disagreements regarding eastern Europe, postwar economic aid, the division of Germany, and atomic energy. Leftist nationalist movements threatened the status quo throughout Europe and elsewhere, raising anxieties in Washington. Faced with an apparently hardening American line, the Soviets seemed determined to strengthen their own position wherever possible. Eastern Europe was most important to Moscow, but Russian action in China indicated to Americans a possible Soviet challenge in Asia as well.

As early as October 1945, Moscow began to obstruct the Nationalists in Manchuria. Closing several ports to Jiang's troops and to the American transport ships that carried them, the Soviets may have been signaling their dissatisfaction with MacArthur's go-it-alone attitude in Japan. Certainly Stalin, who was never one to encourage other strong leaders or movements within his geographic or ideological spheres of influence, had not as yet shown much real interest in supporting the CCP. By late November, when the Council of Foreign Ministers reconvened in Moscow, Soviet policy still seemed more concerned with Japan than with China. In fact, once a compromise was worked out which the Soviets believed would ease tensions in Japan, they seemed to agree that U.S. troops might stay in China longer than originally planned. Many Americans believed that the Soviet acquiescence in China was in response to their acceptance of the Russian sphere in eastern Europe. Soviet penetration in Outer Mongolia and in Sinkiang province may have affected Moscow's willingness to bide its time elsewhere as well. In any event, it was clear to General Marshall that he must soothe the long-standing conflicts between the CCP and the Kuomintang, but that Soviet-American tensions would influence whatever solution, if any, he could achieve.

In the long run, the Marshall mission failed primarily because of Jiang's understanding of U.S. domestic politics. Rightfully believing that his friends in Washington could arouse the Truman administration to continue to support him, the Kuomintang leader refused to compromise with the CCP. Skillfully playing off an ambiguous Soviet offer of aid against Marshall's threats of withdrawing U.S. support, Jiang frightened conservatives in Congress into keeping the dollars flowing. As a consequence, although a truce was officially agreed upon for a time during Marshall's stay in China, the Nationalists never took it seriously. When Marshall returned to Washington for a briefing in March 1946, for example, Jiang launched an ill-planned attempt to displace the CCP from Manchuria. Certain that Washington would continue its financial aid, he refused Marshall's attempts to reinstate the truce upon his return to China. In disgust, Marshall returned to the United States at the end of the year.

Six months later Washington tried once again to influence the situation in China. A new fact-finding mission headed by General

Albert C. Wedemeyer seemed more disposed to support the Nationalists. Although he could not deny the inefficiency of Jiang's program, Wedemeyer nonetheless saw China as part of a wider problem facing the Western powers. If, as Truman had argued in March 1946, containing indigenous Communists in Greece called for large U.S. expenditures, was not the same policy necessary in China? When he vetoed Wedemeyer's advice to increase aid to the Kuomintang, now Secretary of State Marshall implicitly made a distinction in U.S. policy which would hold until it was widely criticized two years later. For Washington and the Truman administration, there was a qualitative difference between the civil wars in Greece (or, for that matter, elsewhere in Europe) and in China. A land war in Asia had long been held untenable, even by the conservative American military establishment. In addition, further U.S. involvement in Asia might encourage increased Soviet adventurism in Europe. It was a risk that the United States was unwilling to take at the time.

As a consequence and despite Wedemeyer's advice, the United States did not intervene directly in the Chinese civil war. Continuing to send advisers, arms, ammunition, and dollars, Marshall and Truman nonetheless refused to take the decisive action that might have helped the Kuomintang to hold on a little longer. When in December 1949 Jiang and his supporters fled to Formosa, Washington carefully explained the Nationalist defeat in terms laid out earlier by the new secretary of state, Acheson. Although admitting Kuomintang corruption, Acheson's letter accompanying the August 1949 *China White Paper* could not resist reference to the CCP's "subservience to foreign power, Russia" and overlooked the influence of China's history and social structure on the revolution. In the face of the near hysteria induced by the China lobby at this outcome, the Truman administration hardened its anti-Communist rhetoric but took no real action against the newly established People's Republic of China.

Still unready to extend to the whole world the actual policy outlined by the theory of containment and the Truman Doctrine, U.S. policymakers turned their attention to Japan. From 1947 on, under the almost continuous guidance of Yoshida Shigeru, Japan had resumed a policy goal of peaceful economic expansion. Supported by the new constitution with its renunciation of war "as a means of settling international disputes," Japanese leaders and American occupation directors agreed that the interests of both their countries could best be served by reestablishing Japanese sovereignty, maintaining Japanese national security by the use of American military strength, and encouraging economic expansion through a close trade relationship with the United States. After the Nationalist defeat in China, the achievement of these goals seemed even more essential to the Truman administration. From the perspective of the Cold War mind-set, Asia had become one more sphere within which Western forces must be marshaled against Soviet expansionism. As evidence that U.S. policies in regard to China and Japan were inextricably linked and greatly influenced by attitudes toward the USSR, the U.S.-Japanese peace treaty, long under consideration, received much more serious attention after early 1950.

Signed in September 1951 the treaty restored Japan's full sovereignty in exchange for its recognition of the independence of Korea and its renunciation of the Pacific islands which it had acquired in the twentieth century. In addition, Japan was required to give up its special rights and interests in China; to renounce war, although it could enter into collective security agreements, to negotiate reparations for its part in World War II, and to establish most-favored-nation trade agreements with the Allied powers. Significantly, the Soviet Union was not one of the fifty signatories to the treaty. Of even greater significance was the fact that within five hours after the signing of the multilateral agreement, the United States and Japan agreed upon a mutual security pact that allowed for the stationing of U.S. troops and military equipment throughout the island nation. After more than a century of "dreaming of the China market," the United States had finally settled for a military and economic alliance with the more amenable Japanese.

China, Japan, the United States, and the USSR were not the only nations shaping Asia in the early postwar years. At least two other developments were of equal significance: the conflict that would become known as the Korean War and the less noted, but perhaps even more important, nationalist revolutions in Malaya, Indonesia, and Indochina.

Although the United States had been interested in Korea since the end of the nineteenth century, it had acquiesced in Japanese annexation of the Hermit Kingdom in 1910 in order not to upset Japan's willingness to balance Russian expansionism in the area. Between 1910 and 1945 the world outside seemed little interested in Korea's future, and whenever World War II conferences focused on the Pacific, Korean independence was mentioned only in general terms. To postpone a decision that was likely to displease one or the other of the Allies, a five-year, four-power trusteeship was finally proposed in 1945 and presented to the Koreans as a fait accompli. Denied an opportunity to manage their own political and economic destinies for over four decades, individual Korean leaders had served Japanese, Chinese, Soviet, or American masters during World War II to derive whatever power they could. It is not surprising, therefore, that at war's end these potential indigenous leaders were sharply divided regarding which international alliances, ideologies, and strategies would be most advantageous. Two distinct coalitions gradually emerged: the Korean Communists and left-wing nationalists, united around the leadership of Soviet-trained Kim Il-sung and the strongly anti-Communist conservatives who followed Syngman Rhee after his return from exile in the United States in October 1945. The next decade of Korean history was shaped by the interplay between these domestic foes and the alliances established within the now more clearly defined international Cold War that supported them. During this period, as Okonogi Masao has argued, in Korea "domestic politics were 'internationalized' and international politics 'internalized.'" When the war ended, the nation was divided temporarily at the 38th parallel. It soon became obvious that the factions involved in the domestic power struggle would not cooperate in the proposed trusteeship.

As the conflict between the United States and the USSR widened and grew more acrimonious during the next five years, the groups struggling for power in Korea identified their domestic interests with the international positions of their allies, and the division of the long-subjugated nation became institutionalized. Despite UN efforts to ensure nationwide elections, by 1948 a Soviet-supported government headed by Kim took shape in the North, and Rhee had won control of the South. Both leaders warded off domestic political competition by calling for armed unification and promising that the ideologies which they espoused would ultimately win out. Such a climate encouraged armed conflicts, and clashes occurred regularly along the 38th parallel. When word finally came of the outbreak of war on June 25, 1950, many wondered which antagonist had moved first. That Kim had instigated the long-threatened war is usually attributed to the fact that in a policy statement to the National Press Club in January 1950, Secretary of State Acheson had explained that Korea was outside the "defensive perimeter" for which the United States felt militarily responsible.

In order to understand this clarification of U.S. policy, it is necessary to look more closely at both European and domestic American developments at the end of the 1940s. Despite pressure from the China lobby after Jiang's defeat, Truman and Acheson seemed determined to stand by their established priority favoring Europe over Asia. Although supported by the Joint Chiefs of Staff as a much more feasible position militarily, Acheson's statement regarding the U.S. defense perimeter seemed to contradict other mainstays of American foreign policy. One of these, the Truman Doctrine, argued that the United States could only ensure its own security by coming to the assistance of "free peoples [wherever they were] resisting . . . armed minorities or . . . outside pressures." The other, the famous "containment doctrine," first promulgated by Kennan in 1947, argued that the United States must "confront the Russians with unalterable counterforce at every point where they show signs of encroaching upon the interest of a peaceful and stable world." Since U.S. policymakers believed the South Koreans to be "free peoples" and commonly assumed that Kim would never have acted without Soviet approval, both theories seemed applicable. When this contradiction was made obvious by the outcries of the Asia-firsters, and when the president reconsidered his party's domestic position in the face of increasing accusations of being "soft on communism," his choice was clear. The United States would urge that UN forces, constituted mostly of American troops, come to the aid of the beleaguered South Koreans. Since at the moment the Soviet Union was boycotting the UN Security Council in response to the U.S. refusal to allow delegates from the People's Republic to assume China's seat, the international agency agreed to the American proposal.

One more factor encouraged U.S. action. Only six months prior to the outbreak of war in Korea, the Truman administration had asked the State and Defense departments to reconsider American defense policy in view of the responsibilities recently assumed under the NATO treaty. This policy statement, known as National Security Council Paper Number 68 (NSC-68), pictured the United States as menaced by Soviet-inspired threats across the world and concluded that these threats could only be contained by a vast American military buildup. The problem was to convince the taxpayers and their representatives in Congress to pay the price. Although American leaders certainly did not desire or encourage the Korean conflict, they were not opposed to using it to persuade Congress to underwrite the policy outlined in NSC-68. Thus, in the minds of those in power, there were simply more reasons for U.S. involvement in Korea than against it. As a consequence, within five days of the North Korean action at the 38th parallel, MacArthur once again led American forces into battle, this time as commander in chief of the UN forces in Korea.

THE KOREAN CONFLICT. General of the Army Douglas MacArthur, commander in chief in Korea, leads the saying of the Lord's Prayer at ceremonies held on September 29, 1950 at the Capitol Building in Seoul to restore the capital of the Republic of Korea to President Syngman Rhee. (U.S. Signal Corps, National Archives)

At the outset, MacArthur and his supporters in the White House and the Pentagon agreed on war aims. Forcing the North Korean troops back above the 38th parallel seemed task enough in view of their lightning thrust through the South. After mid-September, however, when the general's brilliantly planned and executed landing at Inchon raised American expectations, an offensive to "liberate" the whole peninsula gained support. United Nations forces moved north with remarkable alacrity, and, although Mao Zedong and Zhou Enlai warned both publicly and privately that a drive to the Yalu would force them to respond, neither MacArthur nor his president believed a Chinese counterattack likely. As a consequence, American forces were caught by surprise in late October when they first encountered Chinese troops. Ignoring the warning, MacArthur's command ordered the bombing of all bridges across the Yalu, and on November 24 ground forces began a push northward. Two days later the Chinese kept their promise and, with more than 200,000 troops, intervened in the war.

The next few months were filled with fierce fighting, both in Korea and Washington. Back to prewar positions by early March (Communists above the 38th parallel, UN troops below it), MacArthur insistently demanded more leeway in fighting the war. He hoped to call in the massive air power of the United States, and hints escaped from the general and the president that atomic weapons might be used. However, under pressure from the European allies, which were worried about a wider war, Truman soon retracted his tentative support for this possibility and entered instead into conflict with MacArthur. Always a strong supporter of the Asia-first position in the Cold War debate, the longtime hero of American conservatives began to make public his increasing dissatisfaction with Truman's "appeasement." Never known for patience or tact, the president responded in mid-April of 1951 by firing the five-star general.

Truman's sacking of MacArthur helped to define more sharply the divisions in American public opinion on what was now referred to as "limited war." Just as policymakers were split over the reestablishment of a Europe-first position implicit in Truman's less militant stance, so too were average Americans. Influenced by traditional myths, which described all previous American wars as defensive, victorious, and honorable, and believing that World War II had solved most international problems, Americans were confused over the Korean conflict. To its credit, the Truman administration did not bend to the popular outcry for more decisive action. Instead, influenced by European arguments, it replaced MacArthur with General Matthew B. Ridgway and gradually wound down the war, apparently agreeing with General Omar Bradley's assessment that it was "the wrong war, at the wrong place, at the wrong time, and with the wrong enemy." Peace talks began in July 1951, and, although they would drag on for another two years and require a changing of the guard in Washington before an armistice was achieved, the policy was clear: despite rhetoric to the contrary in Congress and the press, top-level decision makers agreed that the United States would not fully commit itself everywhere militarily. Since this was the case, hard choices had to be made and, at least for the time being (and indeed for the next decade), those choices would emphasize Europe and the NATO alliance as the first bulwark against Soviet communism. In July 1953, when the war finally ended, little had changed politically for the Koreans. Their country was still divided at the 38th parallel and still controlled in the North by a Communist government and in the South by a capitalist regime.

Historians have not been able to prove Soviet complicity in the North Korean invasion, and such questions cannot be answered without access to Soviet and Chinese archives. There are many reasons to believe that, while the Soviets may have approved in general of the North Korean plan, they were taken by surprise by Kim's timing. Nonetheless, most American leaders, then as now, firmly accepted the idea that this crisis also originated in Moscow. As Gaddis Smith has explained,

> James Forrestal, the first American Secretary of Defense, had said a few years before that the principal export of the Soviet Union was chaos. The unstated corollary was that wherever chaos appeared, it must be a Soviet export. Americans were blind to evidence of mankind's capacity all over the world to generate indigenous chaos without regard to the Soviet Union or the United States.

Circumstantially, there is evidence on both sides of the question. Just as Washington responded to the attack because it feared that otherwise its position as leader of the free world would be called into question, the Soviets may have seen Korea as an opportunity to consolidate their control of the Communist world in the face of growing competition from the Maoist regime in China. Kennan argued at the time that the Russians most likely wanted to influence U.S. treaty negotiations with Japan. Whatever the truth, there can be no denying that the conflict had an enormous long-range impact on the United States, both at home and relative to its Cold War policy in Asia.

Although dissatisfaction with the Korean standoff certainly contributed to the election of the first Republican administration in twenty-four years, Truman's arbitrary decision to enter the fight without consulting Congress had the most lasting effect on U.S. foreign policy. Thereafter, in a climate of McCarthyism, which increasingly discouraged bipartisan debate of international issues, presidents would act unilaterally with less and less hesitancy. In addition, the debate set off by events in China in 1949 heightened as a result of the struggle in Korea. Which arena, Europe or Asia, was really the most important in the "fight against communism"? Was the expanded defense budget encouraged by NSC-68 adequate? Could the United States solve all the problems of the world? When stated this baldly, most U.S. policymakers after 1953 would undoubtedly have answered the last question with an unqualified no. Nonetheless, the globalism that Truman encouraged by entering the Korean fray and only partly countermanded when he decided to limit that involvement often attempted just that. Nowhere was this more visible than in the obvious belief of Truman's successors that nationalist movements, wherever they developed, were directed by Moscow. This "lesson" of Korea would ultimately cost the United States far more than the billions of dollars and the thousands of lives the war demanded.

Thus, by 1953 China, Japan, and Korea were to varying degrees important in the continuing quests for world power of the Soviet Union and the United States. Attitudes toward the remaining Asian nations, however, were less clear. Just as the British had assumed responsibility for Southeast Asia during the wartime planning, so in the immediate postwar years the United Kingdom, France, and the Netherlands interested themselves in regaining their colonial holdings in the area. At Yalta there had been talk of trusteeships for colonies invaded by Japan, but the war's abrupt ending precluded this solution. Also, because Indochina, Malaya, and Indonesia in particular drew less attention from the USSR and the United States, their fate was uncertain. As Akira Iriye has pointed out, "The future of the area remained ambiguous, dependent upon the interaction between Chinese and European policies at one level, and between the colonial and indigenous populations' divergent wishes at another." Although both of the major Cold War powers expressed ideological support for nationalist movements, neither gave them tangible assistance in the first few years after World War II.

Throughout 1948, then, events in Southeast Asia for the most part were shaped by Britain and China, buttressed by French and Dutch support as it became available. British policy below the 16th parallel resulted in harsh treatment of indigenous nationalist—and sometimes Communist—forces and emplacement of Dutch troops in Indonesia and French troops in Indochina to maintain the status quo as the Allied occupation forces withdrew. Above the 16th parallel, the Kuomintang originally seemed content to replace nationalist Vietminh leaders with its own Vietnamese allies and establish favorable trading relations with its longtime adversaries. By early 1946, however, faced with increased demands for his troops at home, Jiang sold his interest in Vietnam to France. Thus the Kuomintang, like the British farther south, contributed to the weakening of Ho Chi Minh's Vietminh. Here, as in Indonesia, the nationalists seemed initially willing to "wait and see" what bargaining power their indigenous strength and traditional U.S. and Soviet anticolonial policies would give them. As it turned out, they too would ultimately be controlled by international forces defined in Cold War terms and forced, like the Chinese and the Koreans, to walk a tightrope between the great powers, seeking advantages wherever available.

The story of this process in Indochina is explained elsewhere in this book. As for the rest of Southeast Asia, certain patterns can be discerned in the years between 1946, when the United States granted independence to the Philippines, and 1954, when under the guidance of Secretary of State John Foster Dulles the Southeast Asia Treaty Organization (SEATO) made obvious the post-Korean American vision of this part of the world.

Many nationalist leaders in Southeast Asia and elsewhere believed that the rhetoric of self-determination espoused by the United States since 1776, and particularly after 1916, ensured support for their own independence. After Franklin Roosevelt's death, however, there was little indication that U.S. policymakers meant to act on this principle. This very lack of action heightened the indigenous resentments toward the one Western nation in whom they had faith and thereby encouraged Communists in the independence movements. As a consequence, when the United States began to redefine local anticolonial movements as Soviet-controlled Communist efforts, this development served as justification. European alliances often seemed to hinge on U.S. policy toward colonialism in Asia, and, since Europe was the focus of Washington's post-Korean policy, both the Truman and Eisenhower administrations managed to ignore Wilsonian tenets. Nowhere was this policy more evident than in the early 1950 decision to recognize and give economic aid to the newly proclaimed "free states" of Vietnam, Laos, and Cambodia, all French puppets.

Unhampered by European control or influence in the Philippines, U.S. postwar policy in the archipelago represents perhaps the most logical outgrowth of its own traditions. After a brief foray into territorial colonialism at the turn of the twentieth century, the United States for the most part had solved its need for expansion through policies of free trade (the Open Door) and economic imperialism rather than direct colonial control. Although the Philippines were the major exception to this pattern, most American policymakers in the twentieth century agreed that their long-range goal was to grant independence to the Filipinos once they had achieved the skills necessary for self-government as they were defined in Washington.

Democratic administrations usually believed that these skills were present to a greater degree than did their Republican counterparts. Not surprisingly, therefore, during Roosevelt's New Deal administration a concrete plan for independence finally took shape. Encouraged by those who saw Philippine independence as one way to rid U.S. domestic producers of protected competition, an interim commonwealth government was established in 1935, with independence to be granted a decade later.

World War II interrupted this schedule, and the Republic of the Philippines did not come into being until July 1946. At the time, many Filipinos and Americans alike criticized even this date as precipitous. Arguing that the devastation of war had left the nation less able to govern itself, critics charged that Washington's cutback in aid to Manila was irresponsible. Government leaders on both sides of the Pacific saw the affair differently, however, and their official proclamations were taken as truth by most. In Manila the government of Manuel Roxas granted the United States continuing access to military bases in the archipelago and continued to negotiate for whatever aid it could get. In Washington the Truman administration, when it thought of the Philippines at all, seemed content to use the islands as an illustration of American high-mindedness. Only gradually would it become clear to most Filipinos and a few more Americans that true independence required more than political rearrangements.

In contrast to its action in the Philippines, U.S. policy toward Malaya during these years was almost totally governed by the Cold War alliance with Great Britain. In Malaya, Communist-led guerrillas fought for national independence. Despite their efforts, ethnic diversity and conflict, coupled with harsh British military tactics and a stable and expanding economy, eventually led to the establishment of the Federation of Malaya within the British Commonwealth. The United States showed very little interest in this struggle for self-determination, illustrating perhaps most clearly its denial of Wilsonian tenets and its support of the needs of its European friends.

In Indonesia, as in Indochina, may be found the sharpest example of U.S. vacillation in Asia in the early Cold War. The United States reacted to the August 1945 proclamation of the Republic of Indonesia somewhat erratically. At first, Washington agreed to Dutch attempts to reassert control over the area they had named the Netherlands East Indies some three and a half centuries earlier, on the assumption that Dutch colonial policies would be liberalized. As time went on, however, the conflict between a widely supported, indigenous-led movement for independence and increasingly harsh Dutch attempts to control its growth left the United States in a quandary. As Robert J. McMahon has explained, "American officials had advocated the reform of the imperialist system, not its destruction; they had pressed for gradual, evolutionary changes, not abrupt, revolutionary ones." Nonetheless, by late 1948, when the Dutch once again tried to destroy the republic militarily and world opinion seemed sympathetic to the Indonesian cause, the Truman administration hesitantly persuaded Holland to rethink its policy by threatening to withhold European Recovery Program funds. In 1949 independence was declared once again and this time accepted at The Hague.

The Indonesian independence movement and the government established in Djakarta by Sukarno opposed communism. This factor, more than anything else, explains the U.S. reversal toward the Dutch and places U.S. policy squarely within the boundaries imposed by the Cold War world view. This reflexive anticommunism was supported, or so it seemed, by domestic political realities. Denouncing the Korean policies of the Truman administration and its alleged "softness" on communism, the Eisenhower-Nixon ticket achieved easy victory in 1952. Since this political wisdom neatly dovetailed with the international perspective of the new president and Secretary of State Dulles, it is not surprising that the foreign policy they jointly developed reflected a tougher line against Moscow. In Asia this action was most clearly represented in the assumptions underlying the Korean settlement and the establishment of SEATO, which Dulles hoped to build into the Pacific counterpart of NATO. Significantly and symbolically, only three of the eight members (the United States, Great Britain, France, Australia, New Zealand, Pakistan, Thailand, and the Philippines) were Asian, and only two (Thailand and the Philippines) were properly Southeast Asian. Since these distinctions had never been particularly important to policymakers in Washington, the inconsistency of the membership was overlooked. In Asia, however, only the Philippines of all the newly independent nations became a member.

Within the context of its worldwide policies of "brinkmanship," "massive retaliation," and "more bang for the buck," the Eisenhower-Dulles team seemed determined not to be accused of surrendering any ground to the Communists. In Asia, it increased support for the government of Nationalist China. As the Asian experts in the State Department were steadily purged by the McCarthyite forces, Jiang was "unleashed" and actually encouraged by both words and dollars to move more aggressively against the mainland People's Republic. During the entire two terms of the Eisenhower administration, highlighted by the confrontations over Quemoy and Matsu in 1954–55 and in 1958, policy seemed to reflect the old China lobby view that the Nationalist defeat was only temporary and had resulted from a lack of will in the West rather than from Chinese realities.

The decade following World War II was thus a period in which Cold War attitudes in the United States and the Soviet Union quickly spread from an initially narrow focus in Eastern Europe to the rest of the world and to Asia in particular. In fact, until 1960 the United States in the Far East gradually but steadily redefined what had originally seemed to be many specific postcolonial problems into one major conflict between the two Cold War giants in which the original indigenous participants were relegated to smaller and smaller roles.

The next decade and a half, however, witnessed many changes in this pattern. The Vietnam War certainly encouraged these developments, but other factors, too, were important. A greater desire among many postcolonial nations to protect their recently won independence by remaining neutral was one such influence. Increasing tension between the Soviet Union and China, Japan's growing economic strength, and an American diplomatic turnaround toward the People's Republic of China also contributed significantly to the new picture.

Asian nations viewed American involvement in Vietnam from drastically divergent perspectives. Taiwan, South Korea, the Philippines, and Japan supported Washington to varying degrees. China and Indonesia were very critical. The mainland Southeast Asian countries most directly affected by the war—Thailand, Cambodia, and Laos—were often in such chaos that their responses could not be clearly defined. Nonetheless, even among the nations most directly linked to the United States, the war's expansion provided an ominous warning: superpower "protection" was costly and destructive to the countries that became battlegrounds in the struggle. With this in mind, and perhaps influenced by the mid-1950s direction taken by India and twenty-eight other Third World nations at the Bandung Conference of 1955, "nonalignment" and "regionalism" began to be examined as possible alternatives to alliance with the superpowers. SEATO had gradually diminished in strength as Australia, Britain, France, and Pakistan lessened their commitments. Several other attempts at cooperation foundered in these years because the smaller countries in the area had greater dissimilarities than they had shared interests. Only the Association of Southeast Asian Nations (ASEAN) has survived from its inception in the early 1960s. Consisting of Indonesia, the Philippines, Thailand, Malaysia, and Singapore, the organization has gradually gained acceptance as a legitimate international negotiating body, at least in the field of economics. As Harold C. Hinton points out, despite its weaknesses in areas of organization and military strength, ASEAN "is one reason for not accepting uncritically the notion that Southeast Asia is a 'power vacuum' in which the major external powers can act as they please." Clearly, the Vietnam experience encouraged this hope for ASEAN members.

Still, major external powers, as well as major regional powers, continued to wield extensive influence in the area. Until the mid-1970s the outcome of America's involvement in Vietnam and its neighbors was still not evident. As a consequence, Asian nations were required to adjust their own international policy to this ever-changing situation. In addition, Soviet interaction with Asia remained substantial and only elicited more complex responses after the Sino-Soviet split gradually became obvious during the 1960s. Losing whatever security this always tenuous alliance had provided, Beijing reacted to the split with tentative attempts to rejoin the international community, either diplomatically, as with France in 1963, or economically, as with Japan throughout the decade. As Soviet antagonism increased and the political situation in the United States changed after the election of Richard M. Nixon in 1968, indirect attempts to reestablish relations between Washington and Beijing began. In 1972 these efforts culminated in Nixon's trip to China. Although the relationship is still tenuous, this rapprochement between the People's Republic and the United States significantly altered the Cold War balance of power in Asia.

Ironically, just as Japan's defeat in 1945 set the stage for the first phase of the Cold War in Asia, its resurgence as a major economic power thirty years later is another important influence now. Emerging from the American shadow by the late 1960s, Tokyo pursued policies dictated by its desire for increased trade and hegemony within the region and by U.S. encouragement via the Nixon Doctrine, which urged Asian nations to assume more responsibility for their own defense. As the United States began to cut back some of its economic ties with Tokyo and moved toward better relations with Beijing, the Japanese followed suit. This careful attempt to establish better relations between China and Japan after years of conflict and isolation may be the most significant factor in today's Cold War in Asia. Not only does it reflect the growing strength and independence of the two major Asian powers, but this very increase in autonomy by China and Japan also lessens relatively the power of the non-Asian nations, the United States and the USSR, in that realm. As Donald Lach and Edmund Wehrle have explained,

> In a structural sense, China and Japan have become the key "inner powers" in the Far East, while the two giants have become the two great "outer powers." A balance of sorts has been created with the "inner powers" checking each other's ambitions and the "outer powers" neutralizing each other in the Far East and else-where in the world. At the same time, the "inner powers" can work together in such a way as to restrict the influence of the "outer powers," to limit their intervention to only the most seri-ous crises.

If the two "outer powers" continue to invest their wealth in weapons and the two "inner powers" continue their economic advances, these changing relationships already witnessed in Asia may indicate trends elsewhere in the international Cold War and the world.

Sources and Suggested Readings

Buhite, Russell D. *Soviet-American Relations in Asia, 1945–1954.* Norman, Oklahoma, 1981.

Hinton, Harold C. *Three and A Half Powers: The New Balance in Asia.* Bloomington, 1975.

Hsiung, James C., and Chai, Winberg, eds. *Asia and U.S. Foreign Policy.* New York, 1981.

Iriye, Akira. *The Cold War in Asia: A Historical Introduction.* Englewood Cliffs, New Jersey, 1974.

Lach, Donald F., and Wehrle, Edmund S. *International Politics in East Asia Since World War II.* New York, 1975.

Leifer, Michael. *The Foreign Relations of the New States.* Melbourne, 1974.

McMahon, Robert J. *Colonialism and Cold War: The United States and the Struggle for Indonesian Independence, 1945–49.* Ithaca, 1981.

Meyer, Milton W. *A Brief History of Southeast Asia.* Totowa, New Jersey, 1971.

Rose, Lisle A. *The Roots of Tragedy: The United States and the Struggle for Asia, 1945–1953.* Westport, 1976.

Simmons, Robert R. *The Strained Alliance: Peking, Pyongyang, Moscow and the Politics of the Korean Civil War.* New York, 1975.

Stueck, William W., Jr. *The Road to Confrontation: American Policy Toward China and Korea, 1947–1950.* Chapel Hill, 1981.

Yōnosuke, Nagai, and Iriye, Akira, eds. *The Cold War in Asia.* New York, 1977.
Yung-Hwan, Jo, ed. *U.S. Foreign Policy in Asia: An Appraisal.* Santa Barbara, 1978.

American Nuclear Policy

George T. Mazuzan

The atomic age dawned brilliantly in the sky over the New Mexico desert at Alamogordo in July 1945. Code-named "Trinity," the world's first nuclear device exploded with a force of 19 kilotons of TNT (equivalent to 19,000 pounds of conventional explosives), equaling in destructive power what hundreds of average bombs from American bombers had rained down on Dresden and Tokyo in one single day during World War II. As the only new energy source discovered in the twentieth century, nuclear energy contained dual characteristics. It first demonstrated its destructive side with the 20-kiloton bombings at Hiroshima and Nagasaki in August 1945, but it also presented a potential good if harnessed to peaceful uses. From the beginning, both the military and peaceful applications of nuclear energy have caused concern to those American leaders who have been responsible for developing a policy for its use.

The American policy can be characterized by the broadest use of the term "nonproliferation." Simply defined, nonproliferation means preventing the expansion of nuclear weapons in the world. Both vertical nonproliferation, through decrease in the numbers of strategic nuclear weapons in the possession of the nuclear power, and horizontal nonproliferation, through prevention of the manufacture or acquisition of such weapons by nonnuclear states, were professed American goals in the postwar world. Although the terms were not coined until the 1960s, the United States applied a vertical and horizontal nonproliferation policy from the earliest days of the development of nuclear energy. American leaders first formulated the policy to prevent the nation's rivals from access to nuclear weapons technology. Later they pursued this strategy in order to prevent the diversion of civilian nuclear power to weapons purposes.

ATOMIC BLAST. The mushroom-shaped cloud from the second atomic bomb dropped near the end of World War II rises to a height of 60,000 feet over the Japanese port of Nagasaki on August 9, 1945. (National Archives)

Utmost secrecy surrounded not only the development of the atomic bomb during World War II but also atomic policy in the postwar years. Prior to the employment of nuclear weapons against

Japan, American policymakers sensed that the success of the Manhattan Project would ensure that the United States would emerge from the war as the most powerful military nation in the world. The task facing them in 1945 was how to make sure that bomb-making materials and critical technology were not transferred to America's rivals. As the Cold War emerged between the United States and the Soviet Union, this policy became an increasingly important factor in American foreign relations. Its implementation was exemplified by the Baruch Plan, presented to the United Nations in 1946, and the enactment of the Atomic Energy Act in August of that same year.

Speaking three days after the Hiroshima bombing, President Harry S. Truman publicly set the stage for early American nuclear policy. "We must constitute ourselves," he said, "trustees of this new force, to prevent its misuse and to turn it into the channels of service to mankind. It is an awful responsibility which has come to us. We thank God that it has come to us instead of our enemies, and we pray that He may guide us to use it in His way and for His purposes." At the newly created United Nations, the government proceeded to develop this national trust through presentation of an international plan for atomic energy control. David E. Lilienthal, chairman of the Tennessee Valley Authority, and Undersecretary of State Dean G. Acheson headed a committee that drew up the government's plan in early 1946. Concluding that the chances of nuclear war would be great as long as individual nations could indulge in dangerous nuclear activities leading to the quick adaptation of weapons production—that is, controlling installations that produced uranium 235 and plutonium used in building bombs—they proposed that the nuclear enterprise be placed entirely under international management. They envisaged a supranational authority that would have the exclusive right not only to carry out research on nuclear explosives but also to inspect for clandestine activities. Acheson and Lilienthal also suggested a series of transitional stages to move the United States, the sole possessor of the bomb at that time, from a national to international system of atomic energy control. The nation would progressively hand over to the international authority first its information, then its installations, later its fissionable materials, and finally its weapons.

President Truman chose Bernard M. Baruch, a multimillionaire industrialist and informal adviser to several presidents, to handle the delicate political negotiations to implement the Acheson-Lilienthal plan at the United Nations. Baruch convinced Truman to add an important supplemental clause to withdraw the right of veto on atomic energy matters from the five permanent members of the UN Security Council. The American elder statesman told the General Assembly on June 19, 1946 that "there must be no veto to protect those who violate their solemn agreements not to develop or use atomic energy for destructive purposes." Because the veto had been guaranteed by the UN Charter, this action, in effect, helped doom the American proposal. The chief Soviet delegate to the United Nations, Andrei Gromyko, flatly rejected any tampering with the veto. The Soviet Union viewed the Baruch provision as a flagrant violation of its veto rights in deciding matters of substance under the UN Charter. Some historians have noted that the Baruch Plan was meant to elicit such a Soviet response in order to assure, at least in the short term, American supremacy in the atomic weapons field. Others, less critical of U.S. policy, have viewed the plan, even with the veto, as a magnanimous offer to share with the world the benefits of a new technology while establishing a plan to reduce the horrible implications of a future atomic war. In either view the proposed plan was an early expression of America's nonproliferation weapons policy.

Soviet leaders countered the Baruch Plan with one of their own. Gromyko proposed a treaty that included prohibition of the production and use of atomic weapons and the destruction of all existing weapons within three months of the agreement's ratification. Signatory states would enact legislation, giving themselves the duty to oversee the enforcement of the treaty. In other words, instead of international inspection and control unhampered by a veto, as envisaged by the Baruch proposal, national self-control was the key to the Soviet initiative. There are different interpretations of Gromyko's statement. On the one hand, those remembering Russia's deep-rooted distrust of the outside world have concluded that Gromyko merely pursued the USSR's natural minority position of opposition to outside inspection. On the other hand, close observers of the Soviet system have speculated that the Kremlin attempted to take the initiative from the United States and to use this plan as a smoke screen for its own purposes. The Soviet Union's advocacy of the treaty was a way to gain American atomic disarmament while permitting time for the Soviet Union to develop its own arsenal of atomic weapons undisturbed by international inspection. Accepting either interpretation, when the American and Soviet propositions are placed in the context of Cold War tensions, it becomes apparent that the positions of the two superpowers were irreconcilable. The stage was thus set for the nuclear arms race.

The United States established its formal nuclear policy in the Atomic Energy Act of 1946, which made all questions relating to atomic energy the responsibility of the new civilian Atomic Energy Commission. Everything from uranium ore to nuclear fuel came under the authority of, and became the property of, the commission. The law imposed strict secrecy on atomic energy information, designated "restricted data," and tightly controlled dissemination of this classified information, even to the nation's allies. In reality, the new law sought to protect America's nuclear monopoly by attempting to withhold atomic information, technology, and materials from the rest of the world. It prompted both the Soviet Union and America's two major allies, Great Britain and France, to pursue with greater speed atomic weapons research and production on their own.

As the United States slowly developed its nuclear weapons stockpile (estimates for the period 1945 to 1948 range from less than six weapons to about two dozen), political leaders were stunned to learn in September 1949 that the Soviets had detonated an atomic device. American scientists had predicted in 1945 that the Russians would learn the secret of the technology within three to six years, but government officials, blinded by their faith in America's supposed technical superiority, had ignored these forecasts. The Soviet achievement, helped somewhat by espionage, inaugurated the era of proliferation in the nuclear arms race.

The immediate decision facing the Atomic Energy Commission and President Truman was whether to accelerate the weapons program through the development of a much more powerful thermonuclear or hydrogen bomb. The prestigious General Advisory Committee of the Atomic Energy Commission, headed by the former chief scientific director of the Manhattan Project, J. Robert Oppenheimer, recommended against a crash program to build the "super" on the basis of both moral and technical considerations. But pressure from scientist Edward Teller and other scientific and military advisers convinced Truman in early 1950 to initiate the project. That decision also began a major policy shift that dramatically increased the defense budget. The commission successfully detonated an experimental device on October 31, 1952, with a power equivalent to that of 10 million tons of TNT (10 megatons), nearly 500 times more powerful than the Hiroshima bomb (20 kilotons). Sixteen months later on March 1, 1954 a "true" air-transportable thermonuclear bomb was exploded at America's South Pacific test range. Its yield was 15 megatons, or more than 5 times the total power of all the conventional Allied bombs dropped on Germany during World War II.

Not to be outdone the Soviets accelerated their program and once again, to the surprise of the Americans, exploded their first thermo-nuclear mechanism in August 1953. Given the secrecy surrounding both nations' nuclear enterprises, the Soviet Union's explosion deci-sively showed that its scientists were capable of developing advanced nuclear technology without benefit of espionage. It was yet another political and psychological shock to the Americans, capped two years later when the Soviets exploded a true superbomb with a yield of several megatons. Although the United States possessed more deliverable nuclear weapons than the USSR, an equilibrium of terror had been reached by the two powers as early as 1953. Oppen-heimer summed up the situation in a July 1953 *Foreign Affairs* article. America's lead over the Soviets would mean little as the nuclear stockpiles grew, he wrote. There would be small comfort in the fact that the United States had 20,000 bombs, while the Russians had 2,000. America and the Soviet Union, Oppenheimer stated, may be likened to "two scorpions in a bottle, each capable of killing the other, but only at the risk of his own life."

Even as the nuclear arms race intensified, there was an impulse to employ atomic technology for constructive purposes rather than exclusively for military requirements. President Dwight D. Eisen-hower's address, "Atomic Power for Peace," before the UN General Assembly on December 8, 1953 was the most dramatic statement reflecting the desire to turn atoms into plowshares. Since assuming office the previous January, the president had become increasingly concerned about the growing nuclear arms race and finding a means to make its dangers clear to the American people. The Soviet Union's detonation of its thermonuclear bomb in August had hardened his determination to explain frankly the perils of nuclear war. For months Eisenhower's advisers worked on a speech draft, but the president found them too negative in their emphasis on the destruc-tiveness of nuclear energy. He finally decided on a more positive approach that would point out the horror of nuclear war, while at the same time offering hope by stressing the beneficial uses of nuclear energy.

In his "atoms-for-peace" speech, Eisenhower cited the threat of "human degradation and destruction" but coupled it with a proposal to apply atomic resources and knowledge for more peaceful pur-poses. He called for the creation of an International Atomic Energy Agency to accept contributions of fissionable materials from the nuclear powers. The agency would allocate its supplies for the "peaceful pursuits of mankind" in agriculture, medicine, and electri-cal power. Eisenhower's speech was partly propaganda in that it made a dramatic proposal which would in no way threaten American security if accepted by the Soviet Union. At the same time, it might create a foundation for broader discussions on disarmament. Nonetheless, the president had no plans to reduce the nation's nuclear strength. He wrote in his diary that the United States "could unquestionably afford to reduce its atomic stockpile by two or three times the amounts that the Soviets might contribute to the UN agency and still improve our relative position in the cold war and even in the event of the outbreak of war."

Eisenhower's speech also helped set the stage for a revision of the 1946 Atomic Energy Act. By 1954 a confluence of domestic and international developments led to the end of the government's monopoly on nuclear technology. The technical know-how for building atomic power plants was available, a need for new sources of energy was widely accepted, and a number of private concerns had expressed strong interest in the use of atomic energy if they could gain access to information. Furthermore, the widespread desire to enhance America's international prestige, maintain its world leadership,and promote the beneficial applications of atomic energy infused a heightened sense of national urgency in inaugurating a full-scale private atomic power program. Consequently, the new 1954 Atomic Energy Act established a policy for atomic power development. For the first time the law allowed private ownership of nuclear power facilities, thereby spawning a private American reactor industry that envisioned the sale of its reactors, components, and technology abroad as a promising U.S. market. By the late 1960s this resulted in new foreign policy complications.

Weapons proliferation among the technologically advanced nations continued unabated over the next decade after Eisenhower's 1953 atoms-for-peace proposal. Great Britain had exploded its first nuclear bomb in 1952 and a thermonuclear weapon in 1957. France launched its own military nuclear program and carried out its first test explosion in 1960. In 1964 the People's Republic of China joined the nuclear club. Throughout this period the original two nuclear protagonists continued to test larger weapons, under a military deterrence strategy that amounted to a policy of "mutual assured destruction" (appropriately given the acronym MAD in the 1960s) if a nuclear war ever broke out. Eisenhower's secretary of state, John Foster Dulles, noted in 1954 that the American deterrence policy would be a doctrine of "massive retaliation" that would rely on a "great capacity to retaliate instantly, by means and at times of our own choosing," rather than on using expensive army ground forces.

THE DRESDEN POWER STATION. America's first full-scale, privately financed atomic power facility was dedicated on October 12, 1960. Built by the General Electric Company and owned by the Commonwealth Edison Company of Chicago, the reactor produced 180 megawatts of electricity. (National Archives)

(The fiscally conservative Eisenhower administration also wanted to curb the upward spiral of military spending.) In the popular jargon of the day, it meant "more bang for the buck." Oppenheimer's earlier analogy of the two scorpions in a bottle probably fit best.

With such dependence on nuclear weapons, a worldwide popular movement began in the mid-1950s that focused on the global radiation effects of fallout from increasingly larger atmospheric nuclear weapons tests conducted by the United States, the Soviet Union, and Great Britain. Reacting to this pressure, the nuclear powers, through a series of diplomatic maneuvers beginning in 1957, slowly jockeyed toward a moratorium on testing. In March 1958 a breakthrough came when the Soviets, after completing a major series of tests just before the United States was about to start one, announced that they would prohibit atmospheric tests provided other nations did so. After an international nuclear experts meeting in Geneva, Switzerland, showed that test detection was technically possible, Eisenhower proposed that the three powers then having nuclear capability negotiate a permanent end to nuclear tests. He stated that the United States would abstain from testing for one year from the October 31, 1956 date opening negotiations. Furthermore, the president reserved the right to continue the suspension on a year-to-year basis depending on progress made toward development of an international inspection system as well as on disarmament negotiations. Soviet Premier Nikita S. Khrushchev called the American position a trick because it would take about one year to prepare a meaningful test series. He agreed to negotiate but refused to indicate whether the Soviet Union would suspend tests during the conference. All three members of the nuclear club rushed to complete their test series before meeting in Geneva, making 1958 the "dirtiest" atmospheric fallout year to date. Then began a long, laborious negotiation toward a test ban treaty.

During 1959 the principal clauses of a test ban treaty were adopted. They called for renunciation of future atmospheric weapons testing and forbade assistance to other countries that wished to carry out aerial tests. The negotiators also decided upon the future control organization: the International Atomic Energy Agency already located in Vienna. However, a reheating of the Cold War following the shooting down of an American U-2 spy plane over the Soviet Union in May 1960 brought the discussions to a standstill. The main technical point of difficulty remained the long-standing one of international inspection and control. Although newly elected President John F. Kennedy decided to continue negotiations, a Soviet-American confrontation over Berlin in the summer of 1961 contributed to the increasingly gloomy negotiating environment. Then in September 1961 the Soviet Union, with a series of large aerial explosions, broke the three-year truce on testing. Two weeks later the United States resumed underground testing, and in January 1962 the test ban conference adjourned indefinitely.

In October 1962 the Cold War escalated to unprecedented dimensions during the Cuban missile crisis. The confrontation between the Soviets and the Americans forced both sides to deal with the possibility of nuclear war as a serious political reality, rather than merely as a theory in the minds of nuclear strategists. The crisis emerged out of the nuclear arms race and the attempt by both countries to gain and maintain strategic delivery superiority. Delivery systems had become crucial elements since the two superpowers possessed the actual warheads. Prior to 1957, America's strategic policy of retaliation directly against the Soviet Union relied principally on the fleet of B-52s assigned to the Strategic Air Command. The American

position changed abruptly in August 1957 when the Soviets successfully tested an intercontinental ballistic missile (ICBM), an event
that had as grave implications for the United States as had the 1949
Soviet explosion of an atomic device. Six weeks later the Russians
orbited *Sputnik*, the first earth satellite. The fact that *Sputnik* flew
directly over the United States symbolized in the public mind the
nation's new vulnerability to Soviet technology. Taking advantage of
this situation from 1957 to 1961, Khrushchev increasingly played
upon Americans' fears, stirred up by the media and by a chorus of
Democratic congressmen and senators, that the Soviet Union had
created a "missile gap" in its favor.

The Eisenhower administration privately maintained that the Soviet ICBM force was small and in the short term could not offset the
American strategic advantage. This sanguine and accurate intelligence estimate was based in large part on the data accumulated since
1956 by high-altitude U-2 reconnaissance plane flights over the
Soviet Union. The administration estimated that the current overall
strategic force available to the United States could neutralize any
Soviet threat, at least until 1963. By then the Americans would have
operational their sophisticated Polaris and Minuteman missiles,
thereby giving them an even greater advantage. Even after the May
1960 U-2 plane incident revealed to the Soviets that the Americans
knew the strategic impotence of the Soviet ICBM force, Khrushchev
continued to play his deceptive game. It was not until October 1961,
when the Kennedy administration publicly issued an authoritative
and confident appraisal of the strategic balance in America's favor,
that the claim of a missile gap was thoroughly discredited.

This prepared the ground for Khrushchev's gamble to install
missiles in Cuba. Following the tension-filled days of the crisis, both
Kennedy and Khrushchev redoubled their efforts to control nuclear
arms. Sobered by the gravest threat of thermonuclear war the world
had experienced to date, the two sides apparently realized the
dangers of posturing with nuclear weapons. The crisis made the risks
visible to the world and caused both superpowers to pull back from
this kind of competition. Early in 1963 the two nations resumed talks
on a weapons testing ban. After working out thorny technical points
over detection of underground tests and carrying out inspections to
ensure compliance, the United States, the Soviet Union, and Great
Britain agreed on a limited test ban treaty in the summer of 1963.

The treaty prohibited nuclear weapons tests in the atmosphere, in
space, and under water; underground tests were allowed, however.

The signatories also agreed not to help or take part in any unauthorized test explosion by a nonsignatory nation. By the time the treaty became effective on October 10, 1963, over one hundred nations had signed it. France and China, which were just beginning to build their own nuclear arsenals, maintained that the treaty reinforced the monopoly of the three principal nuclear powers and refused to sign it.

The agreement to halt atmospheric tests marked a watershed in the international control of nuclear arms. It was the first international agreement on nuclear weapons ever, and the United States, the Soviet Union, and Great Britain hoped it would be a step toward more comprehensive nonproliferation agreements. Since the beginning of the atomic age, 300 atmospheric nuclear tests had been carried out by the United States, 180 by the Soviet Union, 25 by Great Britain, and 4 by France. Although less numerous than those of the United States, the Soviet explosions doubled the yield of America's experimental tests. The largest Soviet test was 3,000 times more powerful than the 20-kiloton yields of the bombs dropped at Hiroshima and Nagasaki. The treaty, then, significantly reduced the hazard to human health from radioactive fallout. To date, no signatory nation has violated it.

The treaty also began a movement toward a joint American-Soviet nonproliferation policy. At that time the prohibition of tests was conceived as a way to stop possible military nuclear programs among those countries that had nuclear power programs but did not possess nuclear weapons. Although it was possible for a technically advanced nation to explode an atomic device, it was extremely difficult, without atmospheric tests, to advance to a level of sophisticated and powerful weapons. So the treaty limited, although it did not eliminate, the possibility at least of vertical proliferation among nonnuclear weapons states.

The treaty had no effect, however, on the rate at which the two superpowers expanded and improved their own nuclear weapons systems. As France and China had argued in refusing to sign the treaty, the pact favored the advanced members of the nuclear club. Although it relieved world concerns about radioactive fallout from atmospheric tests, the level and sophistication of nuclear armaments among the superpowers continued to increase greatly. The Soviet Union, in particular, learned a lesson between 1957 and 1961 when it had attempted to create a missile gap through deception. In the years from 1963 to 1968, Soviet leaders accepted the fact that they had to shift resources and develop an advanced delivery system if they wanted to neutralize the American strategic position. Throughout this period, both nations conducted high-technology research on antiballistic missile (ABM) defense systems and on fitting as many as one dozen nuclear warheads to a single ballistic missile (multiple independently targeted reentry vehicle or MIRV). Although the former was defensive and the latter offensive, either system, if successfully deployed, threatened the credibility of the parity in thermonuclear forces reached by both nations in 1968.

Equally important, however, a certain degree of détente between the United States and the Soviet Union had resulted from the sobering experience of the Cuban missile crisis and the limited test ban treaty negotiations. Additional concern by both nations over the increasing level of their military budgets also helped to establish a political atmosphere for starting new discussions on limiting their strategic weapons. From 1968 to 1972 the first Strategic Arms Limitation Talks (SALT I) was conducted. It is noteworthy that only the United States and the Soviet Union were involved in these discussions. The exclusion of their allies underscored both the two-power nature of the world nuclear balance and the military supremacy of the two rivals, compared with other countries.

More significant was the limited nature of the discussions. The agenda concerned only nuclear warheads and their delivery vehicles. It did not, for example, include such matters as production plants for fissionable materials. While a promising start toward disarmament, such a restrictive agenda still assured both nations that they would continue to have enough plutonium and highly enriched uranium to maintain a deterrence posture based on mutual assured destruction. SALT I led to two accords. In a "Treaty ... on the Limitations of Antiballistic Missile Systems," the two nations moved to end the emerging competition in defensive systems and restricted ABMs to two sites (the capital and a zone for missile deployment). In the better known SALT interim agreement, the two superpowers took the first steps to check the rivalry in their most powerful land- and submarine-based offensive nuclear weapons. Limited to a five-year span, the document restricted the United States to 1,054 intercontinental missiles and the Soviet Union to 1,618. Although the numbers seemed unfavorable to the United States, America was comforted by its own technical superiority on the MIRV technique and in missile accuracy and mobility. SALT I, then, was a diplomatic success and a welcome addition to the process of détente and disarmament, but it did little to reduce the ability of each nation to annihilate not only the other but to bring a nuclear winter to the rest of the world as well.

Because the interim agreement was to expire in five years, negotiations on a new accord (SALT II) began in 1973. Both sides reached a preliminary agreement at Vladivostok in 1974 that reestablished a parity of 2,400 intercontinental delivery vehicles (intercontinental missiles, submarine missiles, and strategic bombers). It also restricted ground and seaborne MIRVs to 1,320 for each side. In effect until 1985 the Vladivostok agreement was meant as a temporary measure until a permanent treaty could be finalized.

Continued negotiations led to the signing in June 1979 of the SALT II interim agreement, which reduced the number of missile vehicles from 2,400 to 2,250 and MIRVs from 1,320 to 1,200. But a new wave of military escalation and mutual distrust permeated the diplomatic atmosphere. Senate agreement on the SALT II accord in 1979–80 appeared so uncertain in light of deteriorating American-Soviet relations that, when the Soviets occupied Afghanistan in 1980, President Jimmy Carter withdrew the document from consideration by the upper chamber. The SALT II agreement became an important issue in the 1980 political campaign. Republican candidate Ronald Reagan, strongly opposing the interim measure on the grounds that it favored the Soviet Union, suggested new negotiations instead.

Meanwhile, a shift in American nuclear war policy had begun in the Richard Nixon and Gerald Ford administrations that went beyond the earlier doctrine of mutual assured destruction to a strategy based on fighting and winning a limited nuclear war. President Carter further implemented this countervailing strategy through Presidential Directive 59 (PD 59) issued in July 1980. This internal classified statement emphasized a capability to destroy Soviet command and control facilities as well as the targeting of more enemy military bases. Public announcements from President Reagan appeared to continue the strategy laid out in PD 59. In 1982 he called for the production and deployment of the ICBM known as the MX, and more recently he has emphasized continued research on the novel Strategic Defense Initiative, better known as the "Star Wars" system.

Considered sheer folly by many, the formulation of such doctrines and systems spawned a grass-roots antinuclear movement in the United States, Western Europe, and Japan that was reminiscent of the movement against atmospheric testing in the 1950s. As a result, a growing number of concerned citizens from all walks of life has become increasingly apprehensive about the world's nuclear leaders and whether their technical and military advisers are simply wrong to seek strategic solutions seeming to ignore a real world approach that such a war could destroy civilization.

From 1968 to 1978 the major nations also were working on another extremely complex but not so well-known aspect of nuclear nonproliferation. Civilian nuclear power reactors, which were being built by nonnuclear weapons countries, posed the potential danger of producing certain amounts of plutonium and highly enriched uranium that could be used to manufacture nuclear weapons. After three years of negotiations, most of the major powers signed a nonproliferation treaty in 1968, which went into effect in 1970, that was intended to halt the spread of such weapons or their manufacture to any nation that was not already a nuclear weapons state. Like the limited test ban treaty, all nations were encouraged to sign it. The treaty forbade any signatory nuclear weapons country from transferring nuclear weapons or control over them to any other nation and from assisting any nonnuclear weapons state in the acquisition or manufacture of nuclear devices (for example, the process of separating plutonium used in manufacturing weapons from a power reactor's highly radioactive fuel or the enrichment of the natural uranium used in power reactors to highly enriched uranium used in weapons production). Nations that signed the treaty but did not possess nuclear weapons promised not to accept transfer or control over weapons or nuclear devices, or to utilize the technical process needed to manufacture them. All signatories' nuclear facilities were subject to a safeguards inspection system conducted by the International Atomic Energy Agency. However, inspections could only be conducted with the permission of the inspected nation, and, if violations were discovered, the international agency had little more than moral suasion and world public opinion with which to penalize the offending country. Most nations signed the treaty, although France and China again refused, as did a number of nonnuclear weapons states, including India, Pakistan, Brazil, Argentina, South Africa, and Israel. None of these nations admitted publicly to any interest in weapons acquisition, but each one either possessed or was acquiring the technology to develop them. In addition, each country was accumulating militarily significant amounts of plutonium or highly enriched uranium needed for nuclear explosives.

In 1974 India exploded an underground nuclear device. To nuclear specialists aware of India's advanced nuclear technical progress, the event was no surprise. The nation violated no formal international accords since India was not a signatory to the nonproliferation treaty. The plutonium used in the explosion, however, had been irradiated in a Canadian-built civilian research reactor that was moderated with heavy water supplied by the United States. Use of the facility and materials breached India's bilateral pledge to Canada and the United States that it would not manufacture nuclear explosives, but the real importance of the event lay in the undeniable recognition of the technical convergence of civil and military nuclear programs and in the fact that nuclear weapons technology would undoubtedly proliferate worldwide. In other words, the acquisition of nuclear weapons probably was an irreversible process. The Indian explosion created doubts about the validity of the international rules that had been established to govern the technology.

During the Ford and Carter administrations, the United States used the Indian event to launch a new unilateral nonproliferation effort. First through negotiations with the major supplier nations of nuclear source materials and technology, and then through legislative enactment of the 1978 Nuclear Non-Proliferation Act, the United States attempted to force nonnuclear weapons states to submit their entire nuclear programs to the International Atomic Energy Agency "full scope" safeguards before power reactor fuels and technology would be provided. The American policy aimed for a future nuclear economy that would exclude plutonium. The immediate result, however, was a deterioration in America's relations with several Third World countries as well as with some of its nuclear trading partners. The policy amounted to a noble, if fruitless, attempt to place nonproliferation ahead of the economic interests of the nuclear supplier nations. It also showed that the risks of nuclear weapons proliferation stemmed more from the political intentions of those nations that wanted such weapons than from the basic nuclear capabilities of those countries. In other words, if they wanted nuclear weapons badly enough, they would find a way to acquire them. Consequently, tough, serious diplomacy was needed rather than reliance on technological solutions to prevent the proliferation of nuclear weapons states.

American nuclear policy since 1945 has had mixed results. On the positive side, nuclear weapons have never been used in war since the Japanese bombings. Atmospheric test explosions, the cause of heightened radioactive fallout in the 1950s and early 1960s, have been effectively stopped through adherence by most nations to the 1963 limited test ban treaty. Only six nations have publicly demonstrated the ability to produce a nuclear device that can be used to build nuclear bombs, although several other nations either have the technical capability or are nearly at that stage of development. In a small way, these accomplishments stand as a tribute in part to American nonproliferation policy.

Not so encouraging is the continuing and escalating nuclear weapons race between the United States and the Soviet Union. Those two nations have set the awful pace of the arms race. Furthermore, the United States has been the innovator in nuclear technology and nuclear strategic doctrine. Neither the United States nor the Soviet Union appears satisfied with its current overkill capacity, with each instead believing that it must have more than a defensive capability to ensure deterrence. While a certain amount of uneasy stability has come from this balance of mutual assured destruction, one wonders how much continued faith can be placed in the nuclear strategists on both sides. So far they have been merely theorists who have never seen their worst-case scenarios carried out.

Diplomacy appears as the only palatable solution to this intricate and important state of affairs. By placing limits on the proliferation of overkill capacity, the SALT negotiations offered some encouragement, but those talks can be viewed only as a small first step toward the total disarmament that has been the elusive goal of peaceful men in modern history. To turn mutual assured destruction into mutual assured survival depends on strengthening and stabilizing the relations between the United States and the Soviet Union. Furthermore, both nations must carry out a long-term verifiable arms reduction program. Until that occurs it appears that the world's population will continue to be held hostage to the destructive nuclear strategies that the American and Soviet arsenals support.

Sources and Suggested Readings

Brenner, Michael. *Nuclear Power and Non-Proliferation: The Remaking of U.S. Policy.* New York, 1981.

Divine, Robert A. *Blowing on the Wind: The Nuclear Test Ban Debate, 1954-1960.* New York, 1978.

Freedman, Lawrence. *The Evolution of Nuclear Strategy.* New York, 1981.

George, Alexander L., and Smoke, Richard. *Deterrence in American Foreign Policy: Theory and Practice.* New York, 1974.

Goldschmidt, Bertrand. *The Atomic Complex: A Worldwide Political History of Nuclear Energy.* La Grange Park, Illinois, 1982.

Herken, Gregg. *Counsels of War.* New York, 1985.

_____. *The Winning Weapon: The Atomic Bomb in the Cold War, 1945-1950.* New York, 1980.

Hersey, John. *Hiroshima.* New York, 1946.

Hewlett, Richard G., and Anderson, Oscar E., Jr. *A History of the United States Atomic Energy Commission*. Vol. 1, *The New World, 1939-1946*. University Park, Pennsylvania, 1962.

Hewlett, Richard G., and Duncan, Francis. *A History of the United States Atomic Energy Commission*. Vol. 2, *Atomic Shield, 1947-1952*. University Park, Pennsylvania, 1969.

Kaplan, Fred. *The Wizards of Armageddon*. New York, 1983.

Kennedy, Robert F. *Thirteen Days: A Memoir of the Cuban Missile Crisis*. New York, 1969.

Mandelbaum, Michael. *The Nuclear Question: The United States and Nuclear Weapons, 1946-1976*. New York, 1979.

Pringle, Peter, and Spigelman, James. *The Nuclear Barons*. New York, 1981.

Schell, Jonathan. *The Fate of the Earth*. New York, 1982.

Seaborg, Glenn T. *Kennedy, Khrushchev, and the Test Ban*. Berkeley, 1981.

Sherwin, Martin J. *A World Destroyed: The Atomic Bomb and the Grand Alliance*. New York, 1975.

Williams, Robert C., and Cantelon, Philip L., eds. *The American Atom: A Documentary History of Nuclear Policies from the Discovery of Fission to the Present, 1939-1984*. Philadelphia, 1984.

The Vietnam War

George C. Herring

The Vietnam War had profound consequences for the United States. The American phase of the conflict lasted for twelve years (1961– 1973), longer than any other war in which the nation has been involved. It took the lives of more than 58,000 Americans and cost, by some estimates, more than $613 billion. The war set off a runaway inflation that devastated the U.S. economy in the 1970s. It divided Americans as no other event since their own Civil War a century earlier. It brought fundamental changes in American foreign policy, discrediting the policy of containment, undermining the consensus that supported it, and leaving U.S. foreign policy at least temporarily in disarray.

Understanding Vietnam requires addressing two fundamental questions. First, why did the United States commit billions of dollars and a large part of its military power in an area so remote and seemingly so insignificant? Second, why, despite this huge commitment, did the world's richest and most powerful nation fail to achieve its objective, the preservation of an independent, non-Communist South Vietnam?

The question of causation in war is always complex, and in the case of Vietnam it was especially so. America's direct involvement in Vietnam spanned the quarter century between its decision in 1950 to aid France in suppressing the Vietnamese revolution and the fall of Saigon to the North Vietnamese in 1975. Over a period of years the commitment expanded incrementally from aid to France, to support for an independent South Vietnam after the 1954 Geneva Conference, to the commitment of U.S. military power in 1965. America went to war not from one major decision but rather as the result of a series of separate, seemingly small decisions over the period between 1950 and 1965. Amidst this complexity, it is necessary to try to single out the common threads, the patterns of thought that determined the fateful courses chosen.

In the broadest sense, U.S. involvement in Vietnam stemmed from the interaction of two major phenomena of the post-World War II era: decolonization—the breakup of the old colonial empires—and the Cold War. The rise of nationalism and the weakness of the European colonial powers combined at the end of World War II to destroy a colonial system that had been an established feature of world politics for centuries. Changes of this magnitude do not occur smoothly, and in this case the result was turmoil and, in some areas, war. In Asia the British and Dutch grudgingly recognized the inevitable and granted independence to their colonies within several years after World War II. The French, on the other hand, refused to concede the inevitability of decolonization. They attempted to regain control of their Indochinese colonies and to put down the Vietnamese revolution by force, sparking in 1946 a war that in its various phases would not end until the fall of Saigon in the spring of 1975.

What was unique, and from the American standpoint most significant, about the conflict in Vietnam was that the nationalist movement—the Vietminh—was led by Communists. The father of the revolution, the charismatic Ho Chi Minh, was a longtime Communist operative who had devoted his life to gaining independence and national unity for Vietnam. Well organized and tightly disciplined, the Communists took advantage of the fragmentation among the other nationalist groups to establish their own preeminence. During World War II they exploited popular opposition to the French and to Japanese occupation forces to build support for the revolution, and they moved adeptly to fill the vacuum when the Japanese surrendered in August 1945. During the ensuing war with France, the Vietminh solidified its claim to the mantle of Vietnamese nationalism. In all the former European colonies in Asia, only in Vietnam did Communists direct the nationalist movement, and this would have enormous long-range implications, transforming what began as a struggle against French colonialism into an international conflict of vast proportions.

At the very time the Communist-led Vietminh was engaged in a bloody struggle with France, the Cold War was assuming global dimensions, and from an early stage Washington perceived the war in Vietnam largely in terms of its conflict with the Soviet Union. As early as 1946 Americans viewed Ho and the Vietminh as instruments of the Soviet drive for world domination, directed and controlled by the Kremlin. This view was not seriously questioned in or out of government until the United States was involved in full-scale war in Vietnam.

Reality was much more complex than Americans perceived it. Ho and his top lieutenants were Communists committed to establishing in Vietnam, at the first opportunity, a state based on Marxist-Leninist doctrine. In addition, from 1949 on Communist China and the Soviet Union aided the Vietminh and later North Vietnam in various ways. This being said, the view that the Vietnamese revolution was a mere extension of the Communist drive for world conquest needs qualification at several points. Ho initiated the revolution without explicit direction from Moscow, and he sustained it until 1949 without any external support. The revolution grew in strength because it was able to identify with Vietnamese nationalism, and it had a dynamism of its own quite apart from international communism. Moreover, the support provided by the Soviet Union and China was neither unlimited nor unequivocal, and there is ample evidence that the three nations did not share unanimity of purpose. At the Geneva Conference in 1954, for example, the two major Communist powers, for their own reasons, forced upon the Vietminh a settlement with France that provided for the partition of Vietnam, and they gave nothing more than lip service to the provisions of the Geneva Agreements which called for elections to unify the country.

The Vietnamese were therefore keenly aware that they could not always depend upon their allies. In the case of China, moreover, they feared that dependence could lead to domination. "It is better to sniff French dung for a while than eat China's all our life," Ho had said in 1946, rationalizing his efforts to strike a deal with France and expressing in graphic fashion Vietnam's historic fears of its huge northern neighbor. Thus the relationship between the Vietnamese Communists and their allies appears to have been based on a normal pattern of relations among nation-states rather than on ideological harmony and shared goals. America's assessment of the dynamics of the conflict in Vietnam was wide of the mark.

From 1949 on U.S. policy in Vietnam also was based on the premise that the fall of Vietnam to communism would threaten vital interests. There is more than a bit of irony here, for at least until the 1940s Vietnam had never been of any significance to the United States. To understand why it suddenly became so important, it is necessary to look at the reorientation of U.S. foreign policy after the fall of China to the Communists in 1949 and to the emergence of a world view best expressed in the National Security Council study, NSC-68. Drafted in early 1950 in response to the debacle in China and the Soviet Union's explosion of an atomic weapon, NSC-68 set forth as its fundamental premise that the USSR, "animated by a new fanatical faith," was seeking to "impose its absolute authority on the rest of the world." It already had achieved major conquests in Eastern Europe and more recently in China, and American policy-makers, in the frantic milieu of early 1950, concluded that Soviet expansion had reached a point beyond which it must not be permit-ted to go. "Any substantial further extension of the area under the control of the Kremlin," NSC-68 warned, "would raise the possibil-ity that no coalition adequate to confront the Kremlin with greater strength could be assembled."

In this context of a world divided into two hostile power blocs, a fragile power balance, a zero-sum game in which any gain for com-munism was automatically a loss for the United States, areas such as Vietnam, which had been of no more than marginal importance, suddenly took on great significance. The onset of the Korean War in June 1950 seemed to confirm the assumptions of NSC-68 and also suggested that the Communists were now prepared to use military invasion to upset the balance of power. Faced with this challenge the Truman administration in 1950 extended to the Far East a contain-ment policy that had been restricted to Europe. The first American commitment to Vietnam, a commitment to assist the French in suppressing the Vietminh revolution, was part of this broader at-tempt to contain Communist expansion in Asia.

There were other more specific reasons why U.S. policymakers attached growing significance to Vietnam after 1950. The first, usual-ly called the "domino theory," was the idea that the fall of Vietnam could cause the fall of Indochina and then the rest of Southeast Asia, with repercussions extending west to India and east to Japan and the Philippines. This fear of a chain reaction in Southeast Asia was initially set forth by the Joint Chiefs of Staff in 1950, and events in the late 1940s and early 1950s seemed to give it some credence. Mao Zedong's Communists had just taken over in China. The departure of the colonial powers left a vacuum in Southeast Asia; Indochina, Burma, and Malaya were swept by revolution; and the newly inde-pendent government of Indonesia seemed highly vulnerable. Be-cause of its location on China's southern border and because it appeared in the most imminent danger, Vietnam was considered the most important, "the keystone in the arch," as Senator John F. Kennedy put it, "the finger in the dike." If it fell all of Southeast Asia might be lost, costing the United States access to vital raw materials and strategic bases. Primarily for this reason the United States went to the aid of France in 1950, despite its compunctions about supporting French colonialism, and it stepped into the breach when France was defeated in 1954.

The domino theory was reinforced and in time supplanted by the notion that the United States must stand firm in Vietnam to demonstrate its determination to defend vital interests across the world. Acceptance of this principle of credibility reflected the intensity of the Cold War, the influence of certain perceived lessons of history, and the desire on the part of American policymakers to find means of averting nuclear catastrophe. During the most intense period of Cold War confrontation, American policymakers felt certain that what they did in one area of the world might have a decisive impact in others. If they showed firmness, it might deter Soviet or Chinese aggression; if they showed weakness, the adversary would be tempted to take steps that might ultimately leave no option but nuclear war. The so-called Manchurian or Munich analogy—the idea that the failure of the Western democracies to stand firm against Japanese and German aggression in the 1930s had encouraged further aggression—reinforced the idea of credibility. The fundamental obvious lesson was that, in order to avoid war, a firm stand must be taken at the outset.

Even after the Sino-Soviet split dramatically altered the traditional contours of the Cold War in the mid-1960s, the notion of credibility seemed valid. Of the two Communist powers, China appeared to be the more militant and aggressive, the more deeply committed to world revolution. It was closely allied with North Vietnam, and indeed some U.S. policymakers viewed Hanoi as essentially an instrument of Chinese policy. North Vietnam had to be deterred to prevent the expansion of Chinese influence in Asia. Even in the case of the Soviet Union, which appeared to be passive and generally innocuous in the aftermath of the Cuban missile crisis, there seemed good reason for the United States to display firmness. Rivalry with China might force the Soviets once again to assume an aggressive posture. A firm stand in Vietnam, it was reasoned, would discourage any tendency toward a return to adventurism and reinforce the trend toward détente. It also might discourage other potential troublemakers, such as Cuba's Fidel Castro, from attempting to disrupt world order.

In searching for the roots of commitment in Vietnam, a second factor deserves attention: the assumption shared by administrations from Truman to Johnson that the fall of Vietnam to communism would have disastrous consequences at home. This assumption also stemmed from perceived lessons of history, in this case the rancorous and divisive debate following the fall of China in 1949 and Republican exploitation of it at the polls in 1952. Again, the conclusion was that no administration could survive the loss of Vietnam. Although a Democrat, President Kennedy had attacked Truman for losing China. He had been a participant in the debate and vividly remembered it. He seems to have been sufficiently frustrated by Vietnam in late 1963 that he at least considered the possibility of withdrawal, but he was convinced that he could not do so until after he had been reelected. "If I tried to pull out now," Kennedy said, "we would have another Joe McCarthy Red Scare on our hands." Johnson shared similar fears on numerous occasions, exclaiming that he was not going to be the president who saw "Southeast Asia go the way China went."

In analyzing the sources of American involvement in Vietnam, several comments seem in order. First, Vietnam was not deemed significant in and of itself, for its raw materials, its naval bases, or other tangible reasons. It was considered vital primarily because of the presumed effects its loss would have on other areas and for its symbolic importance. Still, the more American policymakers stressed its significance, the more important it grew until it actually became a test case of U.S. credibility to opponents, to allies, and to the United States itself. The fact that the American commitment became increasingly a matter of prestige had important, although seemingly paradoxical, consequences. On the one hand, it made extrication all the more difficult. Interests may be easier to compromise than prestige. On the other hand, the absence of any compelling intrinsic significance in Vietnam or any direct threat to American security made it more and more difficult to justify the sacrifices the nation was called upon to make. This paradox was at least partially responsible for the division and frustration that accompanied the war.

The containment policy now seems misguided, both generally and in its application to Vietnam. Soviet goals were and remain more the product of traditional Russian nationalism than ideology. The so-called Communist bloc was never a monolith; it was torn by division from the start, and the fragmentation has become more pronounced. There has never been a zero-sum game. What appeared to be a major victory for the Soviet Union in China in 1949, for example, turned out to be something quite different. In most parts of the world, neither the Soviet Union nor the United States has prevailed, and pluralism has been the norm.

In applying containment to Vietnam, the United States drastically misjudged the internal dynamics of the conflict. It attributed to an expansionist communism a war that began as a revolution against French colonialism. It probably exaggerated as well the consequences of nonintervention. There is reason to doubt whether the domino theory would have operated if Vietnam had fallen earlier. Nationalism has proven the most potent and enduring force in recent history, and the nations of Southeast Asia, long suspicious of China and Vietnam, would have resisted mightily. Moreover, by making the war a test case of American credibility, U.S. policymakers may have made its consequences greater than they would have been otherwise. In short, by rigidly adhering to a narrow, one-dimensional world view, without taking into account the nature and importance of local forces, the United States may have placed itself in an untenable position in Vietnam from the start.

This leads directly to the second question: Why, despite its vast commitment in Vietnam, did the United States fail to achieve its objective? It has become fashionable in recent years to argue that it failed primarily because it did not use its military power wisely and decisively. Johnson and Defense Secretary Robert S. McNamara placed restrictions on the military that prevented it from winning the war. Such an argument is shortsighted in terms of the long history of U.S. involvement in Vietnam. It ignores the fact that the military solution sought after 1965 followed fifteen years of policy failure. It is therefore necessary to look to the period from 1950 to 1965 to understand fully America's ultimate failure in Vietnam.

During those years, U.S. policy went through three distinct phases. Between 1950 and 1954 the United States supported French efforts to suppress the Vietminh revolution, to the extent by 1954 of paying close to 80 percent of the war's cost. From 1954 to 1959 America helped ease the defeated French out of Vietnam, served as midwife for the birth of South Vietnam, and, violating the letter and spirit of the Geneva Accords, tried to sustain an independent government below the 17th parallel. From 1959 to 1965, through increased economic and military aid and eventually thousands of military "advisers," the United States tried to help the South Vietnamese government put down the insurgency, which began in the South and by 1965 enjoyed large-scale support from North Vietnam. With each step along the way, policy failed to produce the desired results, leading to escalation of the U.S. commitment. In July 1965, Johnson was left the unpleasant choice of calling in American combat forces or accepting a South Vietnamese defeat.

In the case of the French war, the so-called First Indochina War, the explanation for failure seems reasonably clear. France's goal, the retention of some level of imperial control in Vietnam, ran against one of the main currents of post-World War II history. Throughout Asia and Africa, nationalist revolutions have eventually prevailed, and even when imperial nations were able to win wars against insurgencies, as the French later did in Algeria, they were forced to concede independence. American policymakers understood the problem all too well, but they could find no way to resolve it. They pressed the French to fight on to victory in Vietnam, while at the same time urging them to leave as soon as the war ended. This made little sense from the French point of view, and, when faced with the choice of fighting for Vietnamese independence or withdrawing, the French chose the latter. After their disastrous defeat at the battle of Dienbienphu in May 1954, they agreed at Geneva to a negotiated settlement that provided for their ultimate withdrawal from Vietnam.

While the French were negotiating, the United States was planning ways to create a bulwark against further Communist expansion in Southeast Asia by making permanent the temporary partition of Vietnam. For a variety of reasons this effort to create an independent, non-Communist South Vietnam also eventually failed. First, and probably most important, was the magnitude of the challenge itself. Had the United States looked all over the world, it might not have found a less promising place for an experiment in nation building. The economy of South Vietnam was shattered from ten years of war, the departure of the French had left a gaping political vacuum, and France had destroyed the traditional structure of Vietnamese politics but had left nothing to replace it. As a result, there was no firmly established political tradition, no institutions of government, and no native elite capable of exercising effective leadership. In addition, South Vietnam was fragmented by a multitude of conflicting political, religious, and ethnic groups, and the emigration of nearly 1 million Catholics from North Vietnam after 1954 added to the already complex and conflict-ridden picture. Under these circumstances, there may have been built-in limits to what the United States or any nation could have accomplished in South Vietnam.

Second, American nation-building policies were often misguided or misapplied. In the early years, American advisers concentrated on building a South Vietnamese army to meet the threat of invasion from the North, a logical step in terms of the situation in Vietnam and earlier experience in Korea but one that left the South Vietnamese poorly equipped to cope with the developing insurgency in the late 1950s. By contrast, too little attention was devoted during these years to mobilizing the peasantry and promoting pacification in the countryside. When the United States attempted to deal with these problems in the early 1960s, it applied methods that had worked elsewhere but adapted poorly to Vietnam. The strategic hamlet program, promoted by the Kennedy administration with great enthusiasm, is a case in point. The idea of bringing peasants from isolated villages into settlements where they could be protected from insurgents had worked earlier in Malaya. In Malaya, however, the insurgents were Chinese, and it was relatively easy to guard against infiltration; in Vietnam the insurgents were Vietnamese who had lived and worked with the villagers for years, and the hamlets were infiltrated with ease. In Malaya, moreover, the peasants were resettled without major disruption, but in Vietnam they had to be removed from lands on which their families had lived for centuries and that were regarded as sacred. Sometimes they had to be forcibly removed and their old homes burned behind them. They were left rootless and resentful, easy prey for recruiters from the insurgency.

A third important reason was native leadership, a problem all too clearly revealed in the frustrating and ultimately tragic American partnership with South Vietnam's first president, Ngo Dinh Diem. In terms of his anticommunism and his nationalism, Diem appeared to fit America's needs perfectly, and in his first years in power he seemed to be a miracle worker, stabilizing a chaotic South Vietnam in a way no one had thought possible. In time, however, his deficiencies became all too apparent. It was not simply that his government was corrupt and undemocratic. Such governments have survived for years, and Diem may have had logic and history on his side when he insisted that democracy would not work in Vietnam. The problems were more basic. He was a poor administrator who tolerated far too much from his family, particularly his notorious brother Ngo Dinh Nhu. Most important, Diem lacked any real blueprint for Vietnam. He seemed content simply to preside over the government, but he proved incapable of leading his country, mobilizing the peasantry, or coping with the insurgency.

Diem was also fiercely independent, and this posed a dilemma that the United States never resolved. Americans came in time to see his weaknesses, but they could not persuade him to change, and they could not impose their will on him. They saw no alternative to Diem, however, and feared that if he were removed it would only lead to greater chaos. Thus the United States, with some reluctance, stood by him for nine years as the political and military situations in South Vietnam deteriorated. "Sink or swim with Ngo Dinh Diem," a critical journalist summed up American policy. It was only when Diem's policies produced a full-scale political upheaval among Buddhists in South Vietnam's major cities in 1963, and when it was learned that he and his brother were secretly negotiating with North Vietnam, that the United States finally concluded he must go.

As many had predicted, the overthrow of Diem in November 1963 offered no real solutions, only more problems. The army generals who replaced Diem were, for the most part, Western educated. They lacked close touch with their own people and even less than Diem had the capacity to unify a fragmented society. Divided among themselves, they spent their energy on intrigue, and one coup followed another in such rapid fashion that it was almost impossible to keep up with the daily changes in government. Thus by mid-1965 the United States found itself in a position that it never really had wanted and whose dangers it recognized, that of an imperial power moving in to fill a political and military vacuum.

Focusing on American and South Vietnamese failure provides only a partial picture. It is also necessary to analyze why the South Vietnamese insurgents and their northern supporters had reached the verge of victory by 1965. It is now evident from captured documents that by 1957 Diem had nearly exterminated the remnants of the Vietminh in South Vietnam. Alarmed by their plight and the growing certainty that the elections called for at Geneva would not be held, they began to mobilize to salvage the revolution of 1945. The insurgents effectively exploited the unrest caused by Diem's heavy-handed methods. In many areas they implemented land reform programs and lowered taxes, policies that contrasted favorably with those instituted by the government. They also skillfully employed selective violence by assassinating unpopular government officials. They mobilized the peasantry in a way in which the government had not been able. Organizing themselves into the National Liberation Front in 1960, the insurgents not only controlled large segments of the land and the population but also developed a formidable army.

North Vietnam's part in this remains a matter of controversy. It seems clear that Hanoi did not instigate the revolution in the South, as the U.S. government claimed at the time, nor did it remain an innocent and even indifferent bystander, as American critics of the war have maintained. The revolution did begin spontaneously in the

South, perhaps even against Hanoi's instructions. Once it started, however, Hanoi did not stand by and watch. Fearful that the southern revolutionaries might fail—or succeed—without its help, it began to send cadres into the South to assume leadership of the insurgency. In 1959 the Democratic Republic of Vietnam approved the initiation of "armed struggle" against the Diem regime. In the aftermath of the overthrow of Diem, North Vietnam decided to undertake a major escalation of the conflict, even to the point of sending its own military units into South Vietnam to fight intact. It apparently took this step in the expectation that the United States, when faced with certain defeat, would withdraw as it had in China in 1949, rather than risk its own men and resources.

The North Vietnamese gravely miscalculated. Confronting the collapse of South Vietnam in 1965, Johnson never seriously considered withdrawing. Determined to uphold a commitment of more than a decade's standing, and certain that tiny North Vietnam could not defy the will of the world's greatest power, the president in February 1965 initiated a regular systematic bombing of North Vietnam and then in July made what amounted to an open-ended commitment to use whatever ground combat forces were needed to determine the outcome of the war. In making this latter commitment, Johnson also miscalculated. He rejected the Joint Chiefs of Staff's proposals to mobilize the reserves. To avoid any risk of confrontation with China and the Soviet Union and, more importantly, to prevent what he called that "bitch of a war" from interfering with "the woman I really loved"—the Great Society reform program at home—he escalated the war quietly while imposing the lightest possible burden on the American people. He did so in the expectation that the gradual increase of military pressure on North Vietnam would persuade it to abandon the struggle in the South. "I'm going up old Ho Chi Minh's leg an inch at a time," he explained.

Johnson's strategy of gradual escalation did not work. The United States expanded the tonnage of bombs dropped on North Vietnam, from 63,000 in 1965 to 226,000 in 1967, inflicting an estimated $600 million in damages on a primitive economy. The gradualist approach gave the North Vietnamese time to disperse their vital resources, repair the damages, develop an effective air defense system, and adapt in other ways. It encouraged—and probably permitted—them to persevere, and China and the Soviet Union helped make up the losses they sustained. As a result, the bombing did not decisively affect North Vietnam's will to resist, and its very intensity and the fact that it was carried out by a rich, advanced nation against a poor, small nation gave the North Vietnamese a propaganda card they played with consummate skill. In the United States, and indeed throughout the world, the bombing became a major target of criticism and a symbol of the alleged immorality of American intervention in Vietnam.

The strategy of attrition implemented by General William C. Westmoreland on the ground in South Vietnam also failed. The availability of sanctuaries in Laos, Cambodia, and across the demilitarized zone permitted North Vietnam to control its losses, dictate the pace and intensity of the war, and hold the strategic initiative. If at any point losses became excessive, the enemy could withdraw and take time to recover. If, on the other hand, it wished to step up the war, it could do so at times and places of its own choosing. It had the ability to control even the level of American casualties, and in time this became of considerable importance. The attrition strategy thus represented an open-ended commitment that required increasing manpower and produced growing casualties, without any signs of victory. By the end of 1967 the United States had more than 500,000 troops in Vietnam and nothing to show for it except a bloody stalemate.

VIETNAM, 1966. President Johnson and General William Westmoreland review U.S troops. (Lyndon B. Johnson Library)

At the same time, Americanization of the war was counterproductive in terms of the fundamental goal of building a self-sustaining South Vietnam. The South Vietnamese army was relegated to pacification duty, which many good soldiers considered demeaning. The United States dropped more bombs on South Vietnam than in the North, and the heavy bombing, along with massive artillery fire, laid waste much of the countryside and made refugees of more than one-third of the population. The infusion of hundreds of thousands of men and billions of dollars into a small and backward country had a profoundly destabilizing effect. It was as though the United States was trying to build a "house with a bulldozer and wrecking crane," one American official later observed.

As the war dragged on, opposition in the United States assumed major proportions. "Hawks" protested President Johnson's policy of gradual escalation, urging the use of any means necessary to achieve victory. On the other side, a heterogeneous group of "doves" increasingly questioned the wisdom and morality of the war and began to conduct protest marches and encourage draft resistance and other forms of antiwar activity. The mounting cost of the war was more important than the antiwar movement in causing opposition among the general public. Increased casualties, indications that more troops would be required, and Johnson's belated request for new taxes combined by late 1967 to produce a sharp decline in public support for the war and Johnson's handling of it.

The Tet offensive of 1968 brought Johnson's gradual escalation of the war to an inglorious end. In a strictly military sense, the United States and South Vietnam prevailed, repelling a series of massive Vietcong assaults against the urban areas of South Vietnam and inflicting huge casualties. At the same time, Tet had a tremendous psychological impact in the United States, raising serious questions whether anything could be achieved that would be worth the cost. In March 1968, responding to growing signs of public frustration and impatience, Johnson rejected General Westmoreland's request for an additional 200,000 troops and for expansion of the war, cut back the bombing of North Vietnam, launched a diplomatic initiative eventually leading to peace negotiations in Paris, and withdrew from the presidential race.

It would be seven more years before the war finally ended. Recognizing that public frustration required him at least to scale down U.S. involvement, Johnson's successor Richard M. Nixon pursued an approach he called Vietnamization, initiating a series of phased withdrawals of American troops, while expanding aid to the South

DISCUSSING VIETNAM STRATEGY. President Johnson confers in February 1968 with Special Assistant for National Security Affairs Walt W. Rostow. (Lyndon B. Johnson Library)

Vietnamese army to prepare it to take over the brunt of the fighting. Nixon also escalated the war by authorizing "incursions" into the North Vietnamese sanctuaries in Cambodia and Laos to bolster Vietnamization. When the North Vietnamese in the spring of 1972 launched a major offensive against South Vietnam, he resumed the bombing of North Vietnam and mined Haiphong harbor. Nixon was able to save South Vietnam, but opposition to the war in the United States continued to grow. In 1973, without resolving the fundamental issue of the war—the political future of South Vietnam—he was forced to agree to a settlement permitting extrication of U.S. forces. That issue was settled two years later when North Vietnam launched a massive conventional invasion of the South. By that time, Nixon had resigned as a result of the Watergate scandal, and the United States stood by helplessly while an ally of twenty years went down to defeat.

Although American strategies in Vietnam were clearly flawed, the argument that an unrestricted use of military power could have produced victory at acceptable cost is unpersuasive. The capacity of air power to cripple a preindustrial nation was probably quite limited, and there is considerable evidence to suggest that, even though its cities and industries were destroyed, North Vietnam was prepared to fight on, underground if necessary. Invasion of the sanctuaries and ground operations in North Vietnam might have made the strategy of attrition more workable, but they also would have enormously increased the costs of the war at a time when American resources were already stretched thinly. Neither of these approaches would have solved what was always the central problem of the war: the political viability of South Vietnam. Each ran serious risks of Soviet and Chinese intervention. Also, even if the United States had been able to subdue North Vietnam militarily without provoking outside intervention, it would still have faced the dangerous and costly task of occupying a hostile nation along China's southern border, while simultaneously containing an insurgency in South Vietnam.

In the final analysis, the causes of American failure must be found as much in Vietnam as in Washington. In South Vietnam the United States attempted a truly formidable undertaking on the basis of a very weak foundation. For nearly twenty years, Americans struggled to establish a viable nation in the face of internal insurgency and external invasion, but the rapid collapse of South Vietnam after America's withdrawal suggests how little was really accomplished. The United States could never find leaders capable of mobilizing the disparate population of South Vietnam. It launched a vast array of ambitious and expensive programs to promote sound government, win the hearts and minds of the people, and wage war against the Vietcong. When its client state was on the verge of collapse in 1965, it filled the vacuum by putting in its own military forces. The more it did, however, the more it induced a state of dependency among those it was trying to help. Tragically, right up to the fall of Saigon in 1975, South Vietnamese leaders expected the United States to return and save them from defeat.

The United States also drastically underestimated the determination of its adversary. The North Vietnamese made huge blunders of their own and paid an enormous price for their success. At the same time, they were tightly mobilized and regimented, and they were fanatically committed to their goals. They were fighting on familiar soil and used methods perfected in the war against France. They skillfully employed the strategy of protracted war, perceiving that the Americans, like the French, could become impatient and that, if they bled long enough, they might grow weary of the war. "You will kill ten of our men, but we will kill one of yours," Ho once remarked, "and in the end it is you who will tire." The comment was made to a French general on the eve of the First Indochina War, but it could as easily have been said of the American phase.

The circumstances of the war thus posed a dilemma that the United States never really understood, much less resolved. The attainment of American goals would probably have required the physical annihilation of North Vietnam, a distasteful and extremely costly course of action that held out a serious threat of Soviet and Chinese intervention. The only other way was to establish a viable South Vietnam, but, given the weak foundation it worked from, not to mention the strength of the internal revolution, this was probably beyond its capability. The United States very well may have placed itself in a no-win situation.

For the winners of the war, victory has been at best a bittersweet affair. Despite harsh methods, the Hanoi regime has not been able to integrate the defeated South. More than 900,000 southerners have fled the country, and up to 10,000 remain in "reeducation" camps. Passive resistance is not uncommon, and widespread corruption suggests that the ways of the conquered may be rubbing off on the conqueror. Vietnam's efforts to rebuild its devastated economy have met little success, and it is dependent on aid provided by the Soviet Union. Although it is one of the world's poorest countries, it maintains one of the largest armies, and continued guerrilla resistance in occupied Cambodia compels it to keep 180,000 troops there.

The war has had mixed and as yet uncertain consequences for the United States. The great majority of veterans has adjusted smoothly to civilian life, but the high incidence of divorce, violent crime, and drug and alcohol abuse among a minority suggests the lingering impact of the war. Many veterans still harbor deep resentment against a nation they believe has not recognized their sacrifices. Along with Watergate, Vietnam ended presidential dominance of foreign policy, at least temporarily, and it also challenged, again at least temporarily, a generation of interventionism abroad. One decade after the withdrawal of American troops, however, the nation remains deeply divided on the basic issue of the war. Many Americans have found in Hanoi's aggressive postwar actions and in its close ties with the USSR confirmation of their long-standing view that U.S. involvement was both necessary and moral. Others continue to argue that intervention in an essentially local conflict in an area of marginal national interest was at best unwise, at worst immoral. Debate on the so-called lessons of Vietnam still colors discussion of virtually every major foreign policy issue. Given these unresolved issues and the deep emotions that Vietnam still stirs, it seems likely that the full impact of America's longest war is yet to be felt.

Sources and Suggested Readings

Berman, Larry. *Planning a Tragedy: The Americanization of the War in Vietnam.* New York, 1982.

Caputo, Philip. *A Rumor of War.* New York, 1977.

Duiker, William. *The Communist Road to Power in Vietnam.* Boulder, 1981.

Fall, Bernard B. *The Two Vietnams: A Political and Military Analysis.* New York, 1971.

FitzGerald, Frances. *Fire in the Lake: The Vietnamese and the Americans in Vietnam.* New York, 1972.

Gelb, Leslie H., and Betts, Richard K. *The Irony of Vietnam: The System Worked.* Washington, 1979.

Herring, George C. *America's Longest War: The United States and Vietnam, 1950-1975.* New York, 1985.

Karnow, Stanley. *Vietnam: A History.* New York, 1983.

Lewy, Guenter. *America in Vietnam.* New York, 1978.

Palmer, Bruce, Jr. *The 25-Year War: America's Military Role in Vietnam.* Lexington, Kentucky, 1984.

Summers, Harry G., Jr. *On Strategy: The Vietnam War in Context.* Carlisle Barracks, Pennsylvania, 1981.

Zaroulis, Nancy, and Sullivan, Gerald. *Who Spoke Up? American Protest Against the War in Vietnam, 1963-1975.* New York, 1984.

Latin America from Cuba to El Salvador

Lester D. Langley

In the fall of 1939, as Europe plunged into the Second World War, there existed a surface solidarity in the Western Hemisphere. In the past decade, Herbert Hoover and Franklin Delano Roosevelt had done much to alter the image of the United States as a predatory Anglo-Saxon nation in Hispanic America. Under Hoover the country had dramatically retreated from the empire it had created in the Caribbean after the war with Spain; under Roosevelt it had repudiated intervention as a means of settling its disputes with hemispheric countries and to some degree accommodated its policies to nationalistic Latin American governments seeking greater control over foreign companies operating in their domain. Roosevelt became a popular figure in Latin America. "Some of them," he once declared, referring to Latin Americans, "think they're just as good as we are—and they are!" In 1938 at the Pan-American Conference in Lima, delegates who a decade before had condemned American intervention in Nicaragua supported a vaguely worded resolution calling for a united hemisphere (Canada excepted) to meet any external threat. Shortly after the outbreak of the European war the following year, they met again in Panama to deal with the economic problems brought on by the war, and, following Roosevelt's personal recommendation, to declare the Western Hemisphere south of the 49th parallel off limits to belligerent activity. As Hitler's armies swallowed up western Europe in the summer of 1940, hemispheric conferees met in Havana and announced that European possessions in the Western Hemisphere could not be transferred to a non-American state. Already the United States had undertaken a vigorous defense program for the vulnerable Caribbean and its strategic lifeline, the Panama Canal. After Pearl Harbor yet another special conference was called to line up Latin American nations behind the

United States against its global enemies—Germany, Italy, and Japan. By then most already had broken diplomatic relations with the Axis powers, and they would shortly declare war.

Beneath this apparent harmony there were discordant signs. The United States declared that its purpose in waging war was the elimination of dictatorial regimes, such as Hitler's Germany, Mussolini's Italy, and Hirohito's Japan, yet its Latin American allies were hardly examples of "decent democratic regimes" committed to the Four Freedoms. In the Caribbean, which almost slavishly followed American policy, strong-man governments prevailed in Cuba, the Dominican Republic, and Nicaragua. (About one of America's tropical allies Roosevelt allegedly remarked: "He may be an S.O.B., but he's *our* S.O.B.") In the larger countries, whose commitment was even more crucial to American policy, there were blatantly antidemocratic governments. Although supportive of the war effort to the extent of sending an expeditionary force to Europe, Brazil had in Getulio Vargas what some American observers considered a "Brazilian Mussolini"; Argentina, which did not join the Allies until the war was virtually over, exhibited a defiantly pro-German stance.

Still, all things considered the United States obtained what it wanted from Latin America in World War II: subordinate economies and states in the Caribbean and defense sites from Panama to the bulge of Brazil. In the beginning it had justifiable concerns about Latin America's solidarity behind the American cause, but by the end, when the United States stood militarily and economically supreme, the entire hemisphere appeared to stand solidly behind it. Then the United States committed what in retrospect has been judged a grievous error when it neglected its Latin American allies.

The United States and Latin America emerged from the war with different political perspectives on world affairs and strikingly disparate economic prospects. More concerned with the Soviet challenge in Europe, U.S. policymakers considered Latin America of lesser importance in their global calculations. To be sure, the United States committed itself to regional defense and organization at the Chapultepec Conference in Mexico in 1945, in the Inter-American Treaty of Reciprocal Assistance (Rio Treaty), signed in Rio de Janeiro in 1947, and, one year later in the restructuring of the old Pan-American system in the Organization of American States (OAS) at Bogotá. During the Bogotá meeting there were serious riots in the city (in which Fidel Castro participated) brought on by the assassination of a popular Colombian politician, Jorge Eliécer Gaitán. In the United States the *bogotazo*, as the riots were called, took on little more significance than an isolated case of public unrest in the Hispanic world. To the Latin American left, however, it represented deep dissatisfaction with the continent's economic decline and opportunity for a more drastic solution. The United States, it was argued, had profited by its victory; it was restoring world capitalism and revitalizing its markets abroad and, by the end of the decade, reaping the benefits.

Latin America, which had dutifully subordinated its economies to American interest in the war, had emerged from the global conflict with expectations of sharing in postwar prosperity. Instead, its economies had suffered from wartime inflation and loss of world markets. Expecting something on the order of the Marshall Plan, by which the western European economies had been restored, Latin America received comparatively little public assistance from the United States and considerable advice on how to run its political house. When John F. Kennedy commented in the campaign of 1960 that since 1945 the U.S. government had provided more public aid to Yugoslavia, a socialist state, than to all Latin America, he was making a grim statement on the condition of inter-American affairs in the postwar era.

The U.S. government usually got what it wanted in Latin America during the 1950s: a collection of client states among the smaller countries, and among the larger countries, such as Mexico, Colombia, Venezuela, Brazil, and even Argentina, whose economic nationalism under Juan Perón was not perceived as a Third World challenge, more ambitious governments eager to expand their economies to bring about a more consumer-oriented society on the American model. The adoption of the socialist model by Latin America as an acceptable solution to the economic problems wrought by the war and the "revolution of rising expectations" remained forbidden.

Most Latin American governments played the American game by Washington's rules. Even Mexico, which before the war had antagonized the United States by nationalizing its foreign-owned oil industry, got a businessman's president (Miguel Alemán) and embarked on a vigorous expansion of the national economy that earned the plaudits of New York bankers. Cuba became a marketplace for American goods, and its new leader, Fulgencio Batista, a once lowly sergeant in the Cuban army who had become a general, president-maker, and finally president of his country in 1940, threw out the civilians in a bloodless coup in 1952, turning the country into a reliable and anti-Communist bastion. In the Dominican Republic,

"PRESIDENTS COME AND GO, BUT WE'LL NOT DESERT YOU, SEÑOR!" (*Kansas City Star*)

Rafael Trujillo ruled like the "little Caesar of the Caribbean" in his personal fiefdom, reassuring Washington with his anti-Soviet rhetoric. Nicaragua, another client state, was the domain of the Somoza family, installed in power by the Americans a generation before. The tyrants of the Hispanic world, whom the moralistic Cordell Hull had condemned as "proto-Fascists" before the war and whom the United States, under Latin American liberal pressures, was urged to turn out in 1945, had achieved by the mid-1950s a certain respectability in American judgment. They might still be "S.O.B.'s," to requote Roosevelt, but they were still "our S.O.B.'s."

Perhaps no event of the decade more accurately reflected America's priorities in Latin America than its ouster of the leftist government of Jacobo Arbenz in Guatemala in 1954. Ten years before, a coalition of Guatemalan reformers had turned out the dictator Jorge Ubico. Under Juan José Arévalo (who years later would write a bitterly anti-American manifesto, *The Shark and the Sardines*), Guatemala embarked on an economic and social modernization program. After 1950 when Arbenz took over, the government began moving against the most powerful foreign firm on the isthmus, the United Fruit Company (UFCO). In the process Arbenz had to rely more and more on the Guatemalan trade union and other leftist groups. To Secretary of State John Foster Dulles, who had once been associated with the New York law firm representing UFCO, Guatemala was fast becoming an agent of Soviet imperialism. With President Dwight D. Eisenhower's approval, the Dulles brothers (Allen was CIA chief) crushed Arbenz—John Foster by extracting from the other Latin American governments at the Tenth Inter-American Conference at Caracas a pledge that "communism was incompatible with the hemisphere," and Allen by using the CIA to help finance, under Colonel Carlos Castillo Armas, an anti-Arbenz movement operating out of Honduras. The affair was thoroughly, and inexpensively, carried out. The lesson was not lost on Washington, neither was it lost on a then obscure ideologue of guerrilla war, Ernesto "Ché" Guevara.

The compliant Latin American governments, expecting Washington to be grateful for their support by opening its public coffers, learned shortly afterward from Secretary of the Treasury George M. Humphrey that they must still look to private investment for their needs. The continent received some public aid, but it was a pittance compared to the millions poured into Western Europe. In 1952, when Bolivian revolutionaries took over the country and nationalized the tin mines, the Eisenhower administration subsidized the new government in large part to prevent a sharper turn to the Left. A few years later Eisenhower responded favorably to Panama's pleas for larger economic benefits from the canal. Not until after Vice President Richard M. Nixon was stoned and spat upon by leftist demonstrators at Lima and Caracas in 1959 did the U.S. government finally acquiesce in Latin America's insistence on an inter-American development bank, a proposal it had been making for twenty years.

On January 1 of that year, Castro had triumphed in Cuba. From its beginning, the Cuban revolution became intricately intertwined with U.S. policy toward Latin America. Ultimately, it would dramatically affect the Soviet-American relationship as well. Ironically, when Castro first came to power, many observers of Latin America in this country welcomed the political change. After all, the end of the 1950s in Latin America looked like the "twilight of the tyrants." Perón had fallen in a military coup in Argentina in 1955; Manuel Odría, the Peruvian chieftain, in 1956; and Gustavo Rojas Pinilla and Marcos Pérez Jiménez, Colombian and Venezuelan strongmen, in 1957 and 1958, respectively. Even the supreme tyrant of the Caribbean, "El Benefactor" Trujillo of the Dominican Republic, although still in power in 1959, had virtually exhausted his once considerable influence with Washington. Only the Somozas in Nicaragua seemed secure, having survived the assassination of the patriarch by a madman in 1956 and the opposition of Costa Rican leader José "Pepe" Figueres. Throughout Latin America it appeared that a new generation of civilian leaders, who believed in political honesty and progressive rule, was taking over. Even under Eisenhower and certainly under Kennedy, the United States realized its policies must accommodate these changes. In this view, then, Castro looked very much like the guerrilla warrior fighting for the restoration of constitutional rectitude in a corrupt society.

In Cuba, unlike any other Latin American country, the triumph of the revolution meant ultimately not only a break with the old order but also something more significant: a break with the United States. How this came about is still a controversial story. Castro's detractors— those Americans like then Vice President Nixon, or the professional classes that fled the island in the early 1960s—argued that he was, as he declared in late 1961, always a Marxist-Leninist and fully intended to communize the island. In a variation on this theme, tough-minded liberals who saw Castro as a social reformer contended that he betrayed his own revolution by letting the ideologues like Guevara chart Cuba's course. His defenders in the United States—mostly academics—and elsewhere in Latin America argued just as vehemently that the American decision to use economic, and ultimately military, measures to overthrow him drove Castro into the waiting arms of the Soviets.

Although the United States declared very early on in the Cuban-American controversy and continues to this day to insist that Cuba is a sovereign state and can have any kind of government it wants, Washington closely monitored the course of the revolution from the circus-like public trials of former Batistianos to the succession of economic measures leading inexorably to the nationalization of U.S. companies. Throughout, the official and unofficial American response was one of virtually unqualified disapproval, coupled with a determination to retaliate. Yet in the same era—the first two years or so of the revolution—Castro cleverly exploited in Cuba the latent anti-Americanism wrought by sixty years of dependency and unconscionably drove into exile many thousands of middle-class Cubans who found fault with his revolution. In short, the U.S. government made Castro pay a high price to carry out his revolution, but Castro was determined to pay it in order to alter Cuba internally and to change its relationship with the United States.

At least to realistic Latin American observers of the cyclical shifts of American interest in hemispheric conditions it was clear that the grandiose plans of the Alliance for Progress, a Latin American idea picked up by Kennedy in the 1960 campaign and dramatically set into motion early in his administration, were inseparable from America's fear that the Cuban revolution was exportable. "Those who make peaceful revolution impossible," Kennedy was fond of saying, "will make violent revolution inevitable." He was referring to the fact that in 1961, when so much American attention was directed toward the Western Hemisphere, Latin America was still a rigidly structured society ruled by social and military elites. Kennedy was brutally realistic. While he was extolling the new civilian rulers, such as Rómulo Betancourt in Venezuela, and the Alliance goals of industrialization and agrarian reform, at the same time he seemed determined to punish Castro for defying the United States.

Kennedy inherited the plan, concocted by Nixon in 1959 and transmuted by the CIA and Joint Chiefs of Staff into Operation Zapata, for the invasion of Cuba in April 1961. Although the liberating force was composed mostly of Cuban exiles and Kennedy himself declared that no Americans participated, U.S. involvement in what turned out to be a political and military disaster ran deep. Castro's reputation soared, both in Cuba and the world.

After the Bay of Pigs debacle in 1961, when the CIA believed it could stage "another Guatemala," American prestige plummeted, but Kennedy did not back off. In the summer there was another confrontation, this time outside Montevideo at a plush resort in Uruguay called Punta del Este, where Kennedy's alert crew of Latin Americanists exchanged sharp challenges with Guevara. "Look at Latin America a decade from now," he roared, "and then at Cuba and see which has achieved the goals of the Alliance for Progress!" Delegates went back home, counting proffered American aid and calling it "Fidel's money." Early in 1962 at Punta del Este II, under severe American pressure, they voted Castro's government out of the OAS. During these years, as the Church Committee Report on CIA operations revealed much later, several assassination plots against Castro were linked to the American government.

All the while the Cuban-Soviet connection grew stronger. The first ties, cemented in 1960, were essentially economic agreements whereby the Soviets agreed to take the Cuban sugar that the Americans no longer wanted. One year before, during his visit to the United States, Castro had boasted that his country had no ties with the Soviets, but, in his second, more dramatic sojourn, he and Soviet Premier Nikita Khrushchev had embraced at the United Nations, and the Cuban flew back to Havana aboard a Russian jet. In Washington, the Cuban-Soviet relationship was disquieting, but it produced no serious alarm until the summer of 1962 when Cuban exiles and a prominently outspoken senator, Kenneth Keating, charged that the Soviets were up to suspicious military activity at isolated sites in Cuba.

The missiles destined for these sites—missiles capable of carrying warheads to virtually every major city in the Western Hemisphere—did not arrive until September. They were not discovered until mid-October, but their presence triggered two harrowing weeks in the Cold War during which the two superpowers seemed bent on nuclear annihilation. Cuba lies far from the Soviet Union, however, and the Russians, who still did not possess the sea power to challenge the U.S. Navy, dared not risk a nuclear exchange in which they held an inferior position. Khrushchev, who would pay for this embarrassment two years later with his ouster from power, did secure a pledge from Kennedy that there would be no invasion. Angry over the Soviet-American deal carried out without his approval, Castro refused to let UN observers verify the removal of the missiles. For over a year he flirted with the Chinese, who were vilifying the Soviets as "accommodationists," and dispatched Guevara to Bolivia to create "one, two, many Vietnams," but the Russians atoned for their disgrace by giving Cuba a more important place in the socialist system. At one time after Castro's later involvement in Africa's troubles, the Soviets wearied of his disruptive proselytizing and looked to his more trustworthy brother, Raúl, as their choice for Cuba's Sovietized bureaucracy. Fidel, truly the symbol of the revolution bearing his name, survived, however, by toning down his rhetoric and promoting closer relations with other hemispheric nations, including the United States.

By then Kennedy was dead, and America, mired in a jungle war in Southeast Asia, was rapidly losing interest in Latin America. In his brief presidency, Kennedy had erred often in dealing with hemispheric problems, but his instincts had been right. Even Castro, his rival (and some have said the vengeful plotter of his assassination), recognized that, beyond serving America's strategic and economic interests, the Alliance for Progress, despite its shortcomings, offered hope for the millions of Latin Americans trapped in poverty. Ironically, at the time of Kennedy's death, a French journalist was with Castro in Havana, conveying the latest sentiments from Washington on the prospects for a Cuban-American reconciliation. When Castro received the news from Dallas, he said, "everything has changed."

In the early 1960s Washington's amenable attitude toward military governments and dictators had noticeably cooled. What the United States wanted—what Latin America needed—were left-of-center civilian governments, but there was a limit to how far left a country might shift before it incurred America's displeasure. Kennedy set the priorities early on after the assassination of Trujillo in the Dominican Republic. Our choices, he told an aide, are "a decent democratic regime, a continuation of the Trujillo dictatorship, or a communist takeover. We should strive for the first, but we can't rule out the second until we're sure we can avoid the third." Using such logic he condemned the military when it took over in the Dominican Republic, Honduras, Peru, and Argentina in 1962–63, but in the same period he quietly acquiesced in its seizure of power in Guatemala, where the leftist nemesis Arévalo was on the verge of returning to power, and in British Guiana, scheduled for independence, where the United States had to choose between a popular pro-Soviet leftist, Cheddi Jagan, and an anti-Soviet leftist, Linden Forbes Burnham. Kennedy met with Jagan but remained suspicious and persuaded the British to delay their departure until 1966 when Guyana, with Burnham as leader, became independent.

Kennedy remains one of the few American political leaders still admired by Latin Americans; even the Mexicans, ordinarily cool toward U.S. official visitors, gave him and his beautiful wife a stupendous reception. Not since Franklin Roosevelt's triumphant visit to Buenos Aires in 1936 had an American president been so widely adulated in Latin America. His successor Lyndon Baines Johnson inherited not only Kennedy's Vietnam policy but his hemispheric policy as well, and, as in Southeast Asia, Johnson placed his own peculiar imprimatur on that policy.

Of all recent American leaders, Johnson should have been the best informed about Latin America's political, economic, and social problems, about the Hispanic psyche and its values, and about the U.S.-Latin American relationship. After all, he had grown up in the hill country of south central Texas only one hundred miles or so from the Mexican border in a state heavily influenced by Hispanic culture. Still, his was a warped cultural education; he saw Mexicans harassed for years in a political and economic system that regarded them mostly for their cheap labor and their votes in an election. In the campaign of 1960, Kennedy had won by a razor-thin margin. In Texas, Mexican voters in the southern counties had been hastily corralled by rural Democratic bosses and transported to the polls to give Kennedy and Johnson a victory. In dealing with Hispanics, Kennedy, who had been virtually uninformed about Latin America before the 1960 campaign, was noticeably *simpático*. His successor once laid out his philosophy with, predictably, an anecdote that was vintage Johnson: "I know Mexicans," he declared, "they're good neighbors. But you've got to lay down the rules when they get to the front gate. If you don't, before you know it they're up on the front porch."

Johnson acquired a reputation as a "great persuader" among fence-straddling congressmen on Capitol Hill who had to be threatened, cajoled, and sometimes physically intimidated to approve his programs. He demonstrated much the same approach toward Latin Americans. Only a few months in office, he plunged into a major diplomatic crisis in Panama brought on by age-old resentments over American jurisdiction of the Canal Zone. After a series of riots in 1964, Panama suspended diplomatic relations and took its case to the rest of Latin America. Johnson decided to deal with the Panamanian leader as if he were some recalcitrant Democratic politician: "Get me the president of Panama—what's his name—on the phone!" Months of tedious diplomatic negotiations followed, but in the end Johnson was able to employ his carrot-and-stick approach. On nationwide television, sitting in front of a map of the entire isthmus, he dramatically announced that the United States and Panama were working on new treaties that would one day transfer the existing canal to Panama, provide a new defense agreement, and, more important, arrange for the construction of a new sea-level canal, which, the president said, "may be built in Panama." Three years later, long after Johnson had forgotten about tiny Panama and its monomania, the canal, the three treaties finally appeared, but they were assailed in Washington by the then powerful canal lobby and in Panama by anti-American nationalists.

Johnson had come into political prominence during the bitterest years of the Cold War; he was defiantly anti-Communist and thus, unlike Kennedy, did not make subtle distinctions among varying brands of Latin American leftism. Castro was anathema. America had lost Cuba to the Communists, Johnson said, but under him it would not "lose" another hemispheric country to the Communists. Therefore, in late April 1965, when a reformist element in the Dominican Republic moved to reinstall former President Juan Bosch, whom the generals had tossed out two years before, Johnson acted. Declaring that he was not going to permit "another Cuba" in the Caribbean, the president dispatched 20,000 crack troops into Santo Domingo. Although the force was later expanded to include troops from several other Latin American countries, notably from those with rightist regimes, the United States was clearly in charge when it determined that Bosch, whom American officials considered too tolerant of Communists in his brief presidency, would not be reinstalled in power. Throughout the hemisphere, Johnson was accused of reverting to gunboat diplomacy. If a country in the Western Hemisphere appeared ready to fall to the Communists by violent means, the Johnson Doctrine declared, the United States had the right to intervene to prevent it.

Johnson has been harshly judged by Latin Americans, not only for his role in the Dominican intervention but also for his uncritical response to the military takeover in Brazil in 1964, which demonstrably slowed that country's spiraling inflation but did so at a noticeably severe political price. Investors who had grumbled for years about inefficient Alliance programs and inept leftist governments welcomed Johnson's appointment of Thomas Mann as coordinator of hemispheric policy because Mann had a businesslike approach to Latin American issues. Yet it must be remembered that Johnson maintained American financial commitments to the Alliance, even as the Vietnam War was annually consuming more and more of his budget and time. He could be charitable with

Hispanics, such as at the Chamizal ceremony that took place on a strip of land between El Paso and Juárez that after a century of dispute was being turned over to Mexico, or as spokesman for the International Great Society as he stood under a blazing border sun with the president of Mexico and talked about some vast cooperative program for the Mexican and American peoples, to the noticeable indifference of the Mexican leader.

When Nixon became president in 1969, the country's Latin American policy was in shambles. The Alliance for Progress, essentially still functioning, already had come under harsh congressional scrutiny for its demonstrable failures. Critics were saying that the average Latin American now lived under more repressive regimes and poorer economic circumstances than in 1960 when reformers heralded the Alliance as the hemisphere's salvation. In any event, Nixon seemed determined to kill it off, claiming the Latin Americans really did not want the Alliance anymore. "What they want," said Nixon, echoing the collective sentiment of the Viña del Mar Conference of Latin American leaders, "is trade, not aid." His special emissary to the hemisphere, Nelson Rockefeller, a Venezuelan *hacendado*, already had returned after a whirlwind trip. In his sometimes frankly realistic report, Rockefeller had written that the prospects for upheaval throughout the continent were greater than ever. He recommended the creation of a secretariat of Western Hemispheric Affairs and an inter-American police force. The first never came into being; the second ran afoul of Latin American nationalistic sensibilities, although its rightist regimes were cooperating by exchanging information on leftist organizers and its armies now had a generation of young officers drilled at the counterinsurgency school in the Canal Zone.

Nixon referred to his Latin American policy as the "new partnership." Economic barriers began to fall, as he announced that a new General System of Preferences (GSP) would govern inter-American trade. For the hard-pressed Caribbean nations, which usually exported one or two products, GSP meant greater access to the vital U.S. market. Much of the goodwill was offset, however, when Congress, infuriated over the 1973 oil embargo, took revenge on all members of the Organization of Petroleum Exporting Countries, including Venezuela and Ecuador, by denying them trade preferences. The effect on Venezuelan-American relations was predictably harsh.

Nixon could not readily comprehend how a military government, such as that in Peru, could espouse populist programs, but, when the

Peruvian generals took over an American oil company, he did not invoke the Hickenlooper amendment, which called for shutting off aid to any government that nationalized U.S. companies without adequate compensation. If a Latin American government offered a direct challenge, as did Salvador Allende's socialist regime in Chile, Nixon did not hesitate to retaliate. There was no military crusade against Chile like the one Kennedy had unleashed against Castro, but Nixon used American influence with International Telephone and Telegraph, which had extensive operations in Chile, to disseminate funds to Allende's opponents in the 1970 Chilean presidential election. When Allende won anyway, Nixon undertook a campaign, waged largely through American-dominated international lending institutions, to harass Allende for the next three years. By then Allende's appeals to Chile's lower classes had so frightened the middle class that the country had plunged into civil war, a struggle in which the Chilean military, alert to Washington's disapproval of Allende's socialism, triumphed.

Thus Nixon and Henry Kissinger, who had done so much to reshape U.S. policy elsewhere in the world, relegated Latin America to a secondary position in their global priorities. Retreating from the Asian mainland, the United States appeared to retreat from the Western Hemisphere as well. At important OAS sessions the Latin Americans began meeting privately and, after agreeing among themselves, summoned the U.S. representative to listen. In 1975 under Mexican, Venezuelan, and Cuban guidance, twenty-five Latin American governments founded a separatist hemispheric organization, the Latin American Economic System, which excluded the United States. A former adviser to Kennedy on Latin American affairs, William D. Rogers, noting the growing gulf between this country and Latin America, recommended that the United States pull out of the OAS.

One year or so before Nixon resigned, there was a thaw in Cuban-American relations brought on by Castro's irritation over skyjackers and, more importantly, by Congress's urging. Nevertheless, relations deteriorated just as quickly when Cuba dispatched troops into Angola and Ethiopia. Rebuffed by congressmen alarmed over "another Vietnam," Kissinger announced that Cuba was simply doing Moscow's bidding in Africa. This was only partially correct. True, Cuba had been fully incorporated into the Soviet bloc, but its role in Africa went beyond the carrying out of Soviet designs. Cuba's cultural background is African as well as Hispanic; Castro declared that Cuba must participate in liberating African peoples from the last "grasp of imperialism." (In 1979 the Cubans began dispatching the first contingents of troops to Angola, thus creating a force there eventually reaching to more than 20,000, with half of them black.) To Washington, these words were very much Marxist rhetoric, but they had a noticeable impact on the black Caribbean, where "black power" movements had surfaced in the early 1970s and peoples were becoming more sensitive to their African past. Cuba's relations with the Lesser Antilles, negligible in 1970, grew rapidly in the course of the decade.

Even those countries once considered surrogates defied the United States. Tiny Panama, under Omar Torrijos, threw out the 1967 canal treaty proposals and demanded a new agenda. Torrijos united all Latin Americans against the United States on the canal issue and even brought the UN Security Council to Panama to deliberate on the subject. Although every president since Kennedy had declared that one day the canal should be Panama's, there was still the issue of dealing with the powerful canal lobby. Before the fight was over and President Jimmy Carter and Torrijos were sitting side by side to sign new treaties providing for ultimate Panamanian ownership of the canal, the canal's defenders fought a final battle to preserve the most visible symbol of America's imperial past.

In Panama, Carter did what he thought was right; elsewhere in Latin America he directed U.S. policy toward achieving human rights. The results were mixed. In Brazil, Chile, and especially Argentina, where military governments cracked down severely on political enemies of the regime, even to the point of using torture, American condemnation probably saved lives, but the policy inevitably brought countercharges that the president was not uniform in applying his human rights prescription, and relations with these countries worsened. In Nicaragua, where America traced its considerable influence back to a time before World War I, the ruling Somoza family, overthrown in a sanguinary civil war in 1979, blamed many of its troubles on Carter's insistent pressures for human rights. This was absurd, but Anastasio Somoza did have a point when he protested, even as U.S. Ambassador Lawrence Pezzullo, representing a government sick of the war and of the Somozas, was arranging his retirement, that he had faithfully stuck by the Americans in the Cold War and now they were letting him down.

The overthrow of the Somozas, whom the Americans had put into power a half century before, marked the end of an era in which the United States relied on Caribbean surrogates to keep order and promote economic development along American guidelines. Ironically, it had been in Nicaragua that the policy of military intervention and gunboat diplomacy had succumbed in 1933 to Augusto Sandino's jungle war and a collapsing international capitalist structure.

By 1979 American leadership in the Western Hemisphere had slipped badly. The new rulers in Nicaragua, a curious mixture of socialists and middle-class reformers, were not very impressed by America's arrangement of Somoza's departure and embarked on a course of national economic policy that for Washington resembled too closely Castro's economic experiment in Cuba. When in American estimation the Nicaraguans began helping the guerrillas in El Salvador, where a frightfully bloody civil war broke out, the United States started applying severe pressure on Nicaragua, thereby shutting down the flow of aid to its hard-pressed government and stepping up its military support to the shaky Salvadoran government of José Napoleón Duarte, a Christian Democrat caught between a murderous right wing and a fanatical left, and to Nicaragua's northern neighbor Honduras.

The "loss" of Nicaragua did not figure prominently in Ronald Reagan's defeat of Carter in 1980, but Reagan's North American "continentalists" made it clear that in championing human rights Carter had alienated America's friends. The truth was less palatable: the United States, mired in economic difficulties, its embassy personnel held hostage in Iran, was a wounded giant no longer able to chart the future of the Western Hemisphere. The ultimate proof of its impotence came in the 1982 war over the Malvinas Islands between Argentina and Great Britain when the politically harassed Argentine military government, virtually indifferent to the moral blandishments of Washington, attacked the British-controlled Malvinas in the South Atlantic and Great Britain reacted with force, in the process demanding—and getting—American support.

The Malvinas war, which for a few weeks alerted the American people to the hemispheric crisis, just as quickly passed into obscurity. The dramatic U.S. invasion of Grenada in October 1983, presumably undertaken to prevent over six hundred American medical students from becoming hostages to a radical regime that had seized power from pro-Cuban governments, also did not convince Americans that they must shift away from globalism. These events, however, illustrated the U.S. dilemma in dealing with Latin America. In the late 1930s, as war approached in Europe, the Roosevelt administration had exploited public fears about German influence in Latin America to break down isolationist sentiment. Defense of the hemisphere became a popular theme during the war, but the United States had a different purpose than Latin America in promoting inter-American unity. It was moving toward globalism, and it needed reliable Latin American allies for its future commitment in the world. The country's fundamental political, economic, and cultural interests lay with Western Europe, Americans decided, even as the United States participated in the Rio Treaty and the OAS. Obsessed with the Soviet threat in the postwar years, the United States relinquished much of its commitment to the "Western Hemisphere" idea, the cumulative beliefs of generations that held that the future of the Western Hemisphere lay in republican governments whose goal was the betterment of their own peoples. As Kennedy said, the United States must strive for "decent, democratic regimes." He believed that the American political and economic system, despite its flaws, offered the developing Latin American nations a preferable alternative to Castro's Cuba.

To some critics the American commitment in Central America, reinforced by stern rhetoric during the early years of the Reagan administration, closely resembles a return to the paternalism and, in the case of Sandinista Nicaragua, to the forceful meddling of another era. However, unlike earlier times when the United States, by virtue of its political, economic, and military clout in the Caribbean basin, could determine the destiny of small countries, the nation's modern Central American experience more closely represents a kind of entrapment by historical circumstance. Fearful of what the Sandinista revolution portends, the United States has once more allied itself with political and social elites whose values are, quite frankly, alien to American traditions. Yet it has declared, in the Kissinger Commission Report, that Central Americans deserve a future of expanding liberties and prosperity. The determination of these elites to maintain themselves and the equally fervent demands for social change from those who want power have created a political dynamic in Central America not easily manipulated from the outside, even from a nation as powerful as the United States.

This is not to say that Central America's destiny is inevitably Marxist (or Fascist), but that its problems will ultimately be solved by Central Americans themselves. In the meantime, those rivalrous isthmian elements locked in power struggles will try to maneuver the global superpowers into assisting their respective causes. In so doing they are once more demonstrating the capability of small countries to play on the fears of larger ones.

In the early 1960s the Western Hemisphere reverberated with the rhetorical clashes of the Cuban and U.S. governments. Castro said that the nature of Latin American society and government made revolution inevitable. Kennedy assured the same generation that peaceful revolution was possible. A quarter century of experience has shown that the revolution Castro talked about has been achieved only in Cuba but that Cuba's defiance of American tutelage has been widely admired. This era has demonstrated, just as convincingly, that the "peaceful revolution" Kennedy spoke of—civilian governments achieving power by the ballot and not the bullet and the hope of a better life by the generation then coming of age—is the path most Latin Americans prefer.

What threatens Latin America's future and the U.S. stake in the hemisphere is not so much Soviet meddling or Cuba's export of revolution but economic and social concerns that make the resurgence of civilian governments seem a hollow victory. The staggering public debt of most Latin American countries represents a burden few of them can afford to bear into the next century and which Americans do not wish to absorb. The promotion of a consumer society, a central feature of U.S. policy in Latin America since 1945, along with developmentalist schemes of the hemispheric countries themselves, has wrought a modern urban Latin America. In the process the expectations of peoples for a better life have risen in dramatic proportions, and governments have proved unable to meet these expectations. The most hopeful of them have headed north by plane, boat, or often on foot to fulfill their dreams. Still others form part of a vast narcotics trade. Such disturbing features of the inter-American relationship symbolize, ironically, the triumph of the long-standing U.S. goal that Latin America should follow the Western model of development. Yet their existence poses a troubling portent for the future of the Western Hemisphere.

Sources and Suggested Readings

Baily, Samuel. *The United States and the Development of South America, 1945-1975.* New York, 1976.

Blasier, Cole. *The Hovering Giant: U.S. Responses to Revolutionary Change in Latin America.* Pittsburgh, 1976.

Coleman, Kenneth M., and Herring, George C. *The Central American Crisis: Sources of Conflict and the Failure of U.S. Policy.* Wilmington, Delaware, 1985.

Connell-Smith, Gordon. *The United States and Latin America: An Historical Analysis of Inter-American Relations.* New York, 1974.

Cotler, Julio, and Fagen, Richard R., eds. *Latin America and the United States: The Changing Political Realities.* Stanford, 1974.

Davis, Harold E., et al. *Latin American Diplomatic History: An Introduction.* Baton Rouge, 1977.

Domínguez, Jorge I. *Cuba: Order and Revolution.* Cambridge, Massachusetts, 1978.

Fontaine, Roger W., and Theberge, James D., eds. *Latin America's New Internationalism: The End of Hemispheric Isolation.* New York, 1976.

Frank, Andre Gunder. *Lumpenbourgeoisie: Lumpendevelopment: Dependence, Class, and Politics in Latin America.* New York, 1972.

Gil, Federico G. *Latin American-United States Relations.* New York, 1971.

Haglund, David G. *Latin America and the Transformation of U.S. Strategic Thought, 1936-1940.* Albuquerque, 1984.

Halperin, Maurice. *The Rise and Decline of Fidel Castro: An Essay in Contemporary History.* Berkeley, 1972.

Immerman, Richard H. *The CIA in Guatemala: The Foreign Policy of Intervention.* Austin, 1982.

LaFeber, Walter. *Inevitable Revolutions: The United States in Central America.* New York, 1984.

————. *The Panama Canal: The Crisis in Historical Perspective.* New York, 1978.

Langley, Lester D. *Central America: The Real Stakes.* New York, 1985.

————. *The United States and the Caribbean in the Twentieth Century.* Athens, Georgia, 1982.

Leiken, Robert. *Central America: Anatomy of Conflict.* New York, 1984.

Levinson, Jerome, and De Onis, Juan. *The Alliance That Lost Its Way: A Critical Report on the Alliance for Progress.* Chicago, 1970.

Millett, Richard. *Guardians of the Dynasty: A History of the U.S.-Created Guardia Nacional De Nicaragua and the Somoza Family.* Maryknoll, New York, 1977.

Riding, Alan. *Distant Neighbors: A Portrait of the Mexicans.* New York, 1984.

Schmitt, Karl M. *Mexico and the United States, 1821-1973: Conflict and Coexistence.* New York, 1974.

Welch, Richard M., Jr. *Response to Revolution: The United States and the Cuban Revolution, 1959-1961.* Chapel Hill, 1985.

The Middle East, Oil, and the Third World

James W. Harper

After World War II Americans became accustomed to new words describing the world in which they lived. During the late 1940s they learned that they inhabited a "bipolar world" dominated by the United States and the Soviet Union. In the mid-1950s the phrase "Third World" crowded its way into the headlines. The Third World countries, most of them located in Africa or Asia and most of them former European colonies or spheres of influence, sought a neutral or nonaligned path following neither the United States and its allies nor the Soviet bloc. Dominated by a consuming desire for full national independence, often facing staggering economic problems, and having regional rather than global interests, these nations posed major challenges for American foreign policy.

No region of the globe was more typical of the Third World or more challenging than the Middle East. Before World War II most of the region had been under various forms of European control, and even nominally independent nations such as Saudi Arabia and Iran often felt the pressure of outside influence. Economically most of the region was backward, underdeveloped, and feudal, and it depended on foreign economic assistance. Even the newly discovered oil wealth went largely into foreign hands. After World War II the nations of the Middle East moved rapidly from political dependence to independence, and the formerly subsidized Arab oil states emerged as one of the world's dominant economic forces. Most important, the region's chief political conflict—the Arab-Israeli confrontation—dominated all diplomacy and helped to transform the United States into a Middle Eastern power.

In the last forty years the United States has become the major foreign participant in Middle East affairs. This transformation in policy constitutes one of the most dramatic changes in modern American diplomacy and a major chapter in its relations with the Third World. In 1900, U.S. interests in the Near East were modest. America's limited trade centered on exports of petroleum, chiefly kerosene, to a region whose vast oil deposits had not yet been discovered. Its diplomacy focused on protecting American nationals, securing opportunities for Christian missionaries to proselyte in the Moslem region, and supporting American Jews who wished to spend their last years in Jerusalem. In all matters, political and economic, the nation's diplomacy took a backseat to European activity. Although American involvement increased between 1900 and 1945, as manifested by oil concessions in Saudi Arabia and growing support for a Jewish national homeland in Palestine, the United States deferred to Britain in the region until after World War II.

Several factors intensified American involvement after 1945. One was the growing importance of Middle Eastern oil. Fearing a postwar shortage of oil, State Department officials, during World War II, had moved to increase U.S. influence in the region. The February 1945 meeting between President Franklin D. Roosevelt and Saudi Arabian King Ibn Saud symbolized America's growing interest in this strategic and oil-rich region. Moreover, it became apparent that Britain, weakened by the war, would be unable to perpetuate its dominance in the region after the global conflict. As in other areas of the world, the United States took steps to replace Britain as the stabilizing force.

The Cold War also helped to alter traditional American policy. Tension between the United States and the Soviet Union first occurred in the Middle East during 1946 when Soviet troops refused to honor a wartime agreement to evacuate the northern third of Iran which they had occupied during the war. The Russians demanded oil concessions similar to those Iran had granted Britain, aided Iranian Communists in the Azerbaijan region, and threatened to make the country a Soviet sphere of influence, if not a satellite. The United States moved quickly to support the Iranian government, and eventually the twin pressures of American opposition and Iranian resistance forced a Soviet retreat. For U.S. policymakers, however, the Middle East had become yet another region threatened by Soviet expansion. A second Iranian crisis occurred in the early 1950s when nationalist Premier Mohammed Mossadegh sought to nationalize the British-owned Iranian oil fields. Britain threatened an invasion, and the Western oil companies initiated a boycott of Iranian oil that

ABDUL-AZIZ IBN SAUD (1888–1953), KING OF SAUDI ARABIA. (Saudi Arabian Embassy, Information Office, Washington, DC)

threw the country's economy into crisis. Fearful that Mossadegh was a front for Soviet influence, the United States responded to the crisis with a Central Intelligence Agency intervention that led to the overthrow of Mossadegh. The agency helped to restore Shah Mohammed Reza Pahlavi to power in 1954. Thereafter, American policy was aimed at bolstering the shah as an anti-Communist bulwark in the region. Spurred by visions of reviving Persian greatness, Reza Pahlavi cooperated with the Western powers, working out an oil takeover agreement with the British in 1954 and joining defense arrangements such as the American-supported Central Treaty Organization in 1956.

Perhaps the most important cause of increased U.S. involvement in the region was the creation of Israel in 1947. This dramatic event aroused the deepest animosities of the peoples of the region, caused four major wars and hundreds of incursions and terrorist attacks, and spun a web of diplomatic problems still not untangled. The Holocaust had galvanized Western opinion behind the old idea of a homeland for the Jewish survivors of the ghastly Nazi exterminations. As Seth Tillman has noted, however, this support for Zionism conflicted with America's economic stake in Arab oil and its strategic interests in aligning the Arab states against the Soviet Union. Moreover, when the Palestinians dispossessed by Israel made their own demands for nationhood, they, like the Israelis before them, appealed to the venerable American principle of self-determination.

On November 29, 1947 the UN General Assembly, as a first step toward the creation of a Jewish state, voted to partition the former British mandate of Palestine into Jewish and Arab sections. After some initial opposition within his administration, President Harry S. Truman threw his full support behind Israel, recognizing the state within ten minutes of its proclamation of independence on May 14, 1948. American recognition was followed by a warm reception for Israeli President Chaim Weizmann two weeks later, and within one year the United States had facilitated a $100 million loan to the infant republic.

Bitterly hostile to what they regarded as a new form of Western colonization in their region, the Arab states of Egypt, Syria, Jordan, and Lebanon declared war on Israel. However, the Arab war effort was poorly planned and coordinated. The Westernized, disciplined Israeli army, with its superb leadership, many soldiers who had served in European and American armies, and modern tactics, smashed the Egyptian and Syrian invasions. Israeli units also fought the British-trained Jordanian army to a draw before an armistice ended the fighting in July 1949.

The 1948-49 war caused much turmoil in the Middle East. Huge numbers of Arab refugees either fled Israel or were driven out. Over 200,000 left before May 14, 1948, and by the war's end over 600,000 Palestinians had settled on the West Bank of the Jordan or in the Gaza Strip in Egypt. Despite UN pleas, Israel refused to take back the refugees, preferring to preserve as much land as possible for the large number of new Jewish immigrants. Arab nations demanded a homeland for the Palestinian refugees. This unresolved question has caused, and continues to cause, enormous tension in the Middle East. The humiliation of the Arab states also contributed to increased political instability, and revolutions took place in both Egypt and Syria within the next decade.

In defeat, the Arabs naturally blamed outsiders, especially the United States, for supporting Israel. However, during the five years after 1949 the Arab states were impotent, and crises in China and Korea dominated American attention. Even during this period of relative calm, the American commitment to Israel increased. Although the United States initially refrained from giving military assistance to Israel, public and private economic aid was substantial during the 1950s. In the 1960s the United States began providing substantial direct aid, and by 1980 U.S. military assistance totaled $13 billion and economic aid $5.5 billion. This increasing assistance was supported by large sections of the American population, led by American Jews and fundamentalist Christians.

During the Eisenhower administration, the Middle East became the scene of superpower rivalry. After the death of Joseph Stalin in 1953, the new Soviet leadership began major efforts to increase Russian influence in the underdeveloped world. Apparently the Soviets saw the decline of Western influence in the Third World as an excellent opportunity to enhance their political and ideological standing and to secure strategic and economic gains. The United States faced considerable difficulties in competing for influence. Arab states blamed America for the creation of Israel, a source of humiliation, political instability, and revolution. In addition, the U.S. alliance with Britain and France associated it with past European imperialism. These problems were complicated by the moralistic approach of Secretary of State John Foster Dulles, who suspected Arab nationalist leaders like Gamal Abdel Nasser, who came to power in Egypt in 1954, of being tools of the Soviets. Dulles failed to understand why Arab nationalists did not share his fear of Russia and communism.

Initially, Eisenhower and Dulles sought to use Britain and France as the leaders in organizing the region against the Communist menace. The three nations continued their Tripartite Declaration to limit arms shipments to the belligerents of the 1948–49 Arab-Israeli War. More dramatically, Dulles encouraged Britain and France to form a defensive alliance—a Middle Eastern NATO—called the Baghdad Pact or the Central Treaty Organization. This link of Britain, France, Turkey, Iran, and Pakistan secured the membership of only one Arab state, Iraq, and excited fears in Syria, Egypt, and Jordan that it was simply a device for renewed colonialism. The Arabs were more concerned with Israel and their own internal development than with the Cold War, and their opposition to the Baghdad Pact typified the inclination of most Third World states to stay free of East-West alignments.

The efforts of Eisenhower and Dulles to align the Arab states against the Soviets revealed the preoccupation with the Cold War and the insensitivity to nationalism which typified America's response to the Third World. By the 1950s these "emerging nations" were seeking to act collectively as a third force in a seemingly bipolar world. In 1954 they held a major conference in Bandung, Indonesia. Led by Egypt's Nasser, India's Pandit Nehru, and Yugoslavia's Marshal Tito, they sought to create a collective neutralist posture toward Soviet-American competition. The Soviets were quick to seek favor with the neutralists with a series of showy foreign aid projects and persistent anticolonial rhetoric. The People's Republic of China was perhaps even more effective in this endeavor because it was underdeveloped and nonwhite like the great majority of nonaligned countries. The West also recognized the strategic and economic importance of Third World areas, and the United States and Europe responded with billions in economic assistance to win the support of the neutrals.

The American response to the emergence of the Third World was often ambivalent and contradictory, however. Stemming from its own revolutionary past, the United States had ideological sympathy for countries seeking national independence, but this sympathy was often overridden by strategic and economic concerns. In the era of containment the United States had allied itself with the very European countries that had colonized much of the Third World. While American officials considered economic and military aid to countries like Belgium, Portugal, and France vital to the success of containment in Europe, such assistance was often viewed by newly emerging nations as aimed at keeping them under the European yoke. Even U.S. support of independence movements, such as that in Indonesia in the late 1940s, was obscured by the heavy political commitment to European governments elsewhere. This contradiction in goals was sharpened when the Korean War pushed the United States into a worldwide effort to contain communism.

Secretary Dulles typified the strong inclination in the United States during the 1950s to view communism as immoral and to be distrustful of countries that did not think likewise. To neutralist states far more concerned with removing the last vestiges of colonialism, gaining national self-respect, and seeking rapid economic development, Dulles's rhetoric seemed irrelevant and insulting. Further complicating American efforts was the secretary's tendency to support any government that parroted his anti-Communist line, regardless of how undemocratic, brutal, or corrupt it was.

Many Third World countries, from India to Algeria, eventually turned to a form of authoritarian socialism in the belief that state-directed economic planning would offer the fastest route to modernization. This revolutionary socialism considered foreign business interests as exploitative and in many cases proceeded to nationalize foreign holdings. Such threats to American economic interests did not win U.S. support, and, when revolutionary socialism propagated anti-American rhetoric and behavior in forums like the United Nations, it caused many Americans to see the neutralists as Communists in disguise and to insist on firm anti-Communist credentials as the price for American support. In the Third World some conservatives like Premier Nuri Sa'id of Iraq, King Idris of Libya, and President Ngo Dinh Diem of South Vietnam effectively used anti-Communist rhetoric and policies to gain U.S. support to maintain the status quo in their lands. Over the long haul, however, they all were toppled by authoritarian socialist revolutionaries.

America's domestic racial problems were another obstacle in dealing effectively with the Third World. These nations were largely nonwhite, and during the 1950s and 1960s, when the plight of black Americans gained international attention, racism at home undercut U.S. efforts to pose as the champion of freedom, equality, and democracy around the world. Moreover, racial prejudice, combined with economic and political considerations, made the United States slow to condemn racism in nations like South Africa and contributed to a tendency to disparage Asians and Africans in general. With regard to the Middle East, this attitude could be seen in a consistent and often distorted portrayal of the Arabs in the American press as backward, primitive desert dwellers who were not as entitled to Palestine as the progressive, Westernized Israelis.

The Suez crisis of 1956 and the resultant Anglo-French invasion of Egypt in October of that year ended any American hopes of using England and France as anti-Soviet surrogates in the Middle East. Furious at Nasser's nationalization of the Suez Canal, in part caused by an American refusal to sell Egypt arms or finance the Aswan Dam, England and France plotted a joint invasion of Egypt with Israel. The European states intervened under the pretext of protecting the canal. Israel, eager to avenge escalating guerrilla raids that had been launched from Gaza, invaded and swept toward Suez, but the Anglo-French effort was plagued by poor planning, inept leadership, and uncertain objectives. The invasion foundered when the United States publicly criticized its allies and the Soviet Union threatened to rain rockets on the European invaders.

The Suez fiasco marked the end of Anglo-French power in the region and forced Dwight D. Eisenhower to play a much more active role there. The president took the lead in effecting a British and Israeli withdrawal and, with the Eisenhower Doctrine of 1958 (congressional authorization for the United States to aid any country in the Middle East threatened by communism), sought to enhance his authority to act in the area. Nevertheless, Eisenhower's preoccupation with Soviet intentions caused him to forego any serious effort to negotiate an Arab-Israeli settlement in the wake of Egypt's military humiliation by Israel and Arab appreciation of America's condemnation of the Israeli attack. The result instead was an uneasy truce with UN peace-keeping forces separating the Israelis and Egyptians.

During the remainder of his administration, Eisenhower actively sought to align the United States with the pro-Western governments in Jordan, Saudi Arabia, and Iran. He invoked the Eisenhower Doctrine on only one occasion. This occurred in 1958 in the wake of a successful anti-Western coup in Iraq and an abortive one in Jordan. Later that year the pro-Western Lebanese government claimed that it was threatened by outside aggression. When battle-equipped U.S. Marines hit the beaches near Beirut, however, they found bikini-clad swimmers and hot dog vendors instead of outside aggressors. It became clear that the conflict in Lebanon was a result of internal strife, and the troops were withdrawn. Despite U.S. attempts at peacefully bolstering its influence in the Middle East, by the time Eisenhower left office in 1961 it was apparent that Soviet weight in the area had grown. Russian military advisers had replaced Western ones with the armies of Egypt, Syria, and Iraq. Soviet funds financed the Aswan Dam and propped up the Syrian economy. Moreover, the revolutionary nationalism so loathed by Dulles was a growing force from Algeria to Yemen.

Under John F. Kennedy and Lyndon B. Johnson, American policy toward the Third World changed. Whereas Eisenhower had often granted economic aid in hopes of securing short-term political support in selected neutralist countries, Kennedy and Johnson sought to provide economic assistance with less regard for the recipient's ideology, in the hope that by promoting independence and nationalism Soviet influence might be checked. Both presidents sought to show that American assistance came without strings and was aimed at the betterment of the people. The most dramatic example of this approach was the Peace Corps, which sent thousands of young Americans to underdeveloped areas in an attempt to improve living standards. Also, during the 1960s the commitment of the U.S. government to rights for American minorities blunted much of the earlier criticism of the United States as a racist society. Meanwhile, as Russian contacts with peoples from the Asian and African countries increased, stories of Soviet maltreatment of Third World students and brutish behavior by Russian missions in these areas made Russians appear no more free of racial prejudice than Americans.

During the Kennedy and Johnson years, Middle Eastern developments were overshadowed by the Cuban missile crisis and the Vietnam War. The region was far from calm, however. Israel concentrated on building its economy and military with the support of the more sympathetic Democratic administrations. Beneath the surface Arab resentment seethed, and American dependence on cheap Middle Eastern oil rose during a period of unparalleled economic growth.

The uneasy political status quo was shattered by the Six-Day War of 1967. A variety of events including the removal of UN observers, border incidents, and threats to shipping prompted Israel to launch a full-scale attack on Egypt, Syria, and Jordan. In less than one week (June 5–10), Israeli troops routed all three rivals, seizing Gaza and the Sinai from Egypt, the West Bank and East Jerusalem from Jordan, and the Golan Heights from Syria. Despite massive military aid and training provided by the Soviets, the Egyptians and the Syrians were crushed. Apparently political pressure from the United States and a need to consolidate its conquests stopped Israel from taking the capitals of all three Arab nations. Arab humiliation was complete, leaving a legacy of jokes about Arab incompetence and causing Americans wistfully to contrast the decisiveness of Israel's victory with their own Vietnam quagmire.

In the aftermath of the Six-Day War the UN Security Council on November 22, 1967 enacted Resolution 242. It called for Israel to

KING HUSSEIN OF JORDAN AND PRESIDENT JOHNSON. The two leaders met in 1967 to discuss Middle East affairs. (Lyndon B. Johnson Library)

withdraw from the newly occupied areas and for the establishment of a permanent peace based on the recognition of the prewar boundaries of all nations within the area. Writer Jon Kimche and political scientist William Quandt have argued that a major opportunity for permanent settlement was lost in the aftermath of 1967. Unfortunately, the United States, under Johnson and then Richard M. Nixon, was preoccupied with Southeast Asia, and the Middle Eastern countries distrusted each other too profoundly to formulate a permanent settlement on their own.

On October 6, 1973 a new era began with the Middle East's fourth major war since 1945. Egypt and Syria attacked a surprised Israel, and at first Egyptian forces successfully crossed into the Sinai. Quickly the Israelis counterattacked, bolstered by rush deliveries of over $2 billion worth of U.S. arms. When the resurgent Israeli forces threatened to envelop the entire Egyptian Third Army on the west bank of the canal, the Soviet Union hinted it would intervene. The Watergate-troubled Nixon administration responded with a worldwide alert of American nuclear and conventional forces. Although Nixon may have overreacted for both diplomatic as well as domestic political reasons, the alert caused the Soviets to act more cautiously. A subsequent Israeli pullback and agreement to implement a cease-fire ended the most dangerous big-power confrontation of recent Middle Eastern history.

The October War had profound implications. The initial, temporary Egyptian military success gave a psychological lift to that oft-defeated nation and enhanced the prestige of President Anwar Sadat. The Egyptian president had expelled his Soviet advisers in 1972, apparently because they opposed his plans for a new conflict with Israel and intrigued with his domestic opponents. Free of the stigma of the total defeats of 1948, 1956, and 1967, Sadat first accepted the step-by-step disengagement agreements worked out by the tireless shuttle diplomacy of Secretary of State Henry A. Kissinger and then prepared for his own peacemaking efforts in the late 1970s.

To the average American the most alarming result of the October War was the Arab oil embargo of 1973–74. In reaction to the massive U.S. military resupply of Israel, the Arab oil producers, led by Saudi Arabia, banned oil shipments to states that had supported Israel. Americans soon had to adjust to lines at gasoline stations, changes in speed limits, and lowered thermostats in winter. The embargo lasted only until July 1974, and sizable American oil reserves made its effect less painful in the United States than in Europe or Japan. It was obvious that oil was a new Arab weapon that might threaten traditional American policy.

The embargo highlighted a profound revolution in the control of oil. In the late 1940s the Western oil companies (Anthony Sampson's "Seven Sisters") set the price and quantity of Middle Eastern oil production. The position of the American-owned companies was enhanced by a cozy relationship with the Truman and Eisenhower administrations, which blocked antitrust suits and allowed the oil businesses to count taxes paid to Middle Eastern countries as operating costs. When an oil country like Iran sought to challenge this control, the companies blocked the sale of Iranian oil with such devastating effect that other producers thought twice before considering nationalization.

Slowly during the 1950s and 1960s the Middle Eastern oil producers ended their subservience to Western capitalists. Thousands of young Arabs and Iranians received their education in the West and returned to enter the petroleum industry where they gained experience and expertise. Independent Western oil companies sought new concessions in the region, offering the Arabs higher royalties which the older major companies soon had to match. Middle Eastern efforts to control oil led to the formation in 1959 of the Organization of Petroleum Exporting Countries (OPEC), and during the next decade this group secured information, access to company records, better prices, and most important, cooperation and united action among the producers. However, this activity went largely unnoticed in the West as cheap oil fueled the boom of the 1960s.

In 1968, OPEC began to flex its muscles, obtaining access to accounting records from the majors, limiting the size and number of Western concessions, and creating nationally owned oil firms within each member country. In 1971 the organization pushed through substantial price increases, cost-of-living attachments, and other concessions. Against the united front of OPEC and amidst a burgeoning demand for the 12 million barrels of oil produced by OPEC annually, the Western concessionaires had little choice but to yield. When the Nixon administration sought to counter the oil price increases by devaluating the dollar, the chief oil currency, OPEC retaliated with another round of price increases.

In 1972, OPEC insisted on the right of member nations to buy out the foreign companies. Abetted by rising revenues resulting from higher prices, most members of OPEC had taken control of all their domestic oil industry by 1980. The price of a barrel of oil rose 400 percent in the two years after 1973, and by 1980 it was 1,600 percent greater than the 1960 price. The OPEC revolution closed factories and contributed to record inflation in the United States, put the reins on the European economic boom, and, most dramatically, created a $600 billion oil revenue surplus, thereby giving the OPEC members incredible political power and a stake in the finances of Western countries where the surplus was invested. U.S. conservation efforts, threats of armed intervention, and attempts at collective action by petroleum consumers failed to reverse OPEC's course.

Only rising production and Saudi moderation restrained oil prices until the mid-1980s when producers such as Iraq and Iran increased production levels beyond OPEC limits. By 1985 divisions within OPEC and competition from non-OPEC producers like Britain resulted in increased production and a significant reduction in crude oil prices which declined by as much as 30 to 40 percent from 1980 to 1986. Ironically, the lowering of prices on Middle Eastern crude lessened conservation and exploration efforts outside OPEC and increased dependence on Middle Eastern production.

Oil dependence and the serious confrontation with the Soviets in 1973 sparked major American efforts to serve as peacemaker in the

Middle East. In the immediate aftermath of the October War, Secretary Kissinger initiated a series of diplomatic efforts that produced cease-fire agreements between Israel, Egypt, and Syria and a consequent lifting of the oil embargo. Kissinger excluded the Soviets from any role in the peace process, a diplomatic achievement that bolstered American prestige in the region but one gained at the price of making the United States solely responsible for peacemaking. Perhaps most important, Kissinger's diplomacy paved the way for more dramatic steps.

In November 1977 Egyptian President Sadat stunned the world by flying to Jerusalem to discuss peace with Israeli leaders. Convinced that his country needed to focus on domestic developments, Sadat risked his prestige and the scorn of fellow Arab states by gambling that he could reach an agreement with the Israelis. He was warmly received by hard-line Prime Minister Menachem Begin, a terrorist in the early Arab-Israeli conflict and like Sadat a fighter against the British still earlier. Sadat's trip sparked hopes for a cessation of the hostility between the two principal adversaries of the Arab-Israeli conflict. The Jerusalem visit and a subsequent trip by Begin to Egypt started a process aimed at a comprehensive settlement. Such an agreement had obvious advantages for the United States, and President Jimmy Carter threw his support behind its negotiation. Carter's full energies were required because the issues dividing Egypt and Israel were immense: the time schedule of Israel's withdrawal from Egypt, Israeli security, and the status of the West Bank and Jerusalem.

In the two years following the Sadat visit, negotiations threatened to break down several times, and by mid-1978 many believed the process had failed. At this point President Carter invited Begin and Sadat to Camp David, Maryland, where he jawboned both leaders, especially the irascible, tough Begin, into a preliminary settlement known as the Camp David agreement. When old animosities and new irritants threatened to shatter this preliminary accord, Carter risked his personal prestige in a March peacemaking visit to Israel and Egypt where he attempted to remove obstacles in the path to agreement. The efforts bore fruit on March 26, 1979, when Israel and Egypt signed a formal peace treaty.

The Egyptian-Israeli treaty provided for a phased withdrawal by Israel from all of the Sinai Peninsula, coupled with the establishment of full diplomatic relations between the two nations. The pact invited other Arab states to join in an effort to create a general Arab-Israeli peace. This hope was dashed by Arab suspicions and by a failure of the negotiations to produce a workable settlement of the Palestinian question. Even though the treaty failed in its wider goals, the separate peace between Israel and Egypt was the most important step toward Middle East stability since 1945.

Just as the Egyptian-Israeli treaty was being hailed as a major triumph, American diplomacy suffered a stunning reverse in Iran. After the restoration of the shah in 1954, U.S. relations with Iran had grown closer. The shah seemed like "the kind of Moslem we could live with." His oil flowed west, he joined pro-Western military alignments, and he even maintained diplomatic relations with Israel. Thousands of Iranian students enrolled in American colleges and universities. Even when the shah took positions in conflict with American interests, such as his leadership in establishing OPEC, he compensated by spending much of his oil revenues in the United States. President Nixon was determined to make Iran the linchpin of American Near Eastern policy. The shah was encouraged to purchase huge quantities of the latest U.S. weapons, American businessmen rushed in to build new Iranian cities, and U.S. intelligence agencies placed some of their most important installations in his country. Reza Pahlavi was delighted to cooperate, regarding American support as the key to establishing his country's dominance in the Persian Gulf, if not the entire region.

The shah's newfound prominence obscured the wrenching changes taking place within Iran as oil wealth and foreign development propelled the country from backwardness to modernity within the space of two decades. This rapid change provoked both Iranian leftists and rightists. Leftists, educated in the West, deplored the shah's authoritarian rule and called for a popular-based government. On the Right, Moslem leaders deplored the erosion of traditional values and the secularization that appeared indistinguishable from Westernization. By the end of the 1970s these forces burst forth into what became one of the bloodiest revolutions in modern times. The shah was deposed, and the charismatic Moslem fanatic Ayatollah Khomeini gained control of the Iranian government.

Initially the Carter administration misread the depth of opposition to the shah. As the revolution grew, memories of the Vietnam experience led the United States to refrain from massive intervention in support of the shah and to seek contacts with the revolutionaries. Unfortunately, U.S. ties to the past were all too visible in Iran, and the revolutionary rage was virulent in its anti-Americanism. This rage erupted in November 1979 with the seizure of the American embassy and the kidnapping of over fifty U.S. diplomats and embassy employees. The ensuing hostage crisis poisoned the American mind against Iran. As diplomacy dragged on and a rescue attempt failed, the crisis undermined the ability of the Carter administration to continue the Camp David process. It also played a major role in the defeat of Carter in the 1980 election. When the hostages were finally released, Americans seemed disposed to let the dust settle and await further developments within Iran.

The hostages were released as Ronald Reagan took the presidential oath, thus freeing his administration to return to the central question of Arab-Israeli relations. Although Reagan had campaigned on a platform of closer support for Israel and much of his rhetoric resembled that of Dulles, his administration was soon pursuing essentially the same approach as Kissinger and Carter. Dependence on Arab oil and a desire to support anti-Communist Arab states, such as Egypt, Jordan, and Saudi Arabia, balanced the political commitment to Israel, and the administration began supporting a policy of major arms sales to Egypt and Saudi Arabia as well as to Israel.

Reluctantly the Reagan administration was forced to confront what had become the major block to Arab-Israeli peace—the problem of the Palestinians. The 600,000 refugees of 1948 had become the 4,000,000 Palestinians of 1980 spread throughout the Arab world and vehemently insistent in their demand for their own homeland. The Palestinians had first relied on Arab states like Egypt to champion their cause, but by the end of the 1960s they became more self-assertive. By 1968 the Palestine Liberation Organization (PLO), under Jerusalem-born Yassir Arafat, emerged as the leader of Palestinian nationalism. Dedicated to an Arab state in Palestine and hostile to the very existence of Israel, the PLO resorted to terrorist attacks on Israel and Israelis to gain attention for its cause. By 1974 Arab states recognized the PLO as the sole representative of the Palestinians, and Arafat made a dramatic appeal at the United Nations which accorded his organization observer status during the same year.

Palestinian nationalism forced U.S. leaders to weigh the old American principle of self-determination against the nation's traditional policy for support for Israel. Complicating the foreign policy debate was strong domestic political support for Israel. Well-educated, influential, and with a high voting rate in key states, American Jews consistently pressured the legislative and executive alike on behalf of Israel's position and contributed impressive amounts of private financial support to Israel. By the 1980s, American Jews were joined by American Protestant fundamentalists who saw the Jewish state as a fulfillment of biblical prophecy and joined to urge virtually unquestioned support for Israel.

Bolstered by such powerful allies in America, successive Israeli governments refused even to consider negotiations with the PLO, and American leaders who sought to support, or even establish contacts with, the PLO risked encountering the full fury of politically powerful Israeli supporters within the United States. Still, increasingly in the 1980s some Palestinian settlement seemed a keystone of any durable Middle Eastern peacemaking.

The Palestinian issue led directly to the Lebanese crisis of 1982. The once peaceful nation of Lebanon had become the major base of the PLO in the late 1970s. Palestinian raids, Israeli retaliation, and fragile cease-fires followed one another in rapid succession. Quickly Lebanese sovereignty succumbed to raids by Palestinian guerrillas against Israel and strong Israeli counterstrikes against guerrilla bases in Lebanon. Moslem-Christian hostility in Lebanon ignited into a new round of bloody civil war, and a Syrian occupation—originally aimed at ending the civil strife—became itself a source of instability. The final blow came in June 1982 when Israel, determined to end the use of Lebanon as a base for terrorism and seeking to defuse growing Palestinian unrest on the West Bank, launched a full-scale invasion of Lebanon and drove all the way to Beirut. The resultant civilian deaths caused by American-made Israeli weapons and the massacre of Palestinian civilians by Israel's Christian Lebanese allies prompted a major U.S. negotiating effort under Ambassador Philip Habib and the dispatch of American marines to Lebanon as part of an international peace-keeping force.

Neither the Israeli invasion nor American participation in the peacekeeping brought peace to Lebanon. Cease-fires, truces, conferences, and fighting followed in seemingly endless succession. Unable to bring its power to bear and stung by incidents, such as the terrorist bombing of the Beirut marine headquarters in April 1983, the United States withdrew its forces in 1984. Israel, failing to link its withdrawal to a broad settlement, did likewise in 1985. By 1986 the legacy of the Lebanon invasion appeared to be a weakened PLO, humiliated and further fractionalized by the Israeli invasion and a resultant increase in terrorist incidents against the United States and Israel. In 1984 and 1985 terrorism was so rampant that *Time* magazine considered the masked terrorist as its symbolic Man of the Year in 1984, and in the latter year Americans died in terrorist attacks on airplanes, ocean liners, and airports. Angry rhetoric and countermeasures were largely as ineffective as the intervention in Lebanon, and by 1986 the possibility of terrorist action spawned in the Middle East was a major concern of American leaders.

Increasingly there were calls for a peace in the region which might undercut the festering of terrorism, and in 1986 optimists took encouragement from signs that the PLO might be close to dropping its long-standing refusal to recognize Israel's existence, and that some type of an agreement, perhaps linking the Palestinians to Jordan, might be possible. Pessimists, however, recalled other lost opportunities and wondered if the Palestinians had sufficient unity to negotiate and if the Israelis had the commitment, unity, and confidence to take chances for any major breakthrough.

Although the possibility of peace in the Middle East remains uncertain at this time, the acknowledged primacy of the United States in the diplomacy of peacemaking underscores how deeply America has become embroiled in the region since World War II. The limited interests of 1945 have been replaced by a recognition that the United States has a major economic, political, and strategic stake in the area. Lack of involvement in the region gave way to a major superpower confrontation in 1973 and the fear that the Middle East had become the most likely touchstone of a third world war. This concern was accentuated in 1980 when the Carter administration intimated that it might use nuclear weapons if Soviet intervention threatened the oil supply of the Persian Gulf. Even interest in oil, recognized in 1945, had assumed vastly greater importance by the 1980s. Some elements in Middle Eastern diplomacy are unique, notably Israeli relations in which political and emotional commitments conflict with strategic and economic interests. Yet in other areas such as Iran the American experience has been typical of Third World diplomacy. Americans had fostered and sought to control change only to emerge as the victims and villains in that process of change. Vital, complicated, and dangerous, major U.S. involvement in the Middle East seems likely to continue for the rest of the century.

By 1986 the very concept of the Third World appeared less valid. The enormous divergence of economic status, national interests, and political alliances in the nonaligned nations makes generalizations difficult and concerted policy toward them all but impossible. Nonaligned countries still gather at meetings and seek unified common policies in international bodies, but local conflicts often override common global positions. Wars and boundary disputes between countries like Iran and Iraq and Ethiopia and Somalia are far more important to these nations than maintaining identical positions on

Israel, nuclear arms, and economic development. The U.S.-Chinese rapprochement of the 1970s also has blunted common positions as China denounced, with invectives as intense as its anti-American diatribes of the 1950s, Soviet attempts at hegemony in the region. In areas as far apart as Angola, Kampuchea, and Afghanistan, the United States and China found common cause in opposing Soviet activities.

The 1970s success of OPEC, whose members had claimed emerging nation status, created economic rifts within the Third World. Talk of common economic interests between oil-rich Saudi Arabia and destitute Bangladesh is ludicrous. Indeed, the rampant worldwide inflation of the 1970s, caused in large measure by the astronomical OPEC price hikes, produced greater economic hardship in developing countries than in the West. The very economic fragility of many nonaligned countries also undermined attempts at collective positions because nations in that group were increasingly more concerned with their own internal problems than with worldwide neutralist positions. The collapse of a common OPEC production and pricing agreement in 1985 underscored the divisions even in Third World countries with seemingly common interests.

American attitudes concerning the Third World also have changed. In the aftermath of Vietnam the United States seemed much less interested in massive involvement in the divided and weak Third World. Selected areas like the Persian Gulf might involve vital interests, but in general American policy toward underdeveloped countries has emphasized political activity over military intervention as consideration of intervention in Angola, Iran, and El Salvador encountered fierce opposition cries of "no more Vietnams." The Carter administration downplayed ideology, and even the Reagan administration, whose rhetoric sounded like a return to the days of Dulles, if not John Wayne, and whose actions revealed greater willingness to use military force, seemed reluctant to launch a full-scale U.S. military involvement. The marines rushed to Beirut in 1983 but were withdrawn in the face of a situation beyond American power to control, aid to anti-Communist forces in Angola and Nicaragua remained limited as of 1986, and even the volatile and emotionally charged issue of reaction to terrorism evoked only limited military responses from the United States. Underscoring the diminution of American activity was a leveling off in the amount of American economic assistance to developing countries from the time of Nixon to that of Reagan. The $4.487 billion in foreign assistance budgeted for 1984 in constant dollars amounted to less assistance than the $2.47 billion in 1974. Moreover, the decline was likely to continue as the U.S. government looked for budget reductions in the 1980s. As of 1986 a more pragmatic, less ideological approach to the diverse, fragmented Third World seemed both likely and wise. The impact of this new approach on the tangled web of Middle Eastern diplomacy is yet to be determined.

Sources and Suggested Readings

Blair, John M. *The Control of Oil.* New York, 1976.

Kaufman, Burton I. *The Oil Cartel Case: A Documentary Study of Anti-Trust Activity in the Cold War.* Westport, 1978.

Kimche, Jon. *There Could Have Been Peace: The Untold Story of Why We Failed with Palestine and Again with Israel.* New York, 1973.

Kuniholm, Bruce R. *The Origins of the Cold War in the Near East: Great Power Conflicts and Diplomacy in Iran, Turkey, and Greece.* Princeton, 1980.

LaFeber, Walter. *America, Russia, and the Cold War.* New York, 1976.

Neff, Donald. *Warriors at Suez: Eisenhower Takes America into the Middle East.* New York, 1981.

Pierre, Andrew J. *The Global Politics of Arms Sales.* Princeton, 1982.

Quandt, William B. *Decade of Decisions: American Policy Toward the Arab-Israeli Conflict, 1967–1976.* Berkeley, 1977.

Rubin, Barry. *Paved with Good Intentions: The American Experience and Iran.* New York, 1980.

Sampson, Anthony. *The Seven Sisters: The Great Oil Companies and the World They Shaped.* New York, 1975.

Stookey, Robert W. *America and the Arab States: An Uneasy Encounter.* New York, 1975.

Tillman, Seth P. *The United States in the Middle East: Interests and Obstacles.* Bloomington, 1982.

U.S. Department of State. *Foreign Relations of the United States, 1940–1954.* Washington, 1949–1984.

American Foreign Policy:
Past and Future

During the twentieth century the United States experienced a rise to global preeminence without historical precedent in terms of its rapidity and scope. Until 1941 the nation's emergence was gradual, almost imperceptible, but World War II and the Cold War marked a dramatic change, giving rise to what has been called the Pax Americana of the 1950s and 1960s. The United States emerged from the Second World War the dominant economic power in the world, with its industrial base untouched and its economy functioning full throttle. In terms of military power it reigned supreme, and the atomic monopoly added a new and awesome dimension. In the aftermath of the war, the United States also displayed a willingness to use its power on a global scale. Pearl Harbor destroyed the long-standing illusion that geography guaranteed security, and advances in technology fed the new and radically different notion that changes in the status quo anywhere might endanger American interests. The emergence of the Soviet Union as a perceived threat and the development of the policy of containment in response to that threat provided the basis for global involvement. Those who shaped postwar American foreign policy were certain that national survival required involvement in distant areas, and that the United States had the power to mold the world to its image.

In the aftermath of World War II, therefore, the nation took on all the trappings of great-power status. By the early 1950s it had alliances with more than fifty countries, and its military bases spanned the globe. It maintained a large peacetime military establishment and an annual defense budget in the billions of dollars. In the more innocent time before World War II, intelligence operations had seemed downright un-American: "Gentlemen do not read each other's mail," President Herbert Hoover's Secretary of State Henry L. Stimson had once snarled. By contrast, a government report of the

1950s warned that, in the face of an "implacable" Soviet enemy, "long-standing American concepts of 'fair play' must be reconsidered. We must develop effective espionage and counterespionage services and must learn to subvert, sabotage, and destroy our enemies by more clever, more sophisticated, and more effective methods than those used against us." By the mid-1950s the United States was widely employing clandestine operations to overthrow governments perceived as unfriendly.

In a variety of ways the nation's exercise of power challenged traditional self-images of innocence. To be sure, the Marshall Plan and the reconstruction of Japan were acts of great benevolence as well as self-interest, and foreign aid programs, such as Point Four and the Alliance for Progress, reflected a genuine concern for raising living standards in less developed nations. These programs also supported perceived security interests, however, and in general the United States used its power much as other great nations had in times past. In the realm of atomic energy, it pursued the elusive goal of nuclear superiority, stimulating an arms race that remains unchecked nearly forty years later. Attempting to uphold the status quo in a revolutionary world, it propped up governments that did not stand for its own principles and were not responsive to the needs of their own people. It overthrew elected governments in Iran, Guatemala, and Chile when they seemed to threaten U.S. interests. Ultimately, in the case of Vietnam, it sacrificed more than 58,000 lives and billions of dollars in a futile and destructive effort to keep a friendly, non-Communist government in power.

The Pax Americana also challenged what the British scholar D. W. Brogan has called the illusion of American omnipotence, the belief that the nation could accomplish anything to which it set its mind. Perhaps the fundamental lesson of recent history is that, even at the height of its power, the United States could not work its will throughout the world. It was unable to impose on Stalin's Russia, or even Churchill's Britain, its own vision of the postwar world. It could not prevent, except at a cost deemed unacceptable, the Soviet conquest of Eastern Europe at the end of World War II and the Communist victory in China in 1949. It could not win a traditional military victory in Korea without incurring risks regarded as excessive. Short-term successes in Iran and Guatemala were more than matched at the end of the 1950s by failure in Cuba, a direct challenge in an area of traditional American hegemony.

Inevitably, America's decline from world preeminence was almost as rapid as its rise. To some extent, ironically, the United States contributed to its own demise. The reconstruction of Western Europe and Japan made possible the rise of industrial rivals that by the late 1960s were competing vigorously with the United States in world markets. The Soviet Union recovered rapidly from World War II on its own, and, although it lagged behind the Western nations in productivity and technological advancement, it matched the United States in military and nuclear power. Perhaps, more importantly, in the 1960s the bipolar, Europe-oriented world increasingly gave way to a polycentric world in which numerous nations were able to exert significant power in their own regions. Once compliant Third World nations found new leverage in their control of raw materials, especially energy resources, so desperately needed by the advanced nations.

The debacle in Vietnam brought out into the open the flaws in U.S. globalist policies and thus stands as something of a watershed in the postwar era. American support for various South Vietnamese governments and the lavish and destructive use of American firepower in a small backward country raised, in the most blatant form, basic moral questions regarding the use of American power. The vast commitment of the nation's resources, in an area whose centrality to U.S. interests was at best open to question, exposed fallacies in a globalist policy that failed to set priorities among competing interests. The inability of the United States to achieve its objectives in Vietnam, despite the expenditure of billions of dollars and the use of massive military force, suggested that U.S. power, however great, had distinct limits.

The first post-Vietnam president, Jimmy Carter, made deliberate efforts to adjust to the new world conditions. To restore a moral component to U.S. foreign policy, he vowed to support human rights across the world. Publicly Carter downplayed the Cold War conflict with the Soviet Union, and he sought to enlarge on the arms control agreements negotiated by his predecessors. Carter and his Secretary of State Cyrus Vance openly spoke of the limits of American power, cautiously refrained from intervention in revolutions in Nicaragua and Iran, attempted to reduce the nation's dependence on external sources of energy, and even sought to scale down some of the commitments undertaken during the globalist era.

Carter's foreign policy bore a huge political price tag. Frustrated by failure in Vietnam and increasingly squeezed economically by an inflation that resulted in part from the high price of Middle Eastern oil, Americans were in no mood to hear that they must trim their expectations. The much publicized day-by-day captivity of a group of American hostages by Iranian militants created still deeper anger, and a badly bungled rescue mission added to the sense of frustration. The Soviet invasion of Afghanistan in December 1979 revived the anticommunism that had ebbed in the early 1970s, stirring a mood reminiscent of the early Cold War. Carter quickly adapted. To punish the Soviets, he boycotted the 1980 Moscow Olympic Games, and he imposed an embargo on grain shipments. Emulating Harry S. Truman in 1947, he promulgated the Carter Doctrine, warning that Soviet intrusions into the Persian Gulf would bring a forceful American response. Carter's belated conversion to Cold Warrior was inadequate to save him politically. He unfortunately became a symbol of the national impotence that so vexed Americans in the late 1970s and was defeated overwhelmingly in 1980.

His successor, Republican Ronald Reagan, appeared determined to restore the global containment policy and the glory days of the 1950s. Reagan's speeches extolled traditional American virtues and evoked heroic images from the nation's past. His shrill anti-Soviet rhetoric would have embarrassed John Foster Dulles. Soviet leaders were willing to "commit any crime" to achieve their goal of world domination, Reagan charged. The Soviet Union was an "evil empire" destined for the "ash heap of history." On the all-important issue of arms control, he proclaimed that the United States would negotiate only after it had closed the "window of vulnerability" that had opened under Carter. Reagan proceeded with plans to install new missile systems at home and in Europe, and he launched forth on a huge program of rearmament that by late 1985 had cost $1.2 trillion. Like his Cold War predecessors, he viewed left-wing revolutions throughout the world as mere extensions of Soviet influence. In embattled Central America the administration firmly committed itself to the defense of the right-wing government of El Salvador against leftist insurgents, and it initiated a not-so-covert war to support a group of rebels, which Reagan labeled "freedom fighters," against the leftist Sandinista government of Nicaragua. In 1983 the administration sent troops to tiny Grenada in the Caribbean to unseat a pro-Cuban group that recently had taken power. It even applied Cold War formulas to the political jungle that was the Middle East, sending 200 marines to sustain an inherently unworkable peace in Lebanon.

Reagan's actions did not always agree with his militant rhetoric, however. He moved slowly in Central America, stopping well short of sending U.S. troops. When the situation in Lebanon became hopelessly confused and the marines' position became untenable, he withdrew them. Although he had promised "swift and effective retribution" against international terrorists, Reagan responded to actual terrorist activities with prudence and restraint, at least until his April 1986 attack on Libya. A long-time supporter of the Taiwan government, in office he gradually warmed up to the People's Republic of China, especially after Beijing appeared to shift its internal policies in a capitalist direction. Most important, in his successful 1984 campaign for reelection and afterward, Reagan increasingly spoke the language of coexistence with the "evil empire." Arms talks that had long been stalled were revived, and in the fall of 1985 the old anti-Communist met with new Soviet leader Mikhail Gorbachev in Geneva. No agreements resulted, but a new series of summits were planned, and the Cold War tension that had grown so dramatically since 1979 began to ease at least slightly.

One year past the mid-point of his presidency, the results of Reagan's internationalism remained uncertain. His rearmament program and his rhetoric, along with the economic recovery of the early 1980s, seemed to restore the nation's pride and self-confidence, and in Reagan's own words America was "standing tall" by the middle of the decade. Along with this return of self-confidence, however, were signs of a resurgent nationalism that had potentially ugly manifestations and might prove difficult to keep in check. Reagan's rhetoric might have raised expectations that could not be fulfilled. The superpowers were discussing arms limitation again, but agreement still eluded them, and each year's delay widened the already yawning gap between runaway technology and effective arms control. In Central America the Reagan policies had produced a stalemate, not solutions, and the only thing that seemed certain was more bloodshed. The administration, perhaps wisely, had not even sought solutions in the volatile Middle East. Through luck as much as skill, Reagan thus far had avoided major crises, but he also had not been able to attain major diplomatic successes. Nor had he succeeded in building a new consensus on U.S. foreign policy, and the nation remained deeply divided on such issues as intervention in Third World countries.

On the eve of the twenty-first century, the world seemed less stable than at any time in the past. The proliferation of nuclear weapons; the emergence of a bewildering number of new nations; and the existence of a baffling array of regional, local, and internal conflicts in areas ranging from the Philippines to South Africa all combined to produce a profoundly confusing and volatile world. The uncertain triangular relationship between the United States, the Soviet

Union, and China contributed to the instability. The emergence of dynamic new leadership in Moscow in the form of Gorbachev added a critical element that might result in greater harmony in superpower relations or in new and ominous challenges. A continuing tendency toward stagnation in some of the industrial nations, a spiraling American budget deficit, and a staggering debt in the less developed nations had possibly greater implications for global stability and peace than more traditional diplomatic issues.

The United States remained in the mid-1980s, in a military and economic sense, one of the world's two legitimate superpowers. The most pressing—and to this point unaddressed—question was for what purposes and with what effect American power could and should be employed. What seemed to be needed was a new "internationalism" that would bring into balance the defense of vital interests, with acknowledged limits to U.S. power and to the applicability of American ideals, and a new diplomacy that was astute, subtle, and flexible enough to manage Soviet-American competition at a safe level and influence the outcome of other world issues in a way that would avoid military intervention and sustain support at home. If its own history had poorly prepared it for such a challenging task, the history of twentieth-century American foreign policy suggested the danger and folly of other alternatives.

Lexington, Kentucky   G.C.H.
May 1986

Index

Acheson, Dean G.: 129, 132, 134–35, 149
Adams, Brooks: 49–50
Adler, Selig: 53, 54
Afghanistan: 159, 218, 224
Africa: 2, 3; invaded in World War II, 113;
  Cubans fighting in, 191, 195–96;
  nationalism in, 172, 201
Agent General for Reparations: 60, 61
Agricultural Adjustment Act: 75
Aguinaldo, Emilio: 1, 8
Albania: 85
Alemán, Miguel: 185
Algeria: 172, 207, 208
Allende, Salvador: 195
Alliance for Progress: 189–91, 193–94, 222
Alsace-Lorraine: 42
Alsop, Joseph: 84–86
American Committee for the Outlawry of
  War: 65
American Peace Award: 63
Angola: 195–96, 218
Antiballistic missile (ABM): 158
Anti-Comintern Pact: 79
Anti-Imperialist League: 2
Appeasement: of Hitler, 82, 84–85, 87,
  91–92, 109; of Japan, 102
Arabic (British vessel): 29; *Arabic*
  Pledge, 29
Arab-Israeli wars: in 1948–49, 204, 206; in
  1967, 209–10; in 1973, 210–11, 213, 217.
  See also Suez crisis
Arafat, Yassir: 215
Arbenz, Jacobo: 187
Arévalo, Juan José: 187, 191
Argentina: 99, 160, 184, 185, 188, 191,
  196, 197
Arms race: before World War I, 63; in
  1920s, 63–64; in 1930s, 74, 76–80; in
  atomic weapons, 150, 151, 152–62; in
  1980s, 68, 224

Arms trade (U.S.): to Allies in World War I,
  25–26; and Nye Committee, 77; in
  World War II (*see* Lend-Lease); to
  South Vietnam, 172–73, 177–78; to
  Israel, 210, 215; to Iran, 214; to Egypt,
  215; to Saudi Arabia, 215
Association of Southeast Asian Nations
  (ASEAN): 144
Aswan Dam: 208
Atlantic Charter: 111, 112, 117, 119
Atomic bomb: dropping of, 120–21, 128,
  222 (*see also* Hiroshima; Nagasaki);
  possible use of during Korean War,
  137; in Middle East, 217; development
  of, 147–49
Atomic diplomacy: 122–23, 149–51, 159–61,
  221
Atomic Energy Act (1949): 149, 151, 153
Atomic Energy Act (1954): 153
Atomic Energy Commission: 151
Attlee, Clement R.: 120
Attrition strategy: 176, 179
Austin, Warren R.: 86
Australia: 100, 142, 143
Austria: 42, 44, 82, 91
Azerbaijan: 202

B-17 bomber: 102
B-52 bomber: 155
Baghdad Pact. *See* Central Treaty
  Organization
Baker, Ray Stannard: 39
Bandung Conference: 143, 206
Bangladesh: 218
Bankers (U.S.): and China, 16–17; and
  World War I, 25, 32; in 1920s, 60; in
  1930s, 75; and Nye Committee, 77; and
  Latin America, 185
Bank for International Settlements: 62

Baruch, Bernard M.: 149–50
Baruch Plan: 149, 150
Batista, Fulgencio: 185
Battle of the Bulge: 117
Bavaria: 39
Bay of Pigs incident: 189–90
Beard, Charles A.: 87
Begin, Menachem: 213
Beirut: 208, 216, 218
Belgium: 25, 29, 59, 61, 92, 206
Berlin crisis (1961): 155
Betancourt, Rómulo: 189
Beveridge, Albert J.: 3
Birdsall, Paul: 45
Black Sea straits: 123
Bluefields (Nicaragua): 15
Bogotá: 184
Bok, Edward W.: 63
Bolivia: 187–88, 190
Bolshevik Revolution and bolshevism: 31,
    39, 59, 75, 109
Borah, William E.: 48, 64, 76, 77
Bosch, Juan: 193
Boxers (China): 9
Boyden, Roland: 57
Bradley, Omar N.: 137
Brazil: 160, 184, 185, 193, 196
Briand, Aristide: 65
Brinkmanship: 142
British Guiana: 93, 191. *See also* Guyana
Brogan, D. W.: 222
Bryan, William Jennings: 2
Buddhists: 174
Buenos Aires Conference: 78–81
Bunau-Varilla, Philippe: 11, 13
Bureau of Foreign and Domestic
    Commerce: 66
Burgess, John W.: 2
Burma: 168
Burnham, Linden Forbes: 191
Burns, James MacGregor: 112

Cairo Conference: 127
Cambodia: 140, 143, 176, 178, 180. *See also*
    Kampuchea
Camp David agreement: 213, 215
Canada: 51, 123, 161, 183
Carter, Jimmy: and nuclear weapons, 159,
    161; and Latin America, 196–97; and
    Middle East, 213–15, 217, 218; and new

Cold War, 223–24
Carter Doctrine: 224
"Cash and carry" policy: 79–80, 92, 94
Castillo Armas, Carlos: 187
Castro, Cipriano: 13
Castro, Fidel: 7, 169, 188–91, 193, 195–96,
    198–99
Castro, Raúl: 191
Central Intelligence Agency (CIA): 187,
    189, 190, 204
Central Powers: 37, 38
Central Treaty Organization: 204, 206
Chamberlain, Neville: 80–82, 84, 85, 87
Chamizal ceremony: 194
Chapultepec Conference: 184
Chiang Kai-shek. *See* Jiang Jieshi
Chile: 195, 196, 222
China: U.S. pre-World War I interest in,
    8–10, 15–19, 44, 64; and Sino-Japanese
    War, 75, 81, 93, 100–02, 114, 117; U.S.
    military aid in 1930s, 98, 100, 103; and
    proposed appeasement of Japan,
    102–03; and U.S. assistance during
    World War II, 93; in peacemaking
    discussions after World War II, 115,
    119, 123, 127–29; and USSR, 128–29,
    131; civil war in, 127–32; "fall" of, 132,
    167, 168, 170, 222. For events after
    1949, *see* People's Republic of China;
    Republic of China
China lobby: 130, 132, 134–35
China Market: 4, 7, 8, 133
China White Paper: 132
Chinchou-Aigun Railroad: 17
Church Committee Report: 190
Churchill, Winston: before American entry
    into World War II, 98, 107, 109–12; on
    USSR as ally in World War II, 109–12;
    and second front controversy, 112–14;
    at Tehran, 115–16; at Yalta, 116–17; at
    Potsdam, 119–20; loses election, 120;
    and Truman, 120–21; on postwar
    world, 123
Civilian Conservation Corps (CCC): 75
Clayton, William: 99
Clemenceau, Georges: 39–41, 43–45
Cleveland, Grover: 5, 17
Cold War: World War II and origins of,
    107–24, 221; in Asia, 127–45; and
    Korean War, 134–38; and atomic
    diplomacy, 122, 149–53; and Cuban

missile crisis, 190; and Vietnam, 166–69; and Latin America, 193, 196, 198, 224; and Middle East, 202, 205–06, 208, 210–13, 224–25; exposes limits on American power, 222, 223; in 1980s, 224–26

Colombia: 11–13, 184–85, 188

Communism and Communists: in China, 129–32; in Cuba, 188–89, 193; in Greece, 132; in Indonesia, 142; in Iran, 202; in Korea, 134; in Latin America, 187, 191, 193, 198; in Middle East, 207, 208; in Vietnam, 166–67, 169–71, 173

Congress of Vienna (1815): 46

Containment policy: Truman and, 123–24, 132, 168; and Korea, 135; and Vietnam, 165, 170–71; limitations of, 206–07, 221, 224

Coolidge, Calvin: 55–57, 61, 63, 65, 67

Copper: 92

Costa Rica: 15, 188

Council of Foreign Ministers: 131

Cox, James M.: 72

Credibility: 169–71

Cuba: U.S. economic and political expansion in, 2, 4–8, 13, 16, 18, 19, 66; and Spanish-American War, 4–6; revolution in, 184–85, 188–90, 193, 222; and USSR, 190–91, 195, 198–99; sends troops to Africa, 195–96

Cuban missile crisis: 155–56, 158, 169, 190, 209

Czechoslovakia: 84, 85, 87, 91, 98, 99, 100

Dairen: 128

Daladier, Edouard: 84

Dalleck, Robert: 87–88, 118

Danzig, Free State of: 85, 86

Davis, Norman: 74, 80, 81

Dawes, Charles G.: 60

Dawes Committee: 60

Dawes Plan: 61, 62, 69

D-day (June 6, 1944): 108, 118

DeBenedetti, Charles: 63

Declaration on Liberated Europe: 117, 119

Democratic party (U.S.): 47, 55, 72, 85, 123, 140, 156, 192; and the fall of China, 170; and Vietnam, 170; and Israel, 209

Democratic Republic of Vietnam. *See* North Vietnam

Denmark: 92

Destroyers-for-bases deal: 93

Détente: 69, 158, 169

Díaz, Adolfo: 16

Dienbienphu: 172

Disarmament: in 1920s, 57, 63–64, 67, 68; in 1930s, 74, 78–79; and atomic weapons, 149–50, 152–55, 157–62

Dollar diplomacy: 14–17

Dominican formula: 15–16, 17

Dominican Republic: 14, 15–16, 184, 185–86, 188, 191, 193

Domino theory: 168, 169, 171

Draft, military: 92

Drug abuse and drug trade: 57, 199

Duarte, José Napoleón: 197

Dulles, Allen W.: 187

Dulles, Foster Rhea: 53

Dulles, John Foster: 140, 142, 153, 187, 205–07, 215, 218, 224

Eastern Europe: after World War I, 59; in World War II, 108, 110; in post-World War II peace talks, 115–17, 119; Russian control of, 123, 129, 131, 143, 168, 222

East Manchurian Railway: 17, 128

East Prussia: 85

The Economic Consequences of the Peace (Keynes): 60

Economic diplomacy (U.S.): before World War I, 2–19; in 1920s, 53–69. *See also* Investments (U.S.)

Ecuador: 194

Egypt: 204–06, 209–11, 213–15

Eisenhower, Dwight D.: 140, 142; and China, 143; and atomic power, 152–55; and Latin America, 187–88; and Middle East, 205–06, 208, 211

Eisenhower Doctrine: 208

Elections: in Chile, 195; in Korea, 134; in Vietnam, 167, 174

Elections (U.S.): in 1920, 55, 71–72; in 1928, 72; in 1932, 72; in 1936, 78; in 1940, 87; in 1952, 142, 170; in 1960, 192; in 1980, 197, 215; in 1984, 225

El Salvador: 15, 197, 218, 224

Embargoes (U.S.): of weapons, 27, 77, 78, 82, 85, 86; of iron and steel, 94, 101; of

Embargoes (U.S). *(continued)*
grain, 224
Estrada, Juan J.: 15, 16
Ethiopia: 75, 77–78, 195, 217
Ethnic groups, in U.S.: German-Americans, 24; Irish-Americans, 24; Hispanic-Americans, 192; Jewish-Americans, 24, 202, 205, 215–16; Polish-Americans, 115; Scandinavian-Americans, 24
European Recovery Program. *See* Marshall Plan

Fallout, atomic: 154, 155, 157, 161
Far Eastern Advisory Commission: 129
Fascism: in Spain, 78, 82; in Latin America, 198
Feminists: 63
Figueres, José "Pepe": 188
Finland: 112
Five-Power Treaty: 64, 65
Ford, Gerald R.: 159, 161
Foreign Affairs: 152
Formosa: 132. *See also* Republic of China
Forrestal, James V.: 138
"Four Policemen": 115
Four-Power Treaty: 64
Fourteen Points: 36–38, 40, 43, 44
France: as competitor for empire, 7, 8, 11, 16, 17; in World War I, 31, 32; at Versailles peace talks, 36, 38–45, 49, 51; in 1920s, 59–61, 64, 65; in 1930s, 75, 79, 80; and Spain, 82; and appeasement of Hitler, 84, 85, 92, 109; and Poland, 85, 86, 92; defeated by Germany, 92, 93, 98, 99, 110; liberated, 108, 111, 115, 118; and post-World War II imperialism in Asia, 139; in SEATO, 142, 143; and China, 144; and atomic weapons, 151, 153, 157, 160; and Indochina, 165–69, 171–72, 179; and Middle East, 205–06, 208
Franco, Francisco: 82

Gaddis, John Lewis: 124
Gaitán, Jorge Eliécer: 184
Gasoline: 92, 211
Gaza Strip: 205, 208, 209
General Electric Company: 60
General System of Preferences (GSP): 194

Geneva Accords: 171
Geneva Conference (1927): 65
Geneva Conference (1954): 165, 167, 172
Germany: as competitor for empire, 3, 7, 8, 13, 14, 16, 17, 19; and World War I, 24–33; navy of, 28–30 (*see also* Submarines); and Versailles treaty, 38–39, 41–46, 49, 51; in 1920s, 59–63; and Japan, 79, 94, 96, 101; and Poland, 85, 86, 92, 98; and English and French appeasement, 82, 84–85, 87, 91–92, 109; and 1930s U.S. neutrality, 86, 92, 93; and USSR, 86, 96, 102, 108–11; U.S. views on 1930s expansionism of, 96–101, 104; military strategy of, 113–14
Glass, Carter: 66
Gleason, S. Everett: 87
Golan Heights: 209
Good Neighbor policy: 67, 78
Gorbachev, Mikhail S.: 225, 226
Great Britain: as competitor for empire, 3, 8, 11, 13, 14, 16, 17; and World War I, 23–32; navy of, 27, 28, 94–95, 98, 100, 104; at Versailles peace talks, 36, 38–40, 42–45; in 1920s, 60, 64, 65; in 1930s, 79, 80; and appeasement of Germany, 82, 84–85, 87, 91–92, 109; and Spain, 82; and Poland, 85, 86, 92, 110; declares war on Germany, 86, 92; receives American aid before Pearl Harbor, 92–95, 111; fights in Europe, 92, 93, 108; and Japanese expansionism, 93, 100–01, 128; fears German invasion, 98; and aid to USSR in World War II, 109–11; imperial designs after World War II, 109, 112, 115, 123, 128, 139, 141, 166; in SEATO, 142, 143; and atomic weapons testing, 151, 153, 154, 156–57; and war in Malvinas, 197; and Middle East, 202, 204–08; and oil, 212
Great Depression: 63; U.S. diplomacy during, 71–88
Great Society: 175
Greece: 85, 110, 123, 132
USS *Greer:* 95
Grenada: 197, 224
Gromyko, Andrei: 150
Guam: 1, 6
Guatemala: 187, 191, 222

Guevara, Ernesto "Che": 187, 188, 190
Guyana: 191. *See also* British Guiana

Habib, Philip: 216
Haile Selassie: 78
Haiphong harbor: 178
Haiti: 6, 66
Hamilton, Alexander: 40
Harding, Warren G.: 47, 55, 56, 57, 63, 64
Harriman, W. Averell: 118
Havana: 183
Hawaii: 1, 5, 6, 94, 97, 103
Hawley-Smoot Act: 62
Hay, John M.: 9, 10, 11, 13
Hay-Herrán Treaty: 11
Herrán, Tomás: 11
Hickenlooper Amendment: 195
Hinton, Harold C.: 144
Hiroshima: 122, 128, 129, 147
Hitler, Adolf: 79; and European
    appeasement of, 82, 84–85, 91–92, 108;
    at Munich, 84–85; and Poland, 85, 86;
    and USSR, 86, 96, 108; U.S. views of,
    86, 98–99; on Grand Alliance, 107
Ho Chi Minh: 139, 166, 167, 175, 179
Hoff-Wilson, Joan: 55
Hogan, Michael J.: 58
Holocaust: 204
Honduras: 15, 187, 191, 197
Hong Kong: 93
Hoover, Herbert C.: during World War I,
    39; as secretary of commerce, 55, 56,
    66; as president, 57, 62, 63, 72, 78, 80,
    221; and Latin America, 183
Hopkins, Harry: 119
House, Edward M.: 30, 40, 43, 76
House-Grey Memorandum: 30
Hughes, Charles Evans: 55–58, 64, 67
Hughes Plan: 60
Hukuang Railway: 16
Hull, Cordell: and Great Depression
    diplomacy, 73–75, 77, 78, 81–82,
    84–86; and beginning of World War II,
    91, 93–95, 97, 101–04; and Latin
    America, 187
Humanitarianism and human rights: 5, 67,
    196, 197, 223
Humphrey, George M.: 187
Hungary: 39, 110
Hurley, Patrick J.: 130
Hydrogen bomb: 151

Ibn Saud, Abdul-Aziz: 202
Idris (king of Libya): 207
Imperialism: in 1898–1912, 1–19; affects
    Versailles peace talks, 42, 44; and
    European hopes after World War II,
    109, 112, 115, 123, 128, 139, 141, 166
Inchon: 136
"Independent internationalism": 55, 66
India: 143, 160–61, 168, 207
Indian Ocean: 101
Indochina: 93–94, 96, 127, 133, 139; First
    Indochina War, 172, 179
Indonesia: 127, 133, 139, 141–44, 168, 207
The Inquiry (Wilson commission): 35
Inter-American Treaty of Reciprocal
    Assistance: 184, 198
Intercontinental ballistic missile (ICBM):
    152
International Atomic Energy Agency:
    152–53, 155, 160
International Great Society: 194
International Telephone and Telegraph
    (ITT): 195
Investments (U.S.): in Cuba, 5, 7; in China,
    16; in Caribbean, 18, 66. *See also*
    Bankers (U.S.); General Electric
    Company; International Telephone
    and Telegraph; J. P. Morgan and
    Company; United Fruit Company
Iran: 123; under Mossadegh, 202, 204;
    under Reza Pahlavi, 206, 208, 211, 212,
    214; under Khomeini, 214–15, 217, 218,
    222–24
Iraq: 206, 207, 208, 212, 217
Iriye, Akira: 139
Iron and steel: 78, 97
Isolationism (U.S.): 21, 32; in 1920s, 52, 69,
    71; in 1930s, 72, 76–81, 85–87, 92
Israel: 160, 201–02, 204–11, 213–17
Italy: 13, 64; at Versailles peace talks, 39,
    40, 42, 44; and Ethiopia, 75, 77–78;
    and appeasement, 82, 84; and 1930s
    American neutrality, 86; as Axis
    partner, 94; invaded by Allies, 113

Jagan, Cheddi: 191
Japan: and Western imperialism in Asia, 8,
    9, 10, 16, 17, 18, 19; and Versailles
    peace talks, 42, 43, 44; in 1920s, 64, 65;
    and Nazi Germany, 79, 94; and *Panay*
    incident, 80; and Sino-Japanese War,

Japan *(continued)*
81, 93, 100–03; and road to World
War II, 91–104; U.S. cuts off oil to, 94,
96, 102; and USSR, 96, 102, 114, 120,
121, 127–29; U.S. views on
expansionism of, 96–97, 100–04; navy
of, 98, 103; and Great Britain, 100–01;
and atomic bomb, 122, 147–49; U.S.
involvement in after World War II,
123, 127–29, 132–33; signs peace treaty,
133; and Vietnam, 143, 166, 168; and
People's Republic of China, 143–44;
and Middle East, 211
Jefferson, Thomas: 40
Jerusalem: 209, 213
Jiang Jieshi: 114, 127–32, 139, 142
Johnson, Hiram W.: 76, 77
Johnson, Lyndon B.: and Vietnam, 170–72,
175, 177; and Latin America, 192–94;
and Middle East, 209–10
Johnson Act: 76
Johnson Doctrine: 193
Joint Chiefs of Staff (U.S.): 135, 168, 175,
189
Jordan: 204, 206, 208, 209, 215, 217
Jordan River: West Bank, 205, 209, 213,
216
J. P. Morgan and Company: 61, 62

Kampuchea: 214
Katyn Forest massacre: 110
USS *Kearny:* 95
Keating, Kenneth: 190
Kellogg, Frank B.: 56, 60, 65
Kellogg-Briand Pact: 65, 66
Kennan, George F.: 123, 129, 135, 138
Kennedy, John F.: and atomic power, 155,
156; and Vietnam, 168, 170, 175; and
China, 170; and Latin America, 185,
188–92, 195, 196, 198, 199; and Middle
East, 209
Kerosene: 202
Keynes, John Maynard: 37, 41, 42, 44, 45,
59, 60
Khaki Election (Great Britain, 1918): 42
Khomeini, Ayatollah Ruhollah: 214
Khrushchev, Nikita S.: 155, 156, 190
Kimche, Jon: 210
Kim Il-sung: 134, 135, 138
Kintner, Robert: 84, 85, 86

Kissinger, Henry A.: 46, 195, 211, 213, 215
Kissinger Commission Report on Central
America: 198
Knox, Philander C.: 14–18
Konoye, Fumimaro: 101–02
Korea: 10, 114, 123, 127, 129, 133–34. *See
also* North Korea; South Korea
Korean War: 133–39, 207, 222; "lessons" of,
139–40, 168, 173
Kra, Isthmus of: 104
Kuomintang: 129, 131, 132, 139
Kuril Islands: 128
Kursk, battle of: 108

Lach, Donald F.: 145
La Follette, Robert M., Jr.: 76
Lamont, Thomas W.: 62
Langer, William L.: 87
Laos: 140, 143, 176, 178
Latin American Economic System: 195
League to Enforce Peace: 48
League of Nations: Wilson's view of, 37, 41,
43, 44; historians' views of, 45, 46–47,
53; domestic opposition to, 47–51;
Article X, League Covenant, 48, 50,
51; considered during 1920s, 54, 55;
U.S. participation in, 57; legacy of, 66,
71, 72, 75, 114–15
League of Nations Non-Partisan
Association: 63
Lebanon: 204, 208, 216–17, 224–25
Leffler, Melvyn P.: 53, 59
Lend-Lease: 94, 95, 111, 113, 114, 118,
119, 123
Lesser Antilles: 196
Levermore, Charles H.: 63
Levinson, Salmon: 65Libya: 207, 225
Lilienthal, David E.: 149
"Limited war": 36, 137
Lindbergh, Charles A.: 65
Link, Arthur S.: 46, 51
Lippmann, Walter: 48
Literary Digest: 47
Litvinov, Maxim: 112
Lloyd, Henry Demarest: 2
Lloyd George, David: 39, 44, 45, 51
Locarno treaties: 61, 62
Lodge, Henry Cabot: 47, 48, 49, 50, 51, 55
Lodge, Henry Cabot, Jr.: 86
London Conference (1924): 61

London Naval Conference (1930): 65
London Naval Treaty (1909): 25
London World Economic Conference (1933): 75
Luce, Henry R.: 130
Ludlow Amendment: 80
Luftwaffe: 98
Lusitania: 28–29

MacArthur, Douglas: 113, 129, 131, 135–37
McCarthyism: 130, 138, 142, 170
Machiavelli, Niccolò: 46
McKinley, William: 5–10, 15
McMahon, Robert J.: 142
McNamara, Robert S.: 171
Madriz, José: 15
USS *Maine:* 5
Malaya: 93, 96, 100, 127, 133, 139, 141, 168, 173
Malaysia: 144
Malvinas Islands: 197
Manchu dynasty: 17
Manchuria: 10, 16, 17, 97, 114, 117, 129, 131
Manchurian analogy: 169
Manganese: 100
Manhattan Project: 121, 148–49
Mann, Thomas: 193
Mao Zedong: 17, 129, 130, 136, 168
Marshall, George C.: 130, 131, 132
Marshall Plan: 142, 185, 222
"Massive retaliation": 142, 153
Matsu: 143
May, Glenn A.: 8
Mellon, Andrew: 55–56
Mexican War: 40
Mexico: 15, 31, 67, 97, 185, 192, 194, 195
Micronesia: 129
Middle East: in World War II, 101, 129; and diplomacy of oil, 201–19
Minuteman missile: 156
Missile gap: 156, 157
Missiles. *See* Antiballistic missile; Cuban missile crisis; Intercontinental ballistic missile; Minuteman missile; Multiple independently targeted reentry vehicle; MX missile; Polaris missile
Moley, Raymond: 74, 75
Molotov, Vyacheslav M.: 118
Monroe Doctrine: 14, 66, 79
Morgenthau, Henry, Jr.: 73, 86

Morrow, Dwight: 67
Mossadegh, Mohammed: 202, 204
Multiple independently targeted reentry vehicle (MIRV): 158, 159
Munich analogy: 169
Munich Conference: 84, 85, 87
Mussolini, Benito: 84, 85
"Mutual assured destruction" (MAD): 153, 159, 162
MX missile: 159

Nagasaki: 122, 128, 147
Nasser, Gamal Abdel: 205, 206, 208
National Association of Manufacturers: 3
National Council for Prevention of War: 63
Nationalism: 4, 130; in Latin America, 6, 7, 15, 18, 183, 193, 194; in Cuba, 7; in Philippines, 8; in Europe, 38–39, 42, 180; and League of Nations, 48–51; in Asia, 127–28, 133, 139–41, 171, 172, 201; in Korea, 134; and USSR, 170; and the Cold War, 139; and Vietnam, 139, 165–67, 173; and Africa, 172, 201; in Palestine, 204, 205, 215; in Middle East, 204–09
National Liberation Front: 174, 177, 179
National Recovery Administration: 75
National Security Council. *See* NSC-68
Naval arms limitations: 64–66, 98
Nehru, Jawarharlal: 206
Netherlands: 92, 93, 139, 141–42, 166
Netherlands East Indies: 93–94, 96, 97, 141. *See also* Indonesia
Neutrality (U.S.): in World War I, 21–34; and Kellogg-Briand Pact, 66; and 1930s legislation, 77–80, 82, 84–86, 92, 94
Neutrality Act (1935): 77–78
Neutrality Act (1936): 78–79
Neutrality Act (1937): 79–80
New Deal: 75, 76, 83–84, 85, 88
Newfoundland: 93, 111
New Panama Canal Company: 11
New York Globe: 47
New York Herald Tribune: 84
New York Journal: 5
New York Tribune: 3
New Zealand: 100, 142
Ngo Dinh Diem: 173–75, 207
Ngo Dinh Nhu: 173–74

Nicaragua: and U.S. expansionism before
    World War I, 11, 15, 16; in 1920s,
    66, 67; since World War II, 183, 184,
    188, 196–98; in the new Cold War, 218,
    223, 224
Nicolson, Harold: 40, 42, 43, 46
Nine-Power Treaty: 64
Nixon, Richard M.: 218; in 1950s, 142, 144;
    and atomic power, 159; and Vietnam,
    177–78; and Latin America, 188, 189,
    194–95; and Middle East, 210–12, 214
Nixon Doctrine: 144
Nomura, Kichisaburo: 95
North Atlantic Treaty Organization
    (NATO): 135, 137, 142
North Korea: 134, 135, 136, 138
North Sea: 26
North Vietnam: 167, 169, 171, 174–80;
    bombing of, 177, 178–79
Norway: 92
NSC-68: 135, 138, 168
Nuclear energy: 147–62. *See also*
    Atomic bomb
Nuclear Non-Proliferation Act (1978): 161
Nye, Gerald P.: 76, 77, 78
Nye Committee: 77

October Plan: 82
Odría, Manuel: 188
Oil: 69; imported by Italy, 79; in Asia, 93,
    97; U.S. cutoff to Japan, 94, 96, 102;
    U.S. companies, 211–12; "Seven
    Sisters," 211; and Middle East, 211–19,
    223; embargoed by Arab nations, 211
Okonogi, Masao: 134
Olney, Richard: 5
Olympic Games (1980): 224
Open Door notes and policy: 9, 10, 16–18,
    64, 66, 97–98, 100, 140
Operation Zapata. *See* Bay of Pigs incident
Oppenheimer, J. Robert: 151, 152, 154
Organization of American States (OAS):
    184, 190, 195, 198
Organization of Petroleum Exporting
    Countries (OPEC): 194, 212, 214, 218
Orlando, Vittorio: 39
Osgood, Robert E.: 36
Outer Mongolia: 131

Pakistan: 142, 143, 160, 206
Palestine: 202, 204, 207, 214, 215
Palestine Liberation Organization (PLO):
    215, 216, 217
Panama: 11, 13, 16, 66, 183–84, 188,
    192–93, 195
Panama Canal: 4, 10, 11, 18, 183, 188,
    193, 195
Pan-American Conference (1938): 183
USS *Panay:* 80
Paris Peace Pact. *See* Kellogg-Briand Pact
Paris peace talks (Vietnam War): 177
Parrini, Carl: 53
Peace Corps: 209
Peace movements: 63–64, 66, 67, 80,
    177, 178
Pearl Harbor: 86, 91, 96, 103–04, 221
Peking: 9
People's Republic of China: established,
    132; and Korean War, 136–38;
    Eisenhower and, 142–43; and Vietnam,
    143, 167, 169, 175, 179, 180; and Japan,
    144–45; and USSR, 144, 169; Nixon
    and, 144; and atomic weapons, 153,
    157, 160; and Cuba, 190; and Middle
    East, 206, 218; Reagan and, 225
"Percentage deal" (Churchill-Stalin): 110
Peréz Jimenéz, Marcos: 188
Perón, Juan: 185, 188
Persian Gulf: 214, 217, 218, 224
Peru: 188, 191, 194–95
Pezzullo, Lawrence: 196
Philippine Islands: American control of, 1,
    2, 4, 6–9, 18; during World War II, 96,
    101, 102, 103; independence of, 140–41;
    in SEATO, 142; and Vietnam, 143, 168;
    in ASEAN, 144; internal conflict in,
    225
Pittman, Key: 76, 77
Platt, Orville H.: 6
Platt Amendment: 6, 7, 15
Plutonium: 149, 158, 160, 161
Poincaré, Raymond: 60
Point Four program: 222
Poland: 85, 86, 92, 98, 100; and origins of
    Cold War, 110, 115, 119, 122
Polaris missile: 156
Port Arthur: 128
Portugal: 206

Potsdam Conference: 119-20, 121, 122
Pratt, Julius W.: 46
Preparedness measures (Wilson): 30-31
Presidential Directive 59 (PD 59): 159
Progressive Era: 57, 58
Progressive Movement: 7, 22
Prohibition: 47, 75
Propaganda: 24, 37, 176
Protestant churches (U.S.): 63, 205, 215-26
Public opinion (U.S.): in World War I, 24, 28-29, 31; and Versailles peace talks, 39, 54, 55; and isolationism, 71; and World War II, 87, 100, 111, 112, 115, 117; and Korea, 137; on nuclear energy, 159-60; and Vietnam, 177
Puerto Rico: 1, 6
Punta del Este I (1961): 190
Punta del Este II (1962): 190

Quandt, William B.: 120
"Quarantine" speech (FDR): 81-82
Quemoy: 143

Racism: 2-3, 104, 208, 209
RCA Corporation: 60
Reagan, Ronald W.: 159, 197, 198, 224; and Middle East, 215, 218, 224, 225
Reciprocal trade agreements: 74, 75, 88
Refugees: 177, 205, 215
Reid, Whitelaw: 6
Reparations: after World War I, 38, 41, 43, 44, 60, 61, 62, 63; after World War II, 121, 133
Reparations Commission: 57, 60, 61
Republican party (U.S.): 47; in 1920s, 53-55, 57, 59, 71-72; and FDR, 76, 85; and Korean War, 138; and attitude toward self-government, 140; and China, 170; in 1980s, 224
Republic of China (Nationalist China): 130, 132, 142, 143, 225
USS *Reuben James:* 95
Reza Pahlavi, Mohammed: 204, 205, 214
Rhee, Syngman: 134
Rhineland: 61, 62, 79
Ridgway, Matthew B.: 137
Rio Treaty. *See* Inter-American Treaty of

Reciprocal Assistance
Rockefeller, Nelson A.: 194
Rockhill, William: 10
Rogers, William D.: 195
Rojas Pinilla, Gustavo: 188
Roman Catholic Church: in U.S., 82; in South Vietnam, 172
Romania: 85
Roosevelt, Franklin D.: 67; and isolationist sentiment, 71-88; "quarantine" speech, 81-82; and outbreak of World War II, 87-88, 91-104; and "Europe first" strategy, 111-14; on USSR, 112-14; on Japan, 114; and United Nations, 114-15; at Tehran, 115-16; at Yalta, 116-17, 119, 121; death of, 117, 121; and atomic bomb, 122; and Latin America, 183-84, 187, 192, 197; and Middle East, 202
Roosevelt, Theodore: 1-4, 7, 10-15, 18, 49
Roosevelt Corollary: 14, 66
Root, Elihu: 6, 13, 14, 49, 51
Roxas, Manuel: 141
Royal Air Force (Great Britain): 98
Rubber: 92, 100
Ruhr valley: 60, 61
Russia: 8, 17, 19, 24. For events after the Bolshevik Revolution, *see* Union of Soviet Socialist Republics

Saar valley: 42
Sadat, Anwar: 211, 213
Sa'id, Nuri: 207
Saigon: 165, 166, 179
Sampson, Anthony: 211
Sandinistas: 198, 224
Sandino, Augusto: 197
Santo Domingo: 66, 67, 193
Saudi Arabia: 201, 202, 208, 211, 212, 215, 218
Second front controversy (World War II): 112-14, 116-18
Shafter, William: 8
Shantung: 21, 42, 44
The Shark and the Sardines (Arévalo): 187
Shigeru, Yoshida: 132
Shotwell, James T.: 65, 66

Shuttle diplomacy: 211
Siberia: 21
Sicily: 113
Sinai Peninsula: 209, 213
Singapore: 93, 96, 100, 101, 104, 144
Sinkiang province: 131
Sino-Japanese War: 81, 93
Skyjackings: 195
Smith, Al: 72
Smith, Gaddis: 138
Social Darwinism: 2
Somalia: 217
Somoza, Anastasio: 196
Somoza family: 187, 188, 196–97
Sontag, Raymond: 39
South Africa: 207, 225
Southeast Asia Treaty Organization
    (SEATO): 140, 142, 143
South Korea: 134, 135, 138, 143
South Manchurian Railway: 17, 128
South Vietnam: 165, 171–80, 223; army of,
    172–73, 177–78
Spain: 4–7, 18, 97
Spanish-American War: 4–6
Spanish Civil War: 78, 79, 82
Sputnik: 156
Stalin, Joseph: and Russian front of World
    War II, 108–14; at Tehran, 115–16; at
    Yalta, 116–17, 119, 121, 128; and the
    United Nations, 114–16; at Potsdam,
    119–20, 122; and atomic bomb, 122–23;
    and China, 131
Stalingrad, battle of: 108
Stark, Harold R.: 94–95
"Star Wars." *See* Strategic Defense
    Initiative
Stimson, Henry L.: 67, 103, 122, 221
Stock market crash (1929): 63
Storey, Moorfield: 1
Straight, Willard: 16, 17
Strategic Air Command: 155
Strategic Arms Limitation Talks I
    (SALT I): 158
Strategic Arms Limitation Talks II   II):
    159, 162
Strategic Defense Initiative (SDI): 159
Strategic hamlet program (Vietnam): 173
Stresemann, Gustav: 62
Submarines: in World War I, 24, 26–33, 64,
    65; in World War II, 93, 94, 95; with

nuclear weapons, 158, 159
Sudetenland: 84, 91–92, 98
Suez Canal: 101, 208, 210
Suez crisis (1956): 208
Sukarno: 142
Supreme Council: 57
Sussex (British vessel): 29; *Sussex* Pledge,
    29, 30
Syria: 204–06, 208–10, 213, 216

Taft, Robert A.: 86
Taft, William H.: 10, 13–18, 48
Taiwan. *See* Republic of China
Tariffs and tariff reductions: 62, 69, 72, 73,
    74, 75
Tehran Conference: 115–16
Teller, Edward: 151
Teller Amendment: 6, 7
Tennessee Valley Authority (TVA): 149
Tenth Inter-American Conference: 187
Terrorism: 216, 217, 218, 225
Tet offensive (Vietnam): 177
Thailand: 142, 143, 144
Tillman, Seth P.: 204
Time: 216
Time-Life: 130
Tin: 100, 187
Tito, Josip Broz: 206
Torrejos, Omar: 196
Trachtenberg, Marc: 59
Treaty of Versailles: 35–51, 53, 54, 55, 58,
    60, 62
Trujillo, Rafael: 187, 188, 191
Truman, Harry S.: World War II diplomacy
    of, 117–22; on USSR in World War II,
    118, 121, 224; at Potsdam, 119–20, 121,
    122; and atomic bomb, 121–23; and
    containment policy, 123–24, 132, 168;
    and China, 129–32; and postwar
    Japan, 132; and Korean War, 134–40;
    and the Philippines, 140–41; on
    Indonesian independence, 142; and
    atomic policy, 149, 151; and Indochina,
    168, 169–70; and Middle East, 204, 211
Truman Doctrine: 123–24, 132, 135
Trusteeships: 133, 134, 139
Tumulty, Joseph P.: 55
Turkey: 123, 206
Tyrol: 42, 44

U-2 incident: 155. 156
Ubico, Jorge: 187
Unconditional surrender policy: 114, 127
Union of Soviet Socialist Republics
  (USSR, Soviet Union): and Versailles
  peace talks, 39, 43, 46; in 1920s, 64;
  FDR recognizes, 75; and Germany, 79,
  86, 96, 102, 108, 109, 110, 115; and
  Japan, 79, 114, 115, 116–17, 120–21,
  127–29, 131, 133; in World War II
  grand alliance, 108–14, 119, 120; and
  second front controversy, 108, 112–14;
  and England, 109–11; and origins of
  the Cold War, 107–24; and Poland,
  110, 115, 119; and Lend-Lease from
  U.S., 112, 113, 114, 118; and United
  Nations, 43, 112, 114, 116–17, 119; and
  dropping of atomic bomb on Japan,
  121, 122; and Chinese civil war, 127–31,
  170; and Korean War, 133–35, 138; and
  atomic weapons, 149–50, 151, 152,
  154–58, 162, 168, 223; and *Sputnik*,
  156; and SALT I, 158; and Vietnam,
  167, 169, 175, 179, 180; and Cuba,
  189–91, 199; and Middle East, 202,
  204, 205, 208, 209, 210, 211, 212–13,
  217. *See also* Communism and
  Communists; Eastern Europe
United Fruit Company (UFCO): 187
United Nations: organized, 114–17, 119; and
  Korean War, 134, 135, 136, 137; and
  atomic energy, 149–50, 152–53; and
  Latin America, 190, 196; and Middle
  East, 204, 205, 207, 208, 209–10, 215
United Nations Declaration (1941): 112
United Nations Resolution 242 (1967):
  209–10
Uranium: 149, 151, 158, 160
Uruguay: 190
U.S. Army: 6, 8, 14, 102, 174. *See also
  individual wars*
U.S. Congress: and Cuban annexation, 6;
  and World War I, 22, 23, 31, 32; on
  Versailles treaty and League of
  Nations, 38, 47, 49, 50, 54, 55; in
  1920s, 57, 62, 66, 67, 71; FDR and, 73,
  74, 76–82, 85–87, 92, 95; and
  preparation for World War II, 92, 94;
  and aid to USSR in World War II, 112,
  117; and the United Nations, 115; and

China, 131; and rearmament after
  World War II, 135; and Korean War,
  137, 138; and *Sputnik*, 156; Johnson
  and, 192; and Latin America, 194, 195.
  See also U.S. Senate
U.S. Department of Commerce: 60, 66
U.S. Department of Defense: 135–36
U.S. Department of the Navy: 71, 102, 103
U.S. Department of State: before World
  War I, 11, 16; in 1920s, 55, 57, 60; and
  FDR, 74, 81, 82; and World War II,
  102; and the Cold War, 123, 135;
  and China, 130; falls victim to
  McCarthyism, 142
U.S. Department of War: 102, 103
U.S. Marine Corps: in Latin America, 6,
  15, 16, 66, 67; in Middle East, 208, 216,
  218, 224–25
U.S. Navy: Atlantic Fleet, 94–95; Pacific
  Fleet, 96, 104; aids U.S. expansionism,
  3, 5, 11, 13, 14, 15, 16; in World War I,
  71; at outbreak of World War II, 94,
  95, 96, 102, 103, 104; and Cuban
  missile crisis, 190
U.S. Senate: Foreign Relations Committee,
  47, 76; and pre–World War I U.S.
  expansionism, 14, 16; debates
  Versailles treaty and League of
  Nations, 47, 49, 53, 58, 71; and Paris
  Peace Pact, 65; and isolationist
  sentiment, 76, 77; and SALT II, 159
U.S. Supreme Court: 83

Vance, Cyrus: 223
Vandenberg, Arthur H.: 86
Vargas, Getulio: 184
Vargas Villa, José: 18
Venezuela: 3, 13, 185, 188, 189, 194, 195
Versailles Peace Conference: 35–51. *See
  also* Treaty of Versailles
Versailles Twenty Years After (Birdsall): 45
Vietcong. *See* National Liberation Front
Vietminh: 139, 166, 167, 168, 171, 174
Vietnam: 19, 139, 140. *See also* Indochina;
  North Vietnam; South Vietnam
Vietnamization: 177–78
Vietnam War: 143, 144, 165–80, 191, 193,
  209, 210, 222–23; "lessons" of, 144,
  180, 214, 218

Viña del Mar Conference: 194
Voluntarism: 55, 58–59, 64–65, 67, 69

Wallace, Henry A.: 123
War debts, World War I: 59, 62, 69, 72, 76
War-guilt clause: 44
War Resisters League: 63
Warsaw uprising: 110
Washington Conference (1921–22): 64–65
Watergate: 178, 180, 210
Wedemeyer, Albert C.: 131–32
Wehrle, Edmund S.: 145
Weizmann, Chaim: 204
Welch, Richard E., Jr.: 8
Welles, Sumner: 74, 82, 85
Westmoreland, William C.: 176, 177
White slavery: 57
Williams, William Appleman: 53
Wilson, Francis M. Huntington: 16
Wilson, Woodrow: and U.S. entry into
    World War I, 21–34; and Versailles
    peace talks, 35–51, 55; and post-World
    War I diplomacy, 53, 71; legacy of,
    53–55, 58, 71–72, 80, 88, 128
Winter War (Finland): 112
Wood, Leonard: 6, 7
World Court: 77

World War I: U.S. entry into, 21–34;
    "lessons" of, 57–58, 63, 92, 100, 109,
    128
World War II: 53, 54; U.S. entry into, 86,
    91–104 (*see also* Pearl Harbor); and
    origins of the Cold War, 107–24, 166,
    221; on Eastern Front, 114–15, 117,
    120, 121–23; in Europe, 108, 111,
    112–15, 116, 117, 118; in Pacific, 114–15,
    117, 120, 121–23; and Latin America,
    183–84; and Middle East, 202

Yalta Conference: 116–17, 119, 121,
    127–28, 139
Yalu River: 136
Yemen: 208
Young, Owen D.: 60, 61, 62
Young Committee: 62
Young Plan: 62, 63, 69
Yugoslavia: 42, 110, 185

Zelaya, José Santos: 15
Zhou Enlai: 130, 136
Zimmermann, Arthur: 31
Zimmermann Telegram: 31
Zionism: 204

Contributors

JOHN M. CARROLL received his Ph.D. from the University of Kentucky and is currently professor of history at Lamar University. In addition to lecturing, he has published extensively in numerous journals, including *American Historical Review* and the *Journal of American History,* and is coeditor of *European Traditions in the Twentieth Century* (1979) and *Conflict and Change: America 1939 to Present* (1983).

JOSEPH A. FRY is professor of history at the University of Nevada, Las Vegas. He is the author of *Henry S. Sanford: Diplomacy and Business in Nineteenth-Century America* (1982) and is presently writing a biography of John Tyler Morgan, a leading nineteenth-century southern expansionist.

JAMES W. HARPER holds a Ph.D. from the University of Virginia and is associate professor of history and director of honors at Texas Tech University. His work in diplomatic history includes essays in *Historia Mexicana* and *Arizona and the West* and reviews in *The History Teacher.* Recently he has contributed articles in the history of sports to *Baseball History* and the *Biographical Dictionary of American Sports.*

GEORGE C. HERRING is a specialist in the field of U.S. foreign relations and is currently the editor of the quarterly journal *Diplomatic History.* A professor of history at the University of Kentucky, he has written widely on American foreign policy since World War II, including *America's Longest War: The United States and Vietnam, 1950-1975* (1979) and *The Secret Diplomacy of the Vietnam War: The "Negotiating Volumes" of the Pentagon Papers* (1983).

LESTER D. LANGLEY is professor of Latin American and U.S. diplomatic history at the University of Georgia. His most recent work is *Central America: The Real Stakes* (1985).

GEORGE T. MAZUZAN is historian at the U.S. Nuclear Regulatory Commission in Washington, DC. His most recent book was coauthored with J. Samuel Walker and is entitled *Controlling the Atom: The Beginnings of Nuclear Regulation, 1946–1962* (1984).

ROBERT L. MESSER is associate professor of history at the University of Illinois at Chicago and is the author of *The End of an Alliance: James F. Byrnes, Roosevelt, Truman, and the Origins of the Cold War* (1982). He is now writing a book on Truman's nuclear weapons policy.

CAROL MORRIS PETILLO is associate professor of history at Boston College and the author of *Douglas MacArthur: The Philippine Years* (1981). She is the editor of *The Ordeal of Elizabeth Vaughan: A Wartime Diary of the Philippines*, which was published in 1985.

MELVIN SMALL is the author of *Was War Necessary? National Security and U.S. Entry Into War* (1980) and coeditor of *International War: An Anthology* (1985). He is a professor at Wayne State University's History Department and is presently working on a book on the impact of the antiwar movement on policymaking from 1965 to 1971.

JONATHAN G. UTLEY is associate professor at the University of Tennessee, Knoxville. He is the author of *Going to War with Japan, 1937–1941* (1985) and is currently working on the history of the battleship *Tennessee*, as well as on a study of the relationship between Franklin D. Roosevelt and Cordell Hull from 1933 to 1945.

JANE KAROLINE VIETH earned her Ph.D. from Ohio State University in British history and is currently a professor at the Department of Humanities, Michigan State University. She has published several articles in the *Michigan Academician* and is the author of "Joseph P. Kennedy and British Appeasement," in Kenneth Paul Jones, ed., *U.S. Diplomats in Europe, 1919–1941* (1983).

WILLIAM C. WIDENOR received his Ph.D. from the University of California at Berkeley and is associate professor and chair of the Department of History, University of Illinois at Urbana-Champaign. He is the author of *Henry Cabot Lodge and the Search for an American Foreign Policy* (1980), which won the Organization of American Historians Frederick Jackson Turner Prize in 1981.